AFTER WORLD RELIGIONS

The World Religions Paradigm has been the subject of critique and controversy in Religious Studies for many years. *After World Religions* provides a rationale for overhauling the World Religions curriculum, as well as a roadmap for doing so. The volume offers concise and practical introductions to cutting-edge Religious Studies method and theory, introducing a wide range of pedagogical situations and innovative solutions. An international team of scholars addresses the challenges presented in their different departmental, institutional, and geographical contexts. Instructors developing syllabi will find supplementary reading lists and specific suggestions to help guide their teaching. Students at all levels will find the book an invaluable entry point into an area of ongoing scholarly debate.

Christopher R. Cotter is Co-Editor-in-Chief of the Religious Studies Project and Co-Director of the Nonreligion and Secularity Research Network. His ongoing doctoral research at Lancaster University takes a discursive approach to 'non-religion', 'the secular' and related concepts. He has published journal articles, book chapters, and book reviews in these areas, and co-edited *Social Identities between the Sacred and the Secular* (2013).

David G. Robertson is Co-Editor-in-Chief of the Religious Studies Project and Bulletin Editor for the British Association for the Study of Religion. He teaches at the University of Edinburgh, UK. He has published numerous papers on new religions, millennialism, conspiracy theories and Critical Theory, recently guest-edited a special issue of *Nova Religio* and is the author of *UFOs, Conspiracy Theories and the New Age: Millennial Conspiracism* (2016).

RELIGION IN CULTURE

Available:

AFTER WORLD RELIGIONS

Reconstructing Religious Studies

*Edited by Christopher R. Cotter and
David G. Robertson*

Routledge
Taylor & Francis Group

LONDON AND NEW YORK

First published 2016
by Routledge
2 Park Square, Milton Park, Abingdon, Oxon OX14 4RN

and by Routledge
711 Third Avenue, New York, NY 10017

Routledge is an imprint of the Taylor & Francis Group, an informa business

© 2016 Christopher R. Cotter & David G. Robertson

British Library Cataloguing in Publication Data
A catalogue record for this book is available from the British Library

Library of Congress Cataloging in Publication Data
After world religions : reconstructing religious studies / edited by
Christopher R. Cotter & David G. Robertson. -- 1st ed.
pages cm. -- (Religions in culture)
Includes bibliographical references and index.
1. Religion--Methodology. 2. Religions. I. Cotter, Christopher R., editor.
BL41.A38 2016
200.71--dc23
2015030206

ISBN: 978-1-138-91912-9 (hbk)
ISBN: 978-1-138-91913-6 (pbk)
ISBN: 978-1-315-68804-6 (ebk)

Typeset in Bembo
by Taylor & Francis Books
Printed and bound by CPI Group (UK) Ltd, Croydon, CR0 4YY

CONTENTS

PREFACE

> scholars of religion have a similar challenge in introductory courses to that of their colleagues in linguistics who must teach the analysis of language to a room full of proficient language users. In both cases, instructors must facilitate the leap from the student's pre-existing folk understanding to scholarly analysis.
>
> *(McCutcheon 1997, 102)*

On 25 February 2013, the *Religious Studies Project* (RSP) published an audio interview in which James L. Cox and David G. Robertson discussed the 'World Religions Paradigm' (hereafter and throughout the volume, WRP) – that is, a particular way of thinking about religions which organizes them into a set of discrete traditions with a supposedly 'global' import. Despite the limitations of the podcast format, the interview touches on most of the important issues surrounding the WRP, including the colonial context, implicit ranking in order of importance and the tenacity of the model in both public discourse and pedagogy.

Steven Sutcliffe, a colleague of both Cox and Robertson at the University of Edinburgh, opined that it would be interesting to make an episode which asked if and how we might teach an introductory course in Religious Studies (hereafter etc., RS) *without* utilizing the WRP. Robertson, along with Christopher R. Cotter (the other 'half' of the RSP), then set about recording just such an episode, featuring a number of academics rather than a single interview. The episode, *After the World Religions Paradigm ...?*, was broadcast on 1 March 2013 as a response to the Cox episode, and features a number of contributors to this present volume.

Shortly after the broadcast, Cotter and Robertson were contacted by Russell T. McCutcheon (series editor, along with Craig Martin, of what was then Acumen's 'Religion in Culture' series), who suggested submitting a proposal for an edited volume on the topic. Acumen has since been acquired by Routledge. This is that volume.

The editors would like to thank all who have made it possible. Firstly, our thanks to all the editorial staff at Routledge (and Acumen), and the anonymous reviewers for their constructive feedback. We would also like to express our gratitude to the editors, interviewees and everyone else involved with the Religious Studies Project, for inspiring and supporting this project. The Edinburgh Gang – thanks for all the discussion, company, support and fun. And, of course, Jim, Steve, Russell, Craig and Timothy Fitzgerald for their invaluable help and inspiration. Christopher Cotter would like to thank his wonderful wife Lindsey and his parents for their constant support, and the Cat-Like Crew, who've made this year so much fun. David Robertson would like to thank Aileen Swalwell for everything, and Christine and Gordon for taking the boys to Dobbies all the time.

Thanks for reading.

Christopher R. Cotter and David G. Robertson
Edinburgh, July 2015

CONTRIBUTORS

Tara Baldrick-Morrone is a Ph.D. candidate in Religions of Western Antiquity at Florida State University. Her research focuses on rhetoric, violence, and the body in late antiquity.

Dominic Corrywright is course leader for Religion and Theology at Oxford Brookes University. Dominic taught in secondary education for ten years. His research interests relate to alternative and new age spiritualities, healing and religion, theory and methodology in the study of religions. He teaches BA and supervises Masters and PhD students working in the study of religions and cognate fields.

Christopher R. Cotter is Co-Editor-in-Chief of the Religious Studies Project and Co-Director of the Nonreligion and Secularity Research Network. His ongoing doctoral research at Lancaster University takes a discursive approach to 'non-religion', 'the secular' and related concepts. He has published journal articles, book chapters, and book reviews in these areas, and co-edited *Social Identities between the Sacred and the Secular* (2013).

James L. Cox is Emeritus Professor of Religious Studies in the University of Edinburgh and Adjunct Professor in the Religion and Society Research Centre in the University of Western Sydney. Prior to being appointed to the University of Edinburgh in 1993, he held academic posts in the University of Zimbabwe and Alaska Pacific University.

Carole M. Cusack is Professor of Religious Studies at the University of Sydney. She is the author of *Conversion Among the Germanic People* (1998), *Invented Religions: Imagination, Fiction and Faith* (2010) and *The Sacred Tree: Ancient and Medieval*

Manifestations (2011). She is the former editor of *International Journal for the Study of New Religions* and *Journal of Religious History*.

Michel Desjardins is Professor of Religion and Culture at Wilfrid Laurier University, in Waterloo, Canada. He has taught and published in comparative religions, early Christianity, the academic study of religion, and the scholarship on teaching and learning. His core research is on the role of food in people's spiritual lives. Dr. Desjardins is a Canada 3M National Teaching Fellow.

Michael Graziano is a Ph.D. candidate in American Religious History at Florida State University. His dissertation explores the relationship between the Central Intelligence Agency and American religious institutions during the Cold War.

Craig Martin is Associate Professor of Religious Studies at St. Thomas Aquinas College, and author of *Capitalizing Religion: Ideology and the Opiate of the Bourgeoisie* (2014), *A Critical Introduction to the Study of Religion* (Routledge 2014) and *Masking Hegemony: A Genealogy of Liberalism, Religion, and the Private Sphere* (Routledge 2010).

David W. McConeghy is an Adjunct Faculty member in the Religious Studies department at Chapman University in Orange, California, where he teaches courses on Global Ethics and Living Religions of the World. Recently he has contributed to several scholarly communities online including *Sacred Matters*, *The Religious Studies Project* and *Sacred and Sequential*.

Russell T. McCutcheon is Professor and Chair of the Department of Religious Studies at the University of Alabama. He has published widely on topics related to the history of the study of religion and the implications of categorization. His work can also be found in the public domain at his department's own blog and the blog for the research initiative *Culture on the Edge*.

Suzanne Owen is a Senior Lecturer in departments of Theology and Religious Studies at Leeds Trinity University and the University of Chester, teaching method and theory, anthropology of religion and indigenous religions. Since her monograph *The Appropriation of Native American Spirituality* (2008), she has published papers on religion and indigeneity in native North American and British Pagan contexts.

Steven W. Ramey is a Professor of Religious Studies and directs Asian Studies at the University of Alabama. His book *Hindu Sufi or Sikh* (2008) focuses on the ways communities who identify as Sindhi Hindus contest dominant understandings of identities. His continuing work addresses assumptions embedded in religious labels, building on his participation in the *Culture on the Edge* research collaborative.

David G. Robertson is Co-Editor-in-Chief of the Religious Studies Project and Bulletin Editor for the British Association for the Study of Religion. He teaches at the University of Edinburgh, UK. He has published numerous papers on new religions, millennialism, conspiracy theories and critical theory, recently guest-edited a special issue of *Nova Religio* and is the author of *UFOs, Conspiracy Theories and the New Age: Millennial Conspiracism* (2016).

Brad Stoddard is an Assistant Professor of American Religions at McDaniel College in Westminster, Maryland, and is currently revising his manuscript on Florida's faith-based correctional program.

Steven J. Sutcliffe is Senior Lecturer in the Study of Religion at the University of Edinburgh. He specializes in the study of alternative religion and in the modern history of the academic study of religion. He is the author of *Children of the New Age: A History of Spiritual Practices* (2003) and co-editor (with Ingvild Gilhus) of *New Age Spirituality: Rethinking Religion* (2013).

Teemu Taira is Senior Lecturer in the Department for the Study of Religions at the University of Helsinki, Finland. He is co-author of *Media Portrayals of Religion and the Secular Sacred* (2013, with Kim Knott and Elizabeth Poole) and author of four monographs (in Finnish). He has published widely in edited volumes and journals such as *Religion, Journal of Contemporary Religion* and *Culture and Religion*.

Paul-François Tremlett is a Senior Lecturer in Religious Studies at the Open University. He is currently conducting research as part of an inter-disciplinary project called 'Re-Assembling Democracy: Ritual as Cultural Resource'.

FOREWORD

Before the 'After' in 'After World Religions' – Wilfred Cantwell Smith on the meaning and end of religion

James L. Cox

Writing the Foreword to a book with a title that begins with the word 'After' suggests that I should reflect on what comes 'before' the 'after' in the title. In their Introduction, however, Christopher Cotter and David Robertson have done just that by succinctly and clearly describing the historical background to and the development of the World Religions Paradigm (WRP). This leaves me with the problem as to what I can add in a Foreword to a book in which the Introduction sets out the compelling academic need to analyse, critique and eventually demolish the WRP (although Cotter and Robertson demonstrate that many academics tenaciously resist all efforts to challenge the paradigm and continue to produce books that are devoted to outlining the history and beliefs of the 'big five', or sometimes six, so-called world religions).

I have found a solution to my problem by identifying three points, each inspired by the groundbreaking work of the Canadian Islamicist, phenomenologist of religion and liberal Christian theologian, Wilfred Cantwell Smith. These are: (1) the term 'religion', as it is used in the WRP, is the result of historical processes operating in the West that transformed what is essentially a human experience into a limited number of world 'systems'; (2) the misplaced emphasis in many textbooks on the beliefs of the world's religions reflects the historical transformation of belief from its original sense as performing an active role for religious practitioners into a series of propositions; (3) religions are best taught academically and interpreted publicly by fostering empathetic techniques that enable students to gain an in-depth understanding of the concrete experiences of members of communities whose cultural values and shared symbols are different from their own.

Wilfred Cantwell Smith as a forerunner to the contemporary critique of the WRP

In his landmark work on theory and method in the study of religion, entitled *The Meaning and End of Religion* (1964, first published 1962), Wilfred Cantwell Smith devotes the second chapter, 'Religion in the West', to deconstructing the term 'religion' and its application to the concept of the 'world religions'. Smith (1964, 19) suggests that the academic practice of talking about 'religion' and its 'major forms' in 'Christianity, Buddhism, Hinduism, and so on' is so 'fixed in our minds' that scholars may regard his challenge to this way of thinking as 'obstreperous' or even 'absurd'. But Smith (1964, 23–24) contends that the current way of conceptualizing religion has been developing since the seventeenth century under the influence of the Western Enlightenment. He argues that the term originally derives from the Latin *religio*, which when understood substantively may refer to an outside power or force, but when used adjectivally suggests a quality of life, the manner in which humans perceive the world, a sense of being religious. In other words, the adjectival use of *religio* is linked to human experience rather than regarding religion as referring to an object, such as a deity or an unseen power. Over time, the experiential meaning of religion was transformed into 'a great objective something' (1964, 25), so much so that religion, conceived as a 'theoretical construct', came to dominate how it was understood in the West, resulting in the current widespread description of religion as a 'system of ideas' (1964, 38).

In the first instance, the Christian 'religion' was the intellectual system with which scholars were concerned, but when other 'systems' were discovered, instead of encountering different ways of being religious, the Christian 'religion' as an intellectual construct was compared with other intellectual constructs. Smith (1964, 38–39) argues that as a result 'one gets different religions, in the plural', great systems of thought that can be compared, culminating in what we are now calling the World Religions Paradigm. On this model, rather than speaking of someone as 'being religious' or trying to understand how an individual experiences the world 'religiously', we classify the individual as adhering to a particular organized system of beliefs and practices. When used in this way, Smith (1964, 48) concludes that we are far better dropping the term 'religion' altogether and substituting it with something much closer to its original meaning, such as 'faith' or 'piety'.

In another publication, *Faith and Belief* (1979; reprinted in 1998 as *Faith and Belief: The Difference Between Them*), in a way similar to his analysis of religion, Smith traces the history of the term 'belief' and argues that in early English it meant 'to hold dear, to cherish', as in the phrase, 'to regard as lief' (1998a, 106). To believe in a person, for example, 'was to orient oneself towards him or her with a particular attitude or relationship, of esteem and affection, also trust' (1998a, 107). Smith points out that 'belief' in historic usage was not primarily an intellectual formulation but a relationship, an experience, a choice, an act, what the contemporary sociologist Danièle Hervieu-Léger (1999, 84) calls 'belief in motion'. Smith describes a series of changes in the West outlining how belief became transformed from a verb into a noun, with the focus of the former almost always being a person, but in the latter a proposition. As a result, a second form of reification occurred, similar to the objectifying of religion from an experience into a system: from 'believing in', we came to 'believe that'; for a relationship, we substituted propositional truth (Smith 1998a, 119). Religions then came to be compared, analysed and ranked according to the set of propositions they formulated and advocated as 'true'. If we apply Smith's analysis to the WRP, world religions are systems of thought composed primarily of propositions that can be applied universally or globally rather than locally.

This leads to a third, quite practical, point I want to draw from Cantwell Smith. In a book he first published in 1962 under the title *The Faith of Other Men* (reprinted in 1998 as *Patterns of Faith Around the World*), Smith describes how the reification of the terms 'religion' and 'belief' can be circumvented by identifying a central concept or practice that students of religion can use to gain an understanding of how religious people in identifiable communities experience the world and how they act on their beliefs. Smith's aim was to help those who had no prior exposure to any type of religious experience other than their own to attain a depth of understanding that differs markedly from what they may have learned by studying the so-called objective history and doctrines of 'religious systems'. By isolating and empathetically explaining a key phrase that encapsulates a community's most fundamental identifying characteristic, students could discover a way of entering into and imaginatively experiencing what religious people themselves experience.

Smith suggests that his method was developed to challenge the common teaching of religion in universities 'in which the panorama of human religious life across the world is described under a series of headings: Hinduism, Buddhism, Confucianism, and the like – a number of separate systems, each called a religion' (1998b, 28). Since he was writing his book for a largely Western audience, Smith chose to classify the religious practitioners to whom he attached a central identifying term as 'Hindus', 'Buddhists', 'Muslims' and 'Chinese'. He deliberately personalized these categories rather than attributing an 'ism' to them to emphasize that he was describing 'faith' as experience, rather than religion as a system, and belief as action, rather than belief as a proposition.

I will limit my discussion of this point to Smith's (1998b, 35–48) description of 'Hindus', for whom he chose as a key term the Sanskrit phrase found in the Upanishads, '*tat tvam asi*', which he translated as 'That Thou Art'. He outlined how the often confusing idea, for outsiders, of the Brahman–Atman unity as the path to liberation from the endless cycles of birth and re-birth actually describes the widespread experience whereby an individual merges into a sense of totality, or as it has been put in philosophy, as the uniting of the many into the one. Brahman, in a doctrinal sense as taught in many textbooks on Hinduism, is often described as the universal originator of all that is, the overarching reality or as it is put in the *Oxford Dictionary of World Religions* (Bowker 1997, 163): 'the one supreme, all-pervading Spirit; the impersonal Absolute, beyond attributes, which is the origin and support of the visible universe'. By contrast, the Atman is the Self, residing in the deepest part of the individual. It is the real or true Self and not to be confused with the apparent or empirical self. In classical non-dualist teaching, Brahman and Atman are one; the 'impersonal Absolute' is identical with the deepest reality within the individual. As it is put in the *Chandogya Upanishad* (VI, 13, 3):

> Though you do not see *Brahman* in this body, he is indeed here. That which
> is the subtle essence – in that have all things their existence. That is the truth.
> That is the Self (*Atman*). And that … thou art (*tat tvam asi*).
>
> *(Radhakrishnan 1974)*

Smith wants us to understand that the phrase '*tat tvam asi*' provides the key for
understanding the experience of liberation for Hindus, an experience gained
through the realization that the World Spirit, the one essential reality, is identical
with the true Self found within every individual.

In order to make this more than an intellectual understanding, Smith suggests a
parallel relationship between the universal and particular as commonly portrayed in
Western contexts through the terms the Good, the True and the Beautiful. Each of
these words represents a universal idea. The Good is the overarching type; the ideal
for which humans strive as their end and meaning in life. Yet, the Good as a type
finds its expression only in specific, particular and concrete instances. The universal
Good is located, experienced and manifested primarily in the individual. The Good
is in me; I am in the Good: we are one, or *tat tvam asi*. What can be said for the moral
end of humanity can also be applied to the nature of ultimate Truth and the aesthetic
universal ideal we call Beauty. Smith, of course, does not intend these examples to
be taken in a literal sense, but he uses them as a way of drawing on what is
understood in a typically Western experience of the world in order to facilitate
understanding of the Hindu experience of the Brahman–Atman unity (Smith
1998b, 37–38).

Smith is clear that although experiencing religion is personal, it is not indivi-
dualistic. Because people form communities in which they share common cultural
values and traditions, we can assume their experience of what he called 'personal
faith' is similar (Smith 1964, 141). Of course, such communities are vibrant and
respond to varying outside forces and internal pressures in dynamic ways over time.
This is what Smith (1964, 168–169) termed 'the cumulative tradition' and what I
have meant in various publications when, following Hervieu-Léger, I have spoken
of religion as the transmission of an authoritative tradition that is passed on from
generation to generation (Cox 2007, 79–82; Cox 2013, 312–313; Cox 2015: 10).

When I first taught Comparative Religion to undergraduates, I used Smith's
book to illustrate how the phenomenological stage I called 'empathetic interpolation' can be employed to help students cultivate a feeling for experiences of the
world which are fundamentally alien to them, while at the same time using their
own experience to gain an understanding from the inside of how it feels to be a
believer in a community of such like-minded people (Cox 2010, 52–55). The
method of empathetic interpolation is particularly useful because it asks students of
religion to draw from their own shared values and traditions in order to insert into
their personal understanding corresponding types of experience they imaginatively
reconstruct from an empathetic study of other communities' values and traditions.
Smith's key phrases not only fostered understanding, but worked as a pedagogical
tool which meant students internalized the connection they made between their

own experience of the world and those who formed the focus of their study. This approach is rooted in the phenomenological notion of intersubjectivity (Cox 2006, 28–30), which presupposes that nothing human ultimately is alien to another human (Cox 2014, 135–138).

After Wilfred Cantwell Smith

The subtitle of the present book suggests that its principal aim is to 'reconstruct' religious studies. As a starting point towards achieving this goal, I don't think we can ignore the prescient influence of Wilfred Cantwell Smith because by 1962 he had already contributed significantly to deconstructing the WRP and to suggesting ways in which the study of religion can be reconfigured. His incisive critique of the term religion, followed by his call to move the conception of religion away from doctrines or beliefs towards a dynamic, experiential and inter-subjective study, has practical consequences for how scholars of religion convey to students and to the wider public what it means to study 'religion' as lived experience. The significance of Smith as an important predecessor to later deconstructions and reconstructions of religion was emphasized by Timothy Fitzgerald in his landmark book *The Ideology of Religious Studies* (2000, 43), in which he credits Smith with the 'brilliant intuition ... that religion is a modern western invention'. Fitzgerald (2000, 43) adds that Smith's argument is based on the assumption 'that the distinction between the religious and the secular not only distorts western understanding of the rest of the world but also distorts western self-understanding'.

Although he concluded *The Meaning and End of Religion* by suggesting that his analysis would launch a 'new age' of 'theoretical inquiry' (Smith 1964, 181), it is clear in retrospect that Smith did not resolve definitively the problems attached to the WRP. He still tended to create essential categories, as demonstrated in his descriptions of communities as 'Hindus', 'Buddhists', 'Muslims' and 'Chinese', which we can easily translate into 'Hinduism', 'Buddhism', 'Islam' and 'Confucianism' – although clearly Smith recognized the pitfalls in such universal classifications. More-over, he was guilty of inserting a Protestant Christian bias into his analysis by emphasizing religion as 'personal faith' and insisting that religion is at its core a relationship to persons and to transcendence (Smith 1981, 190–192). Although he claimed not to have stressed the 'faith relationship' over historical, sociological, and social scientific studies of religion (1981, 56–80), his liberal theological stance is not hidden in his analysis of religion, belief and faith.

Despite its limitations, if we take on board Smith's analysis of the relationship of the constructed term religion to individual experiences within identifiable commu-nities, we will have made progress towards dismantling the grip the WRP continues to maintain within many academic circles. We will have become critical of the objectification of 'isms' that are classified as the world's major religions. We will have noted and sought ways to overcome the description of religions according to a list of beliefs, as if they could be studied just like a Christian systematic theology. And we will have understood that religion in the abstract means nothing unless we place it into the contexts in which it is practised on the ground in a myriad of local expressions. If my task in this Foreword has been to suggest what comes 'before' the 'after' referred to in the title of this book, I hope to have shown that reflecting on the significance of Wilfred Cantwell Smith's contribution to this project is a good place to begin.

References

Bowker, John. 1997. "Brahman or Brahma". In *The Oxford Dictionary of World Religions*, edited by John Bowker, 163. Oxford and New York: Oxford University Press.

Cox, James L. 2006. *A Guide to the Phenomenology of Religion. Key Figures, Formative Influences and Subsequent Debates*. London and New York: T and T Clark International.

Cox, James L. 2007. *From Primitive to Indigenous: The Academic Study of Indigenous Religions*. Aldershot: Ashgate.

Cox, James L. 2010. *An Introduction to the Phenomenology of Religion*. London and New York: Continuum.

Cox, James L. 2013. "The Transmission of an Authoritative Tradition: That Without Which Religion Is Not Religion." In *Alternative Voices: A Plurality Approach for Religious Studies*, edited by Afe Adogame, Magnus Echtler and Oliver Freiberger, 308–323. Göttingen: Vandenhoeck and Ruprecht.

Cox, James L. 2014. "Phenomenological Perspectives on the Social Responsibility of the Scholar of Religion." In *New Trends and Recurring Issues in the Study of Religion*, edited by Abraham Kovács and James L. Cox, 133–151. Budapest: L'Harmattan.

Cox, James L. 2015. "Religious Memory as a Conveyor of Authoritative Tradition: The Necessary and Essential Component in a Definition of Religion." *Journal of the Irish Society for the Academic Study of Religions* 2(1): 5–23. Online: http://jisasr.org/current-issue-21-2015

Fitzgerald, Timothy. 2000. *The Ideology of Religious Studies*. Oxford and New York: Oxford University Press.

Hervieu-Léger, Danièle. 1999. "Religion as Memory. Reverence to Tradition and the Constitution of a Heritage of Belief in Modern Societies." In *The Pragmatics of Defining Religion. Contexts, Concepts and Contests*, edited by Jan G. Platvoet and Arie L. Molendijk, 73–92. Leiden: Brill.

Radhakrishnan, S., trans. 1974. *The Principal Upanishads*. London: Allen and Unwin.

Smith, Wilfred Cantwell. 1964 [1962]. *The Meaning and End of Religion. A New Approach to the Religious Traditions of Mankind*. New York: Mentor Books.

Smith, Wilfred Cantwell. 1981. *Towards a World Theology. Faith and the Comparative History of Religion*. Philadelphia: The Westminster Press.

Smith, Wilfred Cantwell. 1998a [1979]. *Faith and Belief: The Difference Between Them*. Oxford: Oneworld.

Smith, Wilfred Cantwell. 1998b [1962]. *Patterns of Faith around the World*. Oxford: Oneworld.

1

INTRODUCTION

The World Religions Paradigm in contemporary Religious Studies

Christopher R. Cotter and David G. Robertson

> Let us take the old saying, *divide et impera*, and translate it somewhat freely as 'classify and conquer.'
>
> *(Müller 1873, 122–123)*

> The history of the study of religion is the dramatic story of the complex relationship between European Enlightenment concepts about the nature of religion and the violent reality experienced by people and cultures all over the world who were conquered and colonized by Europeans.
>
> *(Chidester 1996, xiii)*

Classify and conquer: taxonomies and power

In the Preface to his *The Order of Things* (1973), Michel Foucault – French philosopher, social theorist, literary critic and turtleneck-wearer – cites Jorge Luis Borges' essay 'The Analytical Language of John Wilkins' (1942) in order to problematize scholars' uncritical use of taxonomies. Borges' essay (whose title refers to a seventeenth-century philosopher who proposed a universal language with a grammar based on taxonomic classification) presents an alternative taxonomy, ostensibly drawn from an ancient Chinese encyclopedia, *Celestial Emporium of Benevolent Knowledge*, which organizes animals into fourteen categories:

1. Those that belong to the emperor
2. Embalmed ones
3. Those that are trained
4. Suckling pigs
5. Mermaids
6. Fabulous ones

7. Stray dogs
8. Those that are included in this classification
9. Those that tremble as if they were mad
10. Innumerable ones
11. Those drawn with a very fine camel hair brush
12. *Et cetera*
13. Those that have just broken the flower vase
14. Those that, at a distance, resemble flies

(in Foucault 1973, xv; cf. McCutcheon 2014, 142).

To most, this seems like an arbitrary or even ridiculous system of classification. The point that Foucault is making, however, is that objectively it is no more arbitrary than any other system, simply less familiar because we have not internalized its rules.

If we were to ask the reader for today's date, they would almost certainly reply (at time of writing) 'Friday, the thirteenth of February 2015'.[1] They would be far less likely to reply '23 Rabi II 1436', 'Cycle 78, year 31, month 12, day 25' or '13.0.2.3.4'. Yet none of these 'is' the 'real' date any more than any of the others, but rather they reflect different cultural contexts. Moreover, they encode particular epistemological and cosmological assumptions, and when examined critically, issues of power. According to Critical Theory, the criteria by which such distinctions are made do not describe reality, but rather the assumptions of those making them. These taxonomies therefore represent the intersection of knowledge and power – what Foucault would call a particular 'episteme' (1973, xxii). Such arrangements are neither universal, natural nor eternal, but claim to be – and when fully internalized, will appear to be.

This volume is concerned with perhaps the most obvious example of such a taxonomy in the discourse on religion, the World Religions Paradigm (WRP). The WRP typically includes 'the Big Five' (where does that term come from?) of Christianity, Islam, Judaism, Hinduism and Buddhism – and moreover, almost always presented in that Abrahamocentric order – increasingly with additional 'catch-all' categories such as 'indigenous religions' or 'new religions' included.

The publication of *The Norton Anthology of World Religions* in 2014 demonstrates how entrenched this taxonomy is for both the public and, more problematically, academia. Indeed, with university Religious Studies (RS) departments becoming more and more structured around a series of area studies scholars rather than method and theory specialists or generalists, the question of which 'traditions' are to be represented is arguably more important than ever. In this introduction we lay out, first, the development of the WRP as a classificatory schema, and second, the robust critique that it has sustained in recent decades. This will be necessarily brief, but aims to offer a useful 'potted history' for students and their teachers, while pointing towards the sources through which the critique can be pursued fully. Discussion then turns to contemporary problems with putting this critique into practice within introductions to the academic study of religion, before providing a brief overview of the chapters that follow.

Given that the history of the WRP is intimately tied up with the history of RS itself, it is fitting that we begin our discussion with the development of the category 'religion'.

You can't say 'World Religions Paradigm' without saying 'religion' ...

The WRP is intimately bound up with the development of the category of 'religion'[2] and its 'semantically parasitic' other (Fitzgerald 2007, 54), the 'secular'. A discussion of these categories will help contextualize the way in which the WRP was formed, and explain the origin of the very notion that a plurality of 'religions' existed that could be placed within a paradigm. As Brent Nongbri notes,

> the *particular* concept of religion is absent in the ancient world. The very idea of 'being religious' requires a companion notion of what it would mean to be 'not religious,' and this dichotomy was not part of the ancient world.
>
> *(2013, 4)*

Sweeping through history, the term 'religio' can be encountered in a Roman context, primarily in relation to the rites and traditions connected with the ancestors (King 1999, 35–36). According to Brent Nongbri, it makes an appearance in early Latin comedies, where it appears to mean something more along the lines of 'scruples' or 'manners', and was not associated with gods until around the first century BCE (Nongbri 2013, 27). In the writings of Lucretius (99–c. 55 BCE) for example, 'religio' seems to refer to something almost the same as our modern 'superstition'; people could become overcome by 'religio' because of wrong ideas or 'excessive concern' regarding gods (2013, 28). Among the Latin Christians, Tertullian, etc., we encounter the 'religio' or 'religiones' (worship practice/practices) of Christians, and the religiones of others, where the term is deployed in a manner more akin to a racial or ethnic discourse of the modern day (2013, 29). Augustine's 'de vera religio' – 'on true religion' – is similarly suggestive of a meaning of 'worship'; 'our religio is not the religio of other gods, of idols', 'our religio is the religio of the one god', etc. (2013, 30–31).

In the medieval period, however, we see the emergence of the twin concepts 'religiosus' and 'saecularis' as indicative of different types of ecclesiastical vows (Nongbri 2013, 5). To be 'religious' meant to pursue a monastic life, while 'secular' designated those in the 'ordinary' clergy working within the world outside the monastery (Asad 1993, 39). According to Charles Taylor, this development of a religious/secular binary highlighted a perceived distinction between 'ordinary' or 'profane' time, as opposed to 'spiritual' or 'God's' time, and 'reflected something fundamental about Christendom', the view that 'a less than full embedding in the secular [was ...] essential to the vocation of the church' (1998, 32; in Knott 2005, 64). However, it is at the dawn of the Enlightenment period, and the beginning of the colonial encounter, that these terms begin to take on forms more familiar to us today.

Timothy Fitzgerald's *Discourse on Civility and Barbarity* (2007) features an extended discussion of the writings of an English vicar named Samuel Purchas, which he utilizes – along with other case studies – to build a convincing case that until the early Enlightenment/colonial period 'there was arguably no concept in the English language either of "a religion" or of "secular neutrality"', but that '[r]eligion almost always has meant Christian Truth and civility, and was invariably contrasted with barbaric superstitions' (2007, 283). According to Fitzgerald, in 1615 Purchas had

> not only referred to the 'religions' of India, China, Japan, the Americas, and many other parts of the world, but had attempted to analyse and describe them .... His usage, however, was ironic, since in his understanding 'religion' meant Christian (or more precisely Protestant Christian) Truth, and when applied to others the term 'religions' really meant its opposite, superstitions, and thus pagan and irrational misunderstandings. Yet arguably we can see a wobble in his text between irony and straightforward generic usage.
>
> *(2007, 9)*

Samuel Purchas, then, stands in a long line of male authors who were encountering and theorizing the 'other' for the first time, and from a perspective of normative Christianity. Indeed, in some of the earliest accounts of the 'New World' (see J. Z. Smith 1998, 269) we read of 'natives' who went 'without shame, religion or knowledge of God' (Eden 1553), or who 'observ[ed] no religion as we understand it' (Cieza de León 1553). As Jonathan Z. Smith simply but forcefully states, 'the question of the "religions" arose in response to an explosion of data' (1998, 275) and thus by the late 1700s it made linguistic sense for Thomas Jefferson to state that there are 'probably a thousand different systems of religion' of which 'ours is but one of that thousand' (1787, 267). The seeds had been sown from which the Victorian Science of Religion – and the WRP – would spring, and to which discussion shall shortly turn.

Owing in no small part to the intellectualization and individualization of the Protestant Reformation, at the same time as the notion of distinct 'religions' emerges, we begin to see the emergence of the idea of religion as a private, personal, and individual affair, as a matter between the individual 'believer' and 'God'. We see, for example, in Thomas Hobbes' *Leviathan* (1651) an outspoken example of this 'independent ethic, in which religion in general, and "Christian religion" in particular, was located in the private sphere, the realm of conscience, apart from the public sphere of the state' (Knott 2005, 66). For Hobbes,

> The maintenance of civil society depend[s] on justice, and justice on the power of life and death, and other less rewards and punishments residing in them that have the power of the Commonwealth; it is impossible a Commonwealth should stand where any other than the sovereign hath a power of giving greater rewards than life, and inflicting greater punishment than death.
>
> *(1651, 275)*

Here we begin to see the development of the secular as the 'default' state from which 'religions' deviate, something that will be of particular significance when we discuss the legacy of the WRP below.

'Mixed motivations': the Science of Religion

The Victorian 'Science of Religion' was at its core an attempt to produce a typology of 'religions', as per Linnaeus's classification of the natural world or Darwin's proposition of the evolutionary links between the species. Indeed, '[o]nly an adequate taxonomy would convert a "natural history" of religion into a science' (J. Z. Smith 1998, 276). As F. Max Müller, one of the most influential scholars behind the development of the WRP, framed the question, 'How is the vast domain of religion to be parcelled out?' (1873, 123). Terence Thomas describes the emerging Science of Religion as a 'situation of mixed motivations' (2000, 74), with three significant factors – scientific (and particularly Darwinian), theological and colonialist – which shall each be discussed below.

In popular discourse, and distressingly often academic discourse also, 'science' is constructed as a disinterested, objective account of an underlying reality. This argument originates with Victorian positivists like Auguste Comte, and has been repeated by many RS scholars, who 'claim that the methodologies used in this discipline are objective and neutral in that they neither presuppose nor preclude any particular religious commitment' (King 1999, 47). Twentieth-century philosophy has made it clear, however, that such objectivity is difficult and perhaps impossible to achieve. Indeed, the institution of 'science' itself exists within particular social, cultural and political contexts. The 'Science of Religion' is a perfect case in point. How these scholars defined 'religion' and how these definitions were used to create typologies did not dispassionately describe 'reality', but rather simultaneously reflected and reinforced the presuppositions – and therefore the concerns – of those with the power to make such proscriptions. Their typologies did not disinterestedly describe religions, but implicitly ranked them.

For C. P. Tiele, the 'World Religions' – Buddhism, Islam and, of course, Christianity – were those which had 'found their way to different races and peoples and … profess the intention to conquer the world' (1884, 368). Their supposed dynamism set them apart from the other 'ethical religions', such as Judaism and Taoism, which were characterized by being founded on 'holy' scriptures or laws, but are 'generally limited to a single race or nation' (1884, 366). These were in turn superior to the 'nature religions' which were divided into 'polydaemonistic magical religions', 'organized' or 'unorganized magical religions', and 'anthropomorphic polytheism' (ibid.). For Tiele, the 'ancient faiths and primitive modes of worship' must either 'reform themselves as the model of the superior religion' (i.e. the World Religions), or inevitably 'draw nearer and nearer to extinction' (1884, 369). Tiele's typology is therefore both Darwinian and unambiguously theologically normative.

Müller, however, inverted this evolutionary trajectory, seeing religions as degenerating from the purity of their inspired origins towards populist superstition and mythology, which he described as 'the dialectic life of religion' (1873, 274). He singled Hinduism out for particular criticism, describing it as 'a half-fossilised megatherion walking about in the broad daylight of the nineteenth century' (1873, 279). The emphasis on texts reflected Müller's linguistic training, but perhaps less obviously, his Protestant German upbringing: his insistence on the purity of inspired texts was also an implicit critique of priestly, ritualistic Catholicism and its supposed idolatrous materiality.

Tiele and Müller's versions differ in significant respects from one another, both in the evolutionary trajectories and in which religions were singled out for praise or scorn (Christianity again the exception, with Müller describing Christianity as 'the fulfilment of the hopes and desires of the whole world' (1873, 148–9)). Yet they have in common that each utilized an ostensibly scientific model derived from Protestant Christianity, which prioritized 'belief' and 'doctrine' as preserved in texts as the *sine qua non* of 'religion' (Lopez Jr. 1998, 21). On the colonial frontiers, this meant that either it was thought that there simply was no religion there (Chidester 1996), or these contexts were constructed as exemplifying a 'primal' or 'primitive' form of religion (Cox 2007). In other cases where the traditions could not be so easily marginalized, they would be constructed according to Protestant norms, notably in the case of Hinduism, where the role of the Vedas was exaggerated and the supposed trinity of Brahma, Siva and Vishnu was promoted. For many scholars – as typified perhaps most famously by Mircea Eliade in the middle of the twentieth century – these different religions were seen as exemplars of a *sui generis* 'religion' (see McCutcheon 1997), whereby 'Religion in its essence is one and the same thing. Exceedingly varied as may be the forms which it assumes, it does not itself vary or undergo change' (Jordan 1986 [1905], 19).[3] Echoing Linnaeus, this model – a genus ('Religion') which contains a discrete group of species ('World Religions') distinguished (often implicitly) by textual traditions, a stress on orthodoxy rather than orthopraxy and some degree of universal ambition – was to form the basis of the emerging academic study of religion. Indeed, the knowledge gained in this new academic field could be utilized as 'counter-propaganda' (Thomas 2000, 74). This theologically informed model was used to support the proselytization of Christianity in the colonies, as it was presented as the paragon of religions over what was perceived as 'primitive', or completely absent.

Colonialism forms the third factor impacting the emergence of the WRP. As noted above, '[t]he question of the "religions" arose in response to an explosion of data' (J. Z. Smith 1998, 275) brought about by the colonial encounter. Müller and Tiele were both embedded within countries deeply invested in colonial expansion. The British Empire was the largest empire in history, including one quarter of the world's population at its apex in 1921. The East India Company, who had been granted a special sanction to trade in India, Hong Kong, Singapore and Malaysia and often assisted with administration for the British Empire, acted as patron to Müller, funding his move to Oxford and commissioning his translated edition of the Rig Veda (4 vols, 1849–1874). Regarding Tiele's colonial connections, the Dutch Empire grew steadily from 1602 until 1940, and was similarly operated primarily through privately owned trading companies. So Thomas's observation that 'political motivation [was] at the heart of much study of religions' (2000, 77) is appropriate, as there was in fact a practical, economic purpose for such study. As F. D. Maurice observed in 1847, knowledge of other religions was especially useful if you were 'engaged in trading with other countries, or in conquering them, or in keeping possession of them' (1877, 255; c.f. Huston Smith's *The Religions of Man* (1958) and the Müller quotation at the top of this chapter) – or as Thomas wittily suggests, 'not so much a case of "know thy enemy" as "know thy trading partner"' (2000, 77).[4]

The colonies – or more accurately, subjugated men and women – were rich sources of materials. These included raw materials such as minerals, wood, plants and animals, cultural products such as new flavours, fashions, literature, art, philosophies and religious texts, and until the late nineteenth century, people themselves in the form of slaves. So knowledge of 'native' religions became important, both for jurisdiction through law-making and censuses (the case of 'Hinduism' here being a significant example), and for predicting how the indigenous population would respond to various requests and demands. Ironically, in some cases (most obviously, Hinduism and African religions) the post-colonial response was for these people to normalize and homogenize their traditions of belief and practice into 'World Religions' recognizable to Protestant Christians. In aiming to be treated as an equal, they implicitly restated the perceptions of the oppressor.

Critiques of the WRP

The WRP has been subjected to a sustained and rigorous critique in the academic study of religion for many years[5] and, for our purposes, this critique can be divided into three strands: that the WRP constructs 'religion' according to an ostensibly Protestant Christian model; that it is 'deeply implicated ... in the discourses of modernity, especially ... in technologies of power' (Jantzen 1998, 8); and that it encourages an uncritical *sui generis* model of 'religion'.

The first of these strands can be articulated quite simply: despite its non-partisan and inclusive appearance, the WRP has 'remodelled [non-Christian religions] according to liberal Western Protestant Christian values' (Owen 2011, 258), whereby one's religion 'is imprinted on the heart' in the form of beliefs, and 'manifests itself in outward observances of various kinds, [... such as] rituals, ceremonies, and customs' (Fitzgerald 2007, 216). As Donald Lopez Jr. has noted,

> Belief appears as a universal category because of the universalist claims of the tradition in which it has become most central, Christianity. Other religions have made universalist claims, but Christianity was allied with political power, which made it possible to transport its belief to all corners of the globe ..., making belief the measure of what religion is understood to be. Belief, then, or perhaps the demand that there be belief, is implicated both in the activities

of Christian missionaries and in the 'native' efforts (and those of their invited and uninvited surrogates) to counter them.

(1998, 33)

We see this particularly evidenced in swathes of scholarship on 'African' religions, where one finds African deities described as 'eternal, omnipresent, omnipotent, omniscient', etc., the ultimate argument being 'that African deities have identical attributes with those of the Christian God' (p'Bitek 1990, 80; cf. Cox 2014, 1). Of course, we must not assume that this 'Christianizing' of 'other religions' was the explicit intent of those engaged in their study. Indeed, as Masuzawa details in her discussion of Buddhism, those nineteenth-century scholars who were engaged in the construction or 'discovery' of Buddhism as a 'non-national ... qualitatively universal(istic) ... world religion' seemed to do so quietly and automatically 'without either an express endorsement or an audible objection on the part of the scholars specializing in Buddhism' (2005, 137–138). Many examples can be marshalled against this reification of a belief component to 'religion' – from well-documented self-identifying 'secular Jews' to the 'situational belief' of many 'ordinary' British churchgoers (Stringer 2008) – and one can only speculate as to how different the Science of Religion might have been had it developed in contexts where non-Protestant traditions had been historically dominant.

The entanglement of the WRP with technologies of power has been alluded to throughout our discussion of its development and relationship with Protestant Christianity. For starters, the division of humanity into adherents of the 'Big Five' religions plus miscellaneous 'others' reflects an underlying political and economic discourse on what matters to 'us'. Indeed, a 'world religion' appears to be

a tradition that has achieved sufficient power and numbers to enter our history to form it, interact with it, or thwart it. We recognise both the unity within and the diversity among the world religions because they correspond to important geopolitical entities with which we must deal. All 'primitives,' by way of contrast, may be lumped together, as may the 'minor religions,' because they do not confront our history in any direct fashion. From the point of view of power, they are invisible.

(J. Z. Smith 1998, 280)

These invisible Others most obviously take the form of non-Western religions, or minority and new religions in the West, but the power imbalance of the WRP is not confined to the imbalance of colonial centres and peripheries (Owen 2011, 255); it further prioritizes the accounts of elites within specific traditions and communities. For example, as Owen notes, 'Hinduism as a World Religion does not include Hinduism as a village religion' (2011, 255). We see this in textbooks which distinguish between codified theologies and 'unsophisticated' beliefs on the ground (Weightman 1996, 294). Indeed, the focus on texts itself prioritizes elite accounts over those of the illiterate. Moreover, '[n]either Sanskrit nor Pali are vernacular languages, thus they cannot reflect the religious opinions of the nonliterate masses in anything other than an indirect manner' (King 1999, 66).

However, the West and 'the rest' is not the only imbalance inherent in the WRP. This elitism is further reflected in gender imbalance. Colonialism, the rationalism enshrined by the Enlightenment and the WRP itself are the products of men, as demonstrated by the dominance of male scholars in the history of the field (and, indeed, even continuing into the pages of this book). Feminist critiques throughout the twentieth century contributed significantly to a destabilization of the certainties embedded within the dominant 'enlightened' discourse of the West. This critique was realized in many important works of cultural anthropology, including the work of Mary Douglas, Ruth Benedict and other female scholars whose focus on the colonial periphery helped to significantly undermine the gendered and theologically inherited categories of established scholarly research.

These and other power dynamics are inherent in the act of classifying certain social phenomena as '(world) religions'. Timothy Fitzgerald argues forcefully that '[r]eligion is a modern invention which authorises and naturalises a form of Euro-American secular rationality. In turn, this supposed position of secular rationality constructs and authorises its "other," religion and religions' (2007, 6). He goes on to demonstrate that when scholars project 'religion' on to different contexts and languages, there is ambiguity surrounding whether they are imagining religion to be indistinguishable from culture, radically separated from the 'profane' world, or simply a projection 'of the Western religion–secular dichotomy, whereby religious practices are assumed to be different in kind from political, economic, and technical/instrumental ones' (2007, 104–105). More often than not, the projection of religion onto others – whether within or without our 'own' culture – involves being part of a hegemonic structure whereby politics and economics are constructed as inherently natural and rational. We see this logic at work in the administration of 'religion' through censuses and other state apparatus, where the WRP-inflected presumption is that an individual will be an adherent of a single 'faith' in a simple either–or binary, and that the number of adherents of specific traditions relates in some way to their legitimacy (see Chryssides *et al.* 2012).

Finally, by reifying vast swathes of human thought and activity into discrete 'isms', we present 'religions' as having both essence and agency. In such a model, it is not human beings, but Hinduism, Buddhism, etc. which compete, evolve, engage in dialogue and teach things (Suthren Hirst and Zavos 2005, 5). For example, Jack Miles, General Editor of *The Norton Anthology of World Religions* (Miles 2014a), describes how the volume 'responds to a simple desire … that the six major, living, international world religions speak to readers *in their own words*' (2014b, xli; emphasis added). The idea that such a 'religious essence' exists which can express itself, independent of any human agency, is the *sui generis* model which, in the words of Russell McCutcheon, 'deemphasizes difference, history, and sociopolitical context in favour of abstract essences and homogeneity' (1997, 3). It presumes that the category of religion names a specific and stable set of things in the world set apart from all others. We argue, with Steven Ramey, that religion 'does not have agency to teach or do anything' but is constructed by individuals who interpret practices and texts that they associate with religion/s 'in ways that relate to their particular context and the range of interests that enliven that context' (2014, 109). The WRP is one such construction, but one which has gained the hegemonic status of ahistorical, universal 'common sense'. This makes our mission of deconstruction simultaneously all the more difficult and all the more important. The non-confessional social-scientific study of religion must be self-reflexive and self-critical, and cognizant of the political and social implications of its influence upon media discourse and state apparatus such as censuses (Owen 2011, 260).

To conclude this section, rather than promoting critical thinking, we argue that the continued uncritical use of the WRP fosters a breeding ground for relativistic navel-gazing which has no place in the contemporary research university. Yet in spite of the critiques outlined above becoming an established part of the Religious Studies corpus, the need for scholars to continually remind their colleagues of the efficacy of these critiques has yet to abate (Owen 2011; Taira 2013; Beyer et al. 2013). The following section asks just why it is that the model remains so resiliently entrenched.

'Chairs on the *Titanic*': problems of operationalization of critiques

> An introductory course, then, is a first step in [training in argument about interpretations]. Arguments and interpretations are what we introduce, our particular subject matter serves merely as the excuse, the occasion, the 'e.g.'
>
> (J. Z. Smith 2013, 14)

Arguably, the area in which the WRP has proven most resilient is in pedagogy, and particularly in introductory courses on 'religion' (Owen 2011, 253). These courses may be students' only encounter with university-level Religious Studies, and have a major impact upon public perception of the field itself, and upon teaching throughout primary and secondary education (Geaves 2005). Distressingly, this tendency shows little sign of abeyance. For example, Simon Weightman, writing in John R. Hinnells' *A New Handbook of Living Religions* (1996), a textbook that is still widely used in RS introductory courses in the UK,[6] claims that:

> Hinduism displays few of the characteristics that are generally expected of a religion. It has no founder, nor is it prophetic. It is not creedal, nor is any particular doctrine, dogma or practice held to be essential to it. It is not a system of theology, nor a single moral code, and the concept of god is not central to it. There is no specific scripture or work regarded as being uniquely authoritative. Finally, it is not sustained by an ecclesiastical organization. Thus it is difficult to categorize Hinduism as a 'religion' using normally accepted criteria.
>
> (Weightman 1996, 261)

These criteria apply strictly only to prevalent models of Christianity and Islam, and therefore convey a very limited idea of 'normal'. Sadly, however, this bias is by no means unusual. A North American volume, *Teaching and Learning in College Introductory Religion Courses* (Walvoord 2007), despite a welcome focus on the practical aspects of pedagogy, divides the field into two: 'World Religions' and 'Theology, Bible, Christian Formation'. This not only reinforces the assumption that RS is either 'Christian' or 'Other', subscribing to the WRP explicitly, but seems unaware that RS can interrogate, rather than simply reproduce, such categories. It also problematically assumes that students' 'spiritual development' falls within the purview of RS.

This apologetic or even theological trajectory is also seen in the aforementioned *Norton Anthology*, which aims to assist readers 'to see others with a measure of open-ness, empathy, and good will' because, apparently, the aim of RS is to encourage 'human sympathy and cultural wisdom', and not to dispassionately analyse and critique discourses on 'religion', as these authors would suggest (Miles 2014b, 1). *The Norton Anthology* reproduces Weightman's problematic typology in other ways too; for example, it is explicitly based upon 'foundational' texts (back cover), yet admits that 'no canons existed for the literatures of the world's major religions' (Miles 2014b, xliii), and that the editors would be 'creating for the field of religious studies a first draft of the very canon that it lacked', as though this were the point of such a volume (2014b, xiv). Steven Ramey has recently argued that although we can debate the significance of such problems within many areas of RS, 'the[ir] prevalence … in the textbook market is particularly pronounced' (2014, 110). Textbooks frequently reinforce students' desire to find the 'right answer' concerning others' religious beliefs and practices (ibid.), and can be viewed as participating in a dominant political discourse that promotes sameness whilst marginalizing difference (McCutcheon 1997, 161). Even a more nuanced example, Mark Juergensmeyer's *Teaching the Introductory Course in Religious Studies* (1991), which includes contribu-tions from many of Religious Studies' (then) leading authorities and useful opinion essays on how one should/might teach the introductory course, rather uncritically adopts the very paradigm against which the present volume is designed. Before turning to an overview of the chapters presented within, our case is strengthened by briefly considering three prevalent pedagogical strategies that further shore up the WRP.

As noted above, the WRP as articulated today almost always includes 'the Big Five', although increasingly we see an additional sixth category added, such as 'East Asian traditions' (Confucianism, Daoism, Shinto) (MacWilliams *et al.* 2005, 2), indigenous religions, or less commonly, new or alternative religious movements. This is by no means universal, with *The Norton Anthology* reintroducing Daoism as the sixth-place category and ignoring indigenous and alternative religions altogether. The reasons given for the selection of these traditions are that these six, and no others, are 'major', 'living' and 'international' (2014, xlviii). Obviously, many criticisms might be offered here, such as whether Daoism is living, or Hinduism an international 'equal alongside other world religions' (Weightman 1996, 301), especially given that other textbook authors have advanced the view that 'religions characterized under the rubric of traditional African religion have now attained an international status that qualifies them as members of the world religions' (Gore 2002, 226). The simplest criticism is, of course, that 'major' is quite plainly a value judgement. Moreover, it is stated in passing that the main reason for the omission of African religions is that they lack canonical texts (Miles 2014b, xlviii). In essence, such approaches explicitly reject the category while continuing to use the same typology (see, for example, Juergensmeyer 1991; Woodhead *et al.* 2002; Walvoord 2007). Rearranging 'the deckchairs on the *Titanic*', as Sutcliffe puts it in his chapter in this volume.[7]

Although these moves might seem at first a positive step, what such tinkering does is to further entrench the typology. The expanded WRP adds additional categories which act as 'pressure valves', allowing for voices which otherwise do not fit. Such incorporation essentially forces those traditions to behave like World Religions – for example, encouraging various African systems (plural) to be seen (and to see themselves) as 'African Religion' (singular), homogenizing difference and historical development, prioritizing certain structural features such as texts, institutions and 'high gods', and forcing a distinction between 'religious' and 'secular' systems. In so doing, differences and contradictions which might potentially challenge the presuppositions of the WRP are co-opted in its service, sometimes against the best intentions of authors and teachers constrained by the prevalent logics of textbook construction and use (Larsson 2014, 312), and similar pressures surrounding the construction of introductory courses. Where new syllabi are constructed, 'the approach of the course does not [necessarily] change significantly', remaining 'implicitly, if not explicitly, concerned with examining and comparing' seemingly autonomous 'religions' (McCutcheon 1997, 104).

A second approach is to talk primarily of 'Lived Religion', i.e. 'religion as expressed and experienced in the lives of individuals' (McGuire 2008, 3),[8] rather than in the systematized theologies of male elites. Such approaches, through their focus on the particular and contextual, 'challenge … the "World Religions" approach of religious studies with its focus on discrete, generic traditions, and normative beliefs and practices' by 'starting from the particular rather than the general and focusing on what happens to religion' within specific contexts (Knott 2005, 118–119). However attractive such radical particularism might seem, it creates further pedagogical problems within the context of an introductory course or textbook. For a start, due to the constraints of time and space, a persistent danger is that the particularities become reified to generalities in students' minds – the many 'Christianities' become 'Christianity'. A potentially more serious pitfall, to which the authors can attest, is that this strategy runs the risk of producing a similarly entrenched problem to the generalities of the WRP, whereby students emerge from the introductory course with the attitude that 'anything goes', that all academic theorizing is worthless abstraction, and that subjective interpretations of individuals or local communities are what *really* matters, as opposed to history, tradition, etc.

Closely related to these is the 'Material Religion' approach, primarily promoted by David Morgan (beginning with 1999's *Visual Piety*). The Material Religion approach, which advocates studying specific physical objects involved in religious behaviour, has quickly become one of the most fashionable methodologies in contemporary Religious Studies, with numerous edited volumes, conferences and a journal focusing on it. By prioritizing material products, the argument goes, scholars avoid over-reliance on textual sources and speculation on abstracted 'beliefs', refocusing analysis towards everyday human behaviour – an aim the authors would support. Unfortunately, the Material Religion approach seems to inevitably slide into 'phenomenology by stealth'; as McCutcheon notes, talk quickly turns to how religion 'manifests' itself, or how objects 'embody the sacred' (McCutcheon 2013). Thus a methodology meant to focus only on the immanent turns to the transcendent, and scholars once again repeat the essentialist suppositions of Eliade, Otto and their ilk. Seeking to avoid the WRP, these approaches in fact further entrench the problems inherent in it.

It is worth noting that the accumulation of critique detailed above should not be taken as implying that the WRP – and these flawed attempts to avoid it – have no pedagogical value whatsoever. In fact, as we turn to the chapters contained within this volume, particularly those in the first part, it should become evident to the reader that strategically or subversively employing the WRP in classroom situations can be a rewarding pedagogical technique. The WRP is, after all, a culturally constructed symbol, metaphor, or tool, that functions to simplify, for 'good' or 'ill', areas of human behaviour that have been deemed 'religious', in a manner which efficiently communicates 'key points' to constituents of varied levels of ability and spans of attention. And, as many of the chapters in this volume demonstrate, a 'problematic book or text', for example, can 'be utilized as a pedagogical resource' (Larsson 2014, 312). In a limited sense, then, the WRP performs a service. However, as should be clear from the preceding discussion, problems occur when the WRP and other constructed paradigms are taken as constitutive of reality, and when said 'key points' are reified as *sui generis* 'facts', rather than the agenda- and power-laden intellectual constraints that they are. Thus, in addition to presenting viable approaches to RS which in no way presuppose the WRP, this volume considers possible ways forward for scholars who are required to teach a World Religions course, and reflects on how we can avoid alternative models succumbing to the same uncritical essentialism as the WRP itself.

Outline of chapters

The chapters that follow offer a broad range of innovative theoretical and methodological approaches, and directly address the variety of pedagogical challenges presented in different departmental, institutional and geographical contexts. The first part, 'Subversive pedagogies: data and methods', addresses the fact that for many academics, simply starting from scratch is not an option. Whether this is through institutional pressure, tradition, student preference, political factors or other reasons (cf. McCutcheon 1997, 104), in many cases the only way to reform the system is to employ subversive pedagogies – working with an established World Religions model and critiquing from within. Chapters in this part therefore start with the WRP, suggesting opportunities to interrogate or subvert it.

In the first chapter, 'The problem of "religions": teaching against the grain with "new age stuff"', Steven J. Sutcliffe (University of Edinburgh, UK) describes his experience of teaching sections on 'new age' formations in the context of a WRP-structured introductory course. For many academics, especially in the UK, this is a necessity; however, Sutcliffe argues that such content can 'punch above its weight' by offering a theoretical challenge to the students' received understanding of the self-evident existence of plural 'religions'. Rather, drawing on the work of R.D. Baird and J.Z. Smith, he argues that new age formations can be used as empirical evidence for 'the more theoretically adaptable and resistable concept of "religion"'.

'"Not a task for amateurs": graduate instructors and Critical Theory in the World Religions classroom' offers a different take on the same problem, by focusing on the role of postgraduate tutors and instructors who do not have any power to challenge the structure of introductory courses. Reflecting on their time at Florida State University, USA, Tara Baldrick-Morrone, Michael Graziano and Brad Stoddard argue that such roles nevertheless offer rich possibilities for introducing critical reflection, with the tutor/instructor essentially offering a meta-critique of the course structure itself. They suggest that using the course textbooks as data, contrasting how a particular issue is addressed or ignored by different texts, allows instructors to demonstrate that these books do not simply describe *sui generis* religious entities, but rather reflect the interests and biases of the scholars and academic culture which produced them. Further, they demonstrate how such texts can serve as examples that show how scholars of religion construct homogeneity from heterogenous empirical data.

An interesting further possibility is suggested in Steven W. Ramey's (University of Alabama, USA) chapter, 'The critical embrace: teaching the World Religions Paradigm as data'. While a 'World Religions' class may be an institutional requirement, Ramey suggests using the WRP itself as data. Using a traditional WRP-structured textbook critically allows teachers to introduce critique through a model with which they are already familiar, while exposing how the typology was constructed and reinforced by human beings with specific concerns and contexts. Ramey therefore advocates using the development of the WRP as a way into understanding the power plays behind the contemporary popular and academic discourse on religion.

Assuming that one is in a position to propose introductory courses which do not follow a World Religions model – what options are there? The second part, 'Alternative pedagogies: power and politics', offers theoretical models which can be used to explore and interrogate the category 'religion' without following the WRP. Of particular importance here is the issue of power: who benefits from 'world religions' – or 'religion', for that matter?

The first chapter in this part is Craig Martin's (St Thomas Aquinas College, USA) 'Religion as ideology: recycled culture vs. world religions'. Martin argues that introductory courses can be constructed around a scaffold of theoretical questions, with particular data or content being drawn from various 'world religions' in order to meet students' expectations halfway. Reflecting on his experiences teaching a pairing of seemingly orthodox WRP courses – 'Religions of the West' and 'Religions of the East' – and also the more provocatively titled 'The Evolution of Jesus', Martin demonstrates how one can deliver the basic content students desire, while taking a quasi-Marxist functional approach to show them how those basics are used, reused, and recycled in support of various social agendas in different times and places. He concludes, forcefully, that 'students are better served by courses that promote critical thinking as opposed to the accumulation of historical trivia'.

Teemu Taira's (University of Helsinki, Finland) 'Doing things with "religion": a discursive approach in rethinking the World Religions Paradigm' begins by outlining what taking a discursive approach to 'religion' might mean, arguing that while discourses on 'religion' might operate at all levels of society, their function varies enormously from situation to situation and requires detailed empirical study. Taira's chapter provides a practical guide for instantiating such an approach in the classroom, and argues for greater problematization, denaturalization and historicization of World Religions discourse, the introduction of ethnographic material to disrupt stable, pristine and homogeneous WRP-inflected presentations, and for explicit exploration of the category of 'religion' in the classroom. Finally, Taira presents a substantial overview of readings – some of which are explicitly 'discursive', and others that can be reinterpreted from a discursive point of view – that can be assigned to students or integrated into lectures by those wishing to pursue this approach.

Paul-François Tremlett (The Open University, UK) turns the discussion back to Marx, whose thinking underlies much of this part, and the critical study of religion. 'Looking back on the end of religion: opening re Marx' suggests engaging students in a critical reading of Marx in order to destabilize their assumption of reason as objective and disinterested, and move them towards 'a conception of reason as a social practice beyond the binary of subject-centred reason and experience' as suggested by Marcuse, Adorno, Habermas and others. This is done to demonstrate that the students are themselves implicated in the history of the WRP, and the idea of 'religion' itself.

The final chapter in this part focuses upon the contested category of 'the sacred' as a potentially useful tool for broadening and dissecting WRP-dominated approaches. In 'The sacred alternative', Suzanne Owen (Leeds Trinity University and University of Chester, UK) weaves theoretical discussion with an empirical example from a local Pagan festival in the UK to demonstrate the limitations of both the Durkheimian and Eliadean 'sacred' as an analytical framework in cases where 'religion' is ambiguous. Despite this, Owen argues that a focus on 'making sacred' as a human activity that highlights a group's interests is a useful pedagogical alternative to the WRP.

By this point, the volume has critiqued the WRP, subverted it, and provided alternatives to it – now we need to put these measures into practice. The final part of the volume, 'Innovative pedagogies: methods and media', presents innovative pedagogical techniques that facilitate the twenty-first century introduction to 'religion' and, by their very nature, avoid and problematize the WRP, whilst potentially increasing the transmission and internalization of this critique in the next generation of scholars. Can emergent pedagogical techniques be used alongside the methodological approaches already explored to create new ways to introduce Religious Studies? The following four chapters therefore offer alternative entry-points into conceptualizing 'religion'.

Food is the entry-point in Michel Desjardins' chapter, 'The Desjardins diet for World Religions Paradigm loss', which presents his course as run at Wilfrid Laurier University in Waterloo, Canada. Desjardins suggests that teachers can help students to think differently about 'religion' – and therefore the WRP – not by focusing on theory, but by 'creating learning spaces within a thematic course in which students can arrive at more complex understandings of human culture'. It is therefore an example of how using alternative data can help to destabilize preconceptions in the academic study of religion, allowing students to arrive at theoretical conclusions for themselves.

In 'Narrating the USA's religious pluralism: escaping world religions through media', David W. McConeghy (Chapman University, USA) describes his experiences using the PBS television documentary series 'God in America' as a primary and secondary source, and suggests that introductory students can avoid conventional paradigms that trap material into pre-existing models by deconstructing and closely examining the composition of religious narratives. Examining the trope of the United States as the world's most religiously diverse nation provides a powerful means to subvert the dominance of the WRP in the classroom. This creates many opportunities for students and teachers to reveal more complex lives and worldviews without homogenizing differences.

In 'Archaeology and the World Religions Paradigm: the European Neolithic, religion and cultural imperialism', Carole M. Cusack (University of Sydney, Australia) interrogates the idea that self-contained, boundaried 'World Religions' spread across geographical and temporal locations (via mission, imperialism, and colonialism), and then subjugated the indigenous religions of the dominated societies. Here the alternative entry point is archaeological data from Northern European Neolithic peoples, including the Stones of Stenness and the Ness of Brodgar in the Orkneys, and Stonehenge and Durrington Walls on Salisbury Plain. She argues that by using archaeological data rather than *a priori* religious categories, RS can be redirected towards 'a model that is non-elitist, fluid, and non-normative'.

Dominic Corrywright's (Oxford Brookes University, UK) 'Complex learning and the World Religions Paradigm: teaching religion in a shifting subject landscape' takes the issue of pedagogy head on. Rounding off this part of the book, the chapter aligns post-WRP approaches with emergent pedagogical techniques wherein students and teachers become co-pilots navigating a super-abundant sea of data. Corrywright demonstrates that analysis of categories and their deconstruction can be a core mode of teaching.

The volume is bookended by a Foreword from James L. Cox, whose accessible but nonetheless challenging work on the WRP inspired the editors' interest in the subject, and whose interview for the Religious Studies Project (Cox 2013) started the process which would culminate in this book; and an Afterword by Russell T. McCutcheon, who suggested the book and whose work has influenced many of the chapters herein. Both the Foreword and Afterword offer substantial commentary on the themes of this book, with Cox and McCutcheon bringing their own inimitable styles to bear on the work of Wilfred Cantwell Smith, the (de)classification of the 'planet' Pluto, and more. Our sincere thanks to them and all of the contributors.

Notes

1 That this particular date has symbolic significance reinforces the point. It is also worth noting contextual differences in numerical date formats: in the UK, for example, this date would be referred to as 13/02/2015, whereas in the US the dominant format is 02/13/15.
2 We encourage those interested in this development to seek out Timothy Fitzgerald's *Discourse on Civility and Barbarity* (2007), Tomoko Masuzawa's *The Invention of World Religions* (2005), Brent Nongbri's *Before Religion* (2013), or a number of other seminal works cited throughout this volume.
3 Andrew McKinnon traces this line of thought to the mid-nineteenth century, suggesting that Ludwig Feuerbach 'was the first to argue that "religion" in the generic sense was a single thing with a single essence' (2005, 29).
4 Similarly, in *Trying Leviathan: The Nineteenth-century New York Court Case That Put the Whale on Trial and Challenged the Order of Nature* (2007), D. Graham Burnett describes how the decision about whether a whale was a fish or a mammal came down ultimately to economic factors.
5 See, for example, Fitzgerald (2000; 2007), Lincoln (1992), Masuzawa (2005), McCutcheon (1997), Nongbri (2013) and J. Z. Smith (1978; 1998).
6 The authors are most familiar with textbooks that are utilized in the UK. See McCutcheon (2014) for a critique of some prominent textbooks in the USA – particularly Esposito *et al.* (2002) and Fisher (2003) – and Emanuelsson (2014) for an analysis of representations of Islam in textbooks prominent in Sweden.
7 See also McCutcheon (2014). Or, to continue with the zoological language from earlier in the chapter, as 'formulating the most appropriate accommodation arrangements for the animals on board the Tsimtsum', the Japanese freighter in Yann Martel's *Life of Pi*, a story that provides a useful pedagogical tool to both problematize assumptions about singular 'religious' identifications and the relationship between 'belief' and 'truth'.
8 See also many similar formulations, such as 'Everyday Religion' (Ammerman 2007), 'Folk Religion' (Yoder 1974), 'Vernacular Religion' (Primiano 1995; Bowman and Valk 2012) or 'Popular Religion' (Jolly 1996).

References

Ammerman, Nancy T. 2007. *Everyday Religion: Observing Modern Religious Lives*. Oxford: Oxford University Press.

Asad, Talal. 1993. *Genealogies of Religion: Discipline and Reasons of Power in Christianity and Islam*. Baltimore and London: Johns Hopkins University Press.

Beyer, Peter., James L. Cox, Mark Juergensmeyer, Craig Martin, Suzanne Owen and Steven J. Sutcliffe. 2013. "Podcast: After the World Religion Paradigm ...?" *The Religious Studies Project*, 1 March. http://www.religiousstudiesproject.com/2013/03/01/podcast-after-the-world-religion-paradigm/.

Borges, Jorge Luis. 1942. "The Analytical Language of John Wilkins," edited by Jan Frederik Solem, with Bjørn Are Davidsen and Rolf Andersen. Trans. Lilia Graciela

Vázquez. Available at http://www.alamut.com/subj/artiface/language/johnWilkins.html (accessed 15 May 2015).

Bowman, Marion and Ülo Valk, eds. 2012. *Vernacular Religion in Everyday Life: Expressions of Belief.* Sheffield: Equinox.

Burnett, D. Graham. 2007. *Trying Leviathan: The Nineteenth-century New York Court Case that Put the Whale on Trial and Challenged the Order of Nature.* Princeton: Princeton University Press.

Chidester, David. 1996. *Savage Systems: Colonialism and Comparative Religion in Southern Africa.* Charlottesville: University Press of Virginia.

Chryssides, George D., Christopher R. Cotter, David G. Robertson, Beth Singler, Bettina Schmidt and Teemu Taira. 2012. "Podcast: Religion in the 2011 UK Census." *The Religious Studies Project.* 14 December. http://www.religiousstudiesproject.com/2012/12/14/podcast-religion-in-the-2011-census/.

Cieza de León, Pedro. 1553. *Crónica del Perú.* 4 vols. Seville. Reprint 1918, edited by D. Enrique de Vedia, *Historiadores primitivos des Indias,* 2 vols. Madrid: Imprenta de los Sucesores de Hernando.

Cox, James L. 2007. *From Primitive to Indigenous: The Academic Study of Indigenous Religions.* Aldershot: Ashgate.

Cox, James L. 2013. "James Cox on the World Religions Paradigm." *The Religious Studies Project.* 25 February. http://www.religiousstudiesproject.com/podcast/podcast-james-cox-on-the-world-religions-paradigm/

Cox, James L. 2014. *The Invention of God in Indigenous Societies.* Durham: Acumen.

Eden, Richard. 1553. *A Treatyse of the Newe India.* London.

Emanuelsson, Jimmy. 2014. "Islam and the *Sui-Generis* Discourse: Representations of Islam in Textbooks Used in Introductory Courses of Religious Studies in Sweden." *Method & Theory in the Study of Religion* 26(1): 99–107.

Esposito, John L., Darrell J. Fasching and Todd Lewis. 2002. *World Religions Today.* 4th ed. New York: Oxford University Press.

Fisher, Mary Pat. 2003. *Living Religions.* 5th ed. New York: Prentice Hall.

Fitzgerald, Timothy. 2000. *The Ideology of Religious Studies.* New York and Oxford: Oxford University Press.

Fitzgerald, Timothy. 2007. *Discourse on Civility and Barbarity: A Critical History of Religion and Related Categories.* Oxford: Oxford University Press.

Foucault, Michel. 1973 [1966]. *The Order of Things: An Archaeology of the Human Sciences.* New York: Random House.

Geaves, Ron. 2005. "The Dangers of Essentialism: South Asian Communities in Britain and the 'World Religions' Approach to the Study of Religions." *Contemporary South Asia* 14 (1): 75–90.

Gore, Charles. 2002. "Religion in Africa." In *Religions in the Modern World,* edited by Linda Woodhead with Paul Fletcher, Hiroko Kawanami and David Smith, 204–230. London: Routledge.

Hinnells, John R., ed. 1996. *A New Handbook of Living Religions.* Oxford: Blackwell Publishing Ltd.

Hobbes, Thomas. 1651. *Leviathan.* London. Accessed at http://socserv2.socsci.mcmaster.ca/econ/ugcm/3ll3/hobbes/Leviathan.pdf

Jantzen, Grace. 1998. *Becoming Divine: Towards a Feminist Philosophy of Religion.* Manchester: Manchester University Press.

Jefferson, Thomas. 1787. *Notes on the State of Virginia.* London: Stockdale.

Jolly, Karen Louise. 1996. *Popular Religion in Late Saxon England: Elf Charms in Context.* Chapel Hill: University of North Carolina Press.

Jordan, Louis H. 1986 [1905]. *Comparative Religion: Its Genesis and Growth.* Atlanta: Scholars Press.

Juergensmeyer, Mark., ed. 1991. *Teaching the Introductory Course in Religious Studies: A Sourcebook.* Durham: Duke University Press.

King, Richard. 1999. *Orientalism and Religion: Postcolonial Theory, India and 'The Mystic East'.* London and New York: Routledge.

Knott, Kim. 2005. *The Location of Religion: A Spatial Analysis.* London and Oakville, CT: Equinox.

Larsson, Göran. 2014. "Textbooks and Critical Readings – a Challenge for the Future: A Brief Response to Emanuelsson and Ramey." *Method & Theory in the Study of Religion* 26 (3): 308–314.

Lincoln, Bruce. 1992. *Discourse and the Construction of Society: Comparative Studies of Myth, Ritual, and Classification.* New York: Oxford University Press.

Lopez Jr., Donald S. 1998. "Belief." In *Critical Terms for Religious Studies*, edited by Mark C. Taylor, 21–35. Chicago: University of Chicago Press.

MacWilliams, Mark, Joanne Punzo Waghorne, Deborah Sommer, Cybelle Shattuck, Kay A. Read, Salva J. Raj, Khaled Keshk, Deborah Halter, James Egge, Robert M. Baum, Carol S. Anderson and Russell T. McCutcheon. 2005. "Religion/s Between Covers: Dilemmas of the World Religions Textbook." *Religion Studies Review* 31(1–2): 1–35.

Masuzawa, Tomoko. 2005. *The Invention of World Religions, Or, How European Universalism Was Preserved in the Language of Pluralism.* Chicago: The University of Chicago Press.

Maurice, Frederick Denison. 1877 [1847]. *The Religions of the World and Their Relations to Christianity, Considered in Eight Lectures Founded by the Right Hon. Robert Boyle.* London: Macmillan.

McCutcheon, Russell T. 1997. *Manufacturing Religion: The Discourse on Sui Generis Religion and the Politics of Nostalgia.* New York and Oxford: Oxford University Press.

McCutcheon, Russell T. 2013. "Working, Not Wonking." *Culture on the Edge.* 13 December. http://religion.ua.edu/blog/2013/12/working-not-wonking/. (accessed 20 July 2014).

McCutcheon, Russell T. 2014 [2005]. "The Perils of Having One's Cake and Eating it Too: Some Thoughts in Response." In *Entanglements: Marking Place in the Field of Religion*, by Russell T. McCutcheon, 136–148. Sheffield: Equinox.

McGuire, Meredith. 2008. *Lived Religion: Faith and Practice in Everyday Life.* Oxford: Oxford University Press.

McKinnon, Andrew M. 2005. "Reading 'Opium of the People': Expression, Protest and the Dialectics of Religion." *Critical Sociology* 31 (January): 15–38.

Miles, Jack, ed. 2014a. *The Norton Anthology of World Religions.* 2 vols. New York: W.W. Norton.

Miles, Jack. 2014b. "Preface". In *The Norton Anthology of World Religions. Volume 1: Hinduism, Buddhism, and Daoism*, edited by Jack Miles, with Wendy Doniger, Donald S. Lopez Jr. and James Robson, xli–li. New York: W.W. Norton.

Morgan, David. 1999. *Visual Piety: A History and Theory of Popular Religious Images.* Oakland, CA: University of California Press.

Müller, Friedrich Max. 1873. *Introduction to the Science of Religion: Four Lectures Delivered at the Royal Institution with Two Essays on False Analogies, and the Philosophy of Mythology.* London: Longmans, Green.

Nongbri, Brent. 2013. *Before Religion: A History of a Modern Concept.* New Haven: Yale University Press.

Owen, Suzanne. 2011. "The World Religions Paradigm: Time for a Change." *Arts & Humanities in Higher Education* 10(3): 253–268.

p'Bitek, Okot. 1990. *African Religions in European Scholarship*. New York: ECA Associates.

Primiano, Leonard Norman. 1995. "Vernacular Religion and the Search for Method in Religious Folklife." *Western Folklore* 54(1): 37–56.

Ramey, Steven. 2014. "Textbooks, Assumptions, and Us: Commentary on Jimmy Emanuelsson's 'Islam and the *Sui-Generis* Discourse: Representations of Islam in Textbooks Used in Introductory Courses of Religious Studies in Sweden'." *Method & Theory in the Study of Religion* 26(1): 108–110.

Smith, Huston. 1958. *The Religions of Man*. New York: New American Library.

Smith, J. Z. 1978. *Map Is Not Territory: Studies in the History of Religion*. Leiden: Brill.

Smith, J. Z. 1998. "Religion, Religions, Religious." In *Critical Terms for Religious Studies*, edited by Mark C. Taylor, 269–284. Chicago, IL: University of Chicago Press.

Smith, J. Z. 2013. "The Introductory Course: Less Is Better." In *On Teaching Religion: Essays by Jonathan Z. Smith*, edited by Christopher I. Lehrich, 11–19. Oxford: Oxford University Press.

Stringer, Martin D. 2008. *Contemporary Western Ethnography and the Definition of Religion*. London: Continuum.

Suthren Hirst, Jacqueline, and John Zavos. 2005. "Riding a Tiger? South Asia and the Problem of 'Religion'." *Contemporary South Asia* 14(1): 3–20.

Taira, Teemu. 2013. "Making Space for Discursive Study in Religious Studies." *Religion* 43(1): 26–45.

Taylor, Charles. 1998. "Modes of Secularism." In *Secularism and Its Critics: Themes in Politics*, edited by Rajeev Bhargava, 32–53. New Delhi: Oxford University Press.

Thomas, Terence. 2000. "Political Motivations in the Development of the Academic Study of Religions in Britain." In *Perspectives on Method and Theory in the Study of Religion: Adjunct Proceedings of the XVIIth Congress of the International Association for the History of Religions, Mexico City, 1995*, edited by Armin W. Geertz and Russell T. McCutcheon, 74–90. Leiden: Brill.

Tiele, Cornelius Petrus. 1884. "Religions." In *Encyclopedia Britannica*, 358–371. 9th ed. Vol. 20.

Walvoord, Barbara E. 2007. *Teaching and Learning in College Introductory Religion Courses*. Chichester: Wiley-Blackwell.

Weightman, Simon. 1996. "Hinduism." In *A New Handbook of Living Religions*, edited by John R. Hinnells, 261–309. Oxford: Blackwell Publishing Ltd.

Woodhead, Linda, with Paul Fletcher, Hiroko Kawanami, David Smith, eds. 2002. *Religions in the Modern World*. London: Routledge.

Yoder, Don. 1974. "Toward a Definition of Folk Religion." *Western Folklore* 33(1): 2–15.

PART I

Subversive pedagogies: data and methods

2

THE PROBLEM OF 'RELIGIONS'

Teaching against the grain with 'new age stuff'

Steven J. Sutcliffe

The problem of 'religions'

> An examination of historically oriented works (and this is particularly true of intro-
> ductory textbooks), reveals the fact that the categories [*sic*] of 'the religions' are
> almost universally accepted and seldom if ever questioned.
>
> *(Baird 1971, 134)*

In *Imagining Religion* J. Z. Smith famously claimed that 'while there is a staggering
amount of data ... that might be characterized in one culture or another, by one
criterion or another, as religious – *there is no data for religion*' (J. Z. Smith 1982, xi). His
position was not so new, although he set it in neon in the title of his book and in the
manifesto tone of his italics. His claim in general terms had been anticipated (from a
rather different perspective) by Wilfred Cantwell Smith twenty years earlier, in *The
Meaning and End of Religion* (W. C. Smith 1991 [1962], 12), who argued that
'neither religion in general nor any one of the religions ... is in itself an intelligible
entity'. This was the case because, during the course of its evolution in Western Europe,
a 'process of reification' had set in: 'mentally making religion into a thing, gradually
coming to conceive of it as an objective systematic entity' (1991, 51). J. Z. Smith was
also anticipated by R. D. Baird's *Category Formation and the History of Religions*
(Baird 1971), which accepted W. C. Smith's critique of the plural form 'religions'
but rejected his attack on 'religion'. As Baird puts it: 'there is no point in eliminating
the use of the word "religion" simply because it is ambiguous or has been reified'
(1971, 17). Reviewing the historiographical evidence, and using 'Hinduism' and
'Buddhism' as examples of 'the broad and imprecise designations' inherent in the
concept of 'religions' (1971, 134), Baird argues that religion *simpliciter* is 'an adequate
primary category' (1971, 126) on grounds of its functional (or, better, stipulative)
quality.

Arguably Baird's positivist-inclined religion stands in relationship to Smith's 'relentlessly self-conscious' (J. Z. Smith 1982, xi) 'religion' as modernism to post-modernism. While Smith's conceptual reflexivity seems to be intended largely instrumentally, in terms of coaxing the realization that 'no datum expresses intrinsic interest' (1982, xi), there is a danger that Smith overplays his hand in stating that 'self-consciousness constitutes [the historian of religion's] primary expertise, his foremost object of study' (1982, xi). Since I consider religion rather than my (our) 'self-consciousness' to be my (our) 'foremost object of study', I prefer to see Smith's reflexivity anticipated in Baird's implicitly distanciating process of 'category formation'. I therefore tend toward Baird's position in the religion–'religion' dialectic, preferring his pragmatic use of religion as a category referring to material realities to the endlessly deferring signification of 'religion'. I accept J.Z. Smith's call to 'second order, reflective imagination', but I want to fuse this with the empirical intent demonstrated by Baird. What results is a form of reflexive modernism which I would argue forms a common ground on which Baird and Smith can meet. This means that, in Benavides' (2003) blunt riposte, 'there *is* data for religion' (emphasis added).

That said, it is not so much the heuristic adequacy of religion but the empirical inadequacy of 'religions' that I tackle here, in particular in terms of how to teach this in the classroom. I want to argue that 'religions' is more ideologically contaminated than religion due to being intimately tied up in legitimating the functional differentiation of the modern 'global' system into sealed domains (Beyer 2006), despite its historical virtue of inscribing plurality into what was long represented as unitary Christian truth. In this chapter I will try to show how a theoretical preference for religion over religions can be put to work through classroom exploration of 'new age/holistic spirituality'. For reasons of space my data is less empirical examples than their pedagogical construction, even though, as I have indicated, I want to defend Baird and Benavides against a strong reading of J. Z. Smith in order to claim that religion is most certainly 'out there' rather than 'constructed' (Hacking 1999) in the sense that it indexes 'a social and material arena of practice "done" by embodied others' (Sutcliffe 2004, xxiii–xxiv). I also follow the lead of Russell McCutcheon and 'get my hands dirty' in this chapter by doing my 'fieldwork' as 'a participant-observer-analyst of the scholarly profession of constructing religion[s]' (McCutcheon 1997, 7). My overall aim, then, is to teach 'no religions' while introducing students to the study of religion through analysis of 'new age/holistic spiritualities'. I will simply refer to this as 'new age stuff' to sidestep the complicated definitional debate on the substance and boundary of 'new age'.

The proposition that there are 'no religions' may seem counter-intuitive or even absurd. But as Baird (1971, 136) puts it: 'a study utilising "the religions" … is not historical since "the religions" are categories which, rather than growing out of an examination of historical data, are imposed upon a mass of material prior to its examination'. As I will show, 'world religions' is one common way to impose aprioristically on the 'mass of material', but it is not the only concept to reduce the complexity of the religious 'field', in a Bourdieuan sense, to the structural-functional circulation of authorized entities in a global system (Beyer 2006). Here I will slightly qualify my position by acknowledging a limited place – for example, in non-technical contexts, or perhaps where a more pressing point is at stake (although it is difficult to imagine what could be more pressing than our field's basic theoretical object) – of 'religions' as shorthand for plurality and heterogeneity since these qualities have strategic uses. But in the technical space of the classroom I do not use it since the term is based in the transposition of the abstract noun religion into the specific noun 'a religion'. The latter, pluralized, have come self-evidently to designate rationalized, multi-dimensional, bureaucratic organizations analogous to multi-national corporations whose leaders are effectively CEOs and whose members are obedient employees. This conception of what I call a 'religion entity' constitutes of the building blocks of post-Reformation Christian denominationalism. As a 'business model' it has come to influence 'modernizing' processes in denominational thinking, thus helping to cement the idea of the existence of multiple 'religions' in the modern world from the practitioners' side. But this shaping of the rich data for religion hides the will to power of the managerial classes on both academic and user sides under the cloak of an appealingly modernsounding, empirical, even scientific concept. As such it perpetuates a model of secularized Christian formations in a more insidious fashion than does the more theoretically adaptable and resistable concept of 'religion'.

'World religions' as symptom

In other words, it is the idea of 'religion entities' which legitimates the more familiar 'world religions'. The latter are sub-types of a more foundational concept and thus not the main culprit but certainly vital accessories. The classic modern source is C. P. Tiele's article 'Religions' (Tiele 1884), which introduces both concepts and shows their co-dependence. Tiele's progressive-sounding category 'religions' has been both a blessing and a curse: the former, because it re-established the crucial idea of plurality in data for religion (which existed in the classical world), helping us to move on from the unitary prototype bequeathed by early modern European history; the latter, because this new plural form, in the same article, gave birth to the familiar 'world' sub-type. In this article the terminology of the modern study of religion is rehearsed in microcosm as Tiele wrestles with various terms, toying with using 'universal' or 'world churches' (a giveaway), even opining that 'world religion' is only a placeholder that in due course 'must be sacrificed' (Tiele 1884, 368). Finally he defends his preferred term in what J. Z. Smith (1998, 191) acknowledges to be 'blunt imperialistic language':

> [T]he term 'world religions' might still be retained for practical use, to distinguish the three religions which have found their way to different races and peoples and all of which profess the intention to conquer the world, from such communities ['national' religions] as are generally limited to a single race or nation, and, when they have extended farther, have done so only in the train of, and in connexion with, a superior civilization. Strictly speaking, there can be no more than one universal or world religion, and if one of the existing religions

is so potentially it has not yet reached its goal. This is a matter of belief which lies beyond the limits of scientific classification.

(Tiele 1884, 368)[1]

Tiele's account usefully attempts, first, to make a distinction between 'science' and 'belief', and second, to represent genealogical and morphological diversity. The irony is that the timing of this representation of plurality coincides with the high-water mark of the Victorian 'science of religion' (Wheeler-Barclay 2010) so that it becomes fused with positivist ideas of entities and boundaries. The result is the scientific attractiveness of the plural form 'religions'. As remarked above, this seems to presuppose the singular form 'a religion'. But here the biological analogy ends, for '(a) religion' – the genus logically inferred in this schema – is not a natural kind but a theoretical concept.

As Fitzgerald (2009, 978) wryly comments: 'no one has ever seen a religion'. The new legitimation of plurality disguised this troublesome epistemological issue and continues to do so. Such has been the political drive to represent plurality in the recent period that in some academic quarters 'Study of Religions' has been championed as a superior disciplinary descriptor to 'Religious Studies' (which may imply that the method is determined by its object) or 'Religion' (an opaque title which lacks methodological relationship to its object).[2] However, this comparatively banal signification of multiplicity and difference comes at the cost of reinscribing an essentially ideological position, as indicated in Tiele's slip of the tongue, that religious formations are by definition self-contained, boundaried and competitive entities. A compromise has been advanced by Engler and Stausberg who, drawing on Stausberg's usage (2010), recommend 'study of religion\s'. In their terms 'the idiosyncratic use of the backslash is meant to index a series of theoretical and meta-theoretical questions regarding the referents and framing of "religion" and "religions"' (Engler and Stausberg 2011, 127 fn. 2). The orthographic intent is attractive, but the backslash is fiddly (why not the forward slash?) and does not convert aurally. From a discursive perspective, von Stuckrad argues that 'religion' is 'an empty signifier' and as such not an appropriate theoretical object. Instead he proposes the study of RELIGION (*sic*), which he defines as '*the societal organization of knowledge about religion*' (von Stuckrad 2013, 17; emphasis in original). This elicits similar aural objections to Engler and Stausberg, unless the block capitals are taken to indicate shouting (as in poor netiquette). It may also imply that religion is a special problem. For example, retitling sociology as 'study of society\ies' or SOCIETY highlights the comparative artificiality of these suggestions.

This quick analysis of category formation shows how the 'World Religions Paradigm' is a symptom of a wider, chronic cognitive disease in which reified entities are represented in a hierarchy in which (to use the analogy of English soccer) the 'world' religions form a premier league, the 'new' religions form a championship, the 'indigenous' religions form a first division, and the 'others' – here, 'new age stuff' – only register as wannabes (Sutcliffe 2013). A quick scan of departments worldwide confirms the persistence of this league table as the primary teaching structure. Since the 1970s, 'new' formations have gained tenure (Arweck and Clarke 1997) as, more recently, have indigenous formations (Cox 2007). However 'new age stuff' remains a Cinderella. But since it is beyond the pale and there is nothing to lose (as it were) it can serve as an experiment in resisting the juggernaut. Strictly speaking, my argument against 'religions' also applies to the various sub-types, for to argue, even strategically, that the taxonomy can be rescued by teaching 'new' and/or 'indigenous' or 'lived' (etc.) types, which is understandably tempting, only reinscribes the underpinning logic in spite of the best intentions of the reformers (see Editors' Introduction). The danger is that this only rearranges the deckchairs on the *Titanic* and 'the band plays on despite the ship taking on water' (McCutcheon 2005, 35).

In practice: teaching 'new age stuff' in the introductory course

Forming a contrast to the 'usual suspects' – the 'isms' such as Hinduism, Judaism, Buddhism, etc. – teaching this stuff can offer a different take on religion. This is not through presenting it as 'exotic' or 'weird' – typically how students are primed to find it – but through teaching it as an example of quite ordinary and commonplace thinking and behaving in late modern secular societies, not only in the Anglophone world or 'the West'.[3] This 'stuff' includes meditation, body practices, self-help therapy, healing rituals, domestic ritual, consumption of literature and ambient music, amongst other data (see examples in Sutcliffe 2003). As such it operates below the radar of 'religion entities' and is often portrayed pejoratively by academics and jour-nalists alike: as ephemeral, faddish and consumeristic – in sum, not 'real' religion. This superficially unlikely data offers a real opportunity to try to teach religion instead of religions. I have tried to do this in a first year course for more than a decade.

Since I hold to the model of teacher-as-researcher, I need to say a few words about how my own research has informed my teaching. Like many of my gen-eration, my approach to the 'data' has been faced with the lessons as well as the excesses of deconstruction and post-structuralism. So in my Ph.D. work I critiqued existing representations of a 'New Age Movement' (NAM),[4] arguing instead that the historical and ethnographic evidence suggested collective engagement with ideas and practices, but not membership in a 'movement' as such. The NAM model homogenized and thereby elided more vital and 'elementary' forms of practice.

It was only after completing my Ph.D. that I began to think about developing a more positive angle in the sense of identifying what this 'stuff' *was* rather than what it *wasn't*. This was in part a pragmatic question since I had no 'world religion' to fall back on in the labour market. Because I was committed to a comparative and also a historical approach, I mused on ways to treat this apparently 'new' phenomenon as prototypical for 'grand theorizing' of religion which, warts and all, had been a strength of an earlier period but had gone firmly out of fashion.

In particular this 'new age stuff' seemed to raise disciplinary questions. Decon-struction had problematized the object of the study of religion and critiqued the very rationale of disciplinary formation. But I became convinced that disciplinary formation was key to establishing a secure educational and pedagogical base for the study of religion. To form a viable disciplinary field required three methodological components: a theoretical concern with category formation, engagement with comparative data (working across 'traditions'), and a broadly explanatory programme. How I was teaching 'new age stuff' could illustrate a larger disciplinary model.[5]

Elsewhere I have discussed the history of 'New Age Beliefs and Practices', my advanced undergraduate course (Sutcliffe 2011, 256–262). Here I focus on the even trickier challenge of teaching this 'stuff' within a short section of an introductory course. J. Z. Smith's argument is once again crucial since it is in the introductory course that students learn the ropes (J. Z. Smith 2013a). By the time they reach the advanced courses it is often too late.

For the last ten years my take on the introduction has come as the final three week section of a first year, second semester, course called 'Global Religions'. Many students in a typical enrolment of 80 to 100 are taking this as a core course in a Religious Studies degree. Others take it in a Theology degree, or as an elective in History, Sociology or Anthropology. For the last ten years 'Global Religions' has partnered 'Lived Religions', offered in the first semester and occupying the same timetable slot and classroom allocation. The result is that most students sign up for the pair. This introduces the less visible question of the wider curricular context in which this one section of one particular course is located. The pedagogical value of my 'slot' will not only be tested and compared by students in relation to preceding sections of the same course, but against the further courses – core and elective – which they will take in their various programmes. Within our Religious Studies programme we can anticipate and correct any theoretical dissonances between the introductory course and advanced courses, but it is less easy to keep track of this across programmes administered by other Schools. The goal therefore is to introduce a sense of the relative sophistication of the study of religion so that there is no theoretical shortfall – hopefully even some gain – for students when they come to take their other courses.

Here is how my section of the syllabus for Global Religions looked in 2015, warts and all[6]:

New Religions in Europe (weeks 9–11)
    The decline of traditional forms and institutions of Christianity in Europe, along with secularization of culture and society, has been challenged by the rise of innovative and self-consciously 'alternative' forms of religion, especially from the 1960s. This final section of the course examines new and alternative beliefs and practices in Europe, beginning with a consideration of historical and cultural context, then moving into two empirical case studies: Wicca/neo-pagan witchcraft, and 'new age' or 'holistic' spirituality.
    Week 9: New and alternative religions in Europe
    9 March: Introducing 'new' and 'alternative' religions.
    10 March: De-christianization, secularization and pluralization.

12 March: The 'cultic milieu' and 'seekership'.

13 March: Tutorial.

Week 10: Wicca/Pagan witchcraft

The Pagan revival (neo-paganism) and the development of Wicca: 1950s to the present.

16 March: The Pagan revival – background and overview.

17 March: Old or new religion? The historiography of Wicca.

19 March: Beliefs and practices – the ethnography of Wicca.

20 March. Tutorial.

Week 11: 'New age' spirituality and the 'holistic milieu'

The history and ethnography of 'new age' spirituality, 1960s to the present.

23 March: 'New age' beliefs and practices – an overview.

24 March: Case study 1: the Findhorn colony, Moray, Scotland.

26 March: Case study 2: the 'holistic milieu' in Kendal, England.

27 March. Tutorial.

These final three weeks were preceded by three weeks on Indigenous Religions of Africa and, to begin, four weeks on Religions of South Asia. The first thing to note therefore is that 'New Religions in Europe' follows the prevailing logic of the declension of 'religion entities', however problematized or deconstructed in the lecture room. On the plus side, my blurb speaks of 'forms of religion', 'beliefs and practices' and 'empirical case studies', rather than an 'ism' or 'a religion', and explicitly 'begin[s] with a consideration of historical and cultural context'. By design, my first week is entirely thematic, theoretical and historiographical, and reflexively returns the spotlight from the 'overseas' locations of the earlier sections to the European territory in which I am teaching and from which most of our students come, thus encouraging a de-exoticization of the data for religion and a more radical self-positioning. This first week emphasizes the social and cultural context in which new religious formations emerged. After a brief problematization of the twin assumption that 'new' religions are necessarily 'irrational' and solely modern, I introduce students to Colin Campbell's sociological model of 'seekership' and the 'cultic milieu' (Campbell 1972). I illustrate this biographically with short films of interviews with three practitioners: a member of the International Society for Krishna Consciousness, a member of the Friends of the Western Buddhist Order (now the Triratna Buddhist Community) and an independently practising Buddhist. All three interviewees were born in the post-Second World War 'baby boom' generation and were involved with the post-1960s counterculture, allowing me to relate 'religious' formation to social and cultural change. I further prepare students with three basic concepts: secularization, de-christianization and pluralization.

Having front-loaded the section with history and theory, I use the remaining two weeks for two illustrative case studies: Wicca, created by Gerald Gardner and associates, which I present within the broader Pagan movement from the mid-1950s and in light of the comparative historiography of witchcraft; and in the final week, the Findhorn colony in northern Scotland as a key example of 'new age stuff'. To integrate the first week's theory, I use seekership to model participation in Findhorn, and the concept of the cultic milieu to model the 'holistic milieu' which Heelas and Woodhead (2005) present as a hot spot of contemporary 'spirituality'. I place both case studies in cultural context: the Pagan groups in light of environmentalism and 'green' politics, and Findhorn in light of the secularization debate coupled with continuities in popular religion. Building on the historiographical discussion, this week has recently introduced the concept of 'invented religion' (Cusack 2010) to probe the received wisdom that Wicca, Druidry and other 'Pagan' formations can be considered historical 'revivals'.[7]

I aim in this section practically to teach 'no religions' by inviting students to locate 'religious' beliefs and practices within ordinary (socio-cultural) ideas and behaviour. Apart from the first lecture which, in giving an overview of 'new religions', is admittedly recuperable within the 'religion entities' framework, all my case studies are framed in this way. I do not explicitly theorize to students that what I am doing is teaching against 'religions', but I smuggle in the idea by inference on the back of 'new age stuff'. This is designed to avoid the charge that what I am teaching is 'merely' theoretical and represents my attempt at 'skilful means' to avoid frightening off students who prefer to learn about 'religions'.

More problematically, my section comes last in this course, and it also constitutes the first year's final batch of new material. In these last three weeks of the teaching year, many students are tired, preparing for exams, or planning for the summer. My 'stuff' therefore risks being seen as an afterword to the main business. One possibility is to shift around the sections, but knock-on impact on timetabling has so far prevented this. Also, the section covers too much ground. I still need to learn the tip for good use of examples in J. Z. Smith's epigraph from Lenin: 'better fewer but better' (2013a, 11). Finally, the section in many ways gets off to a rocky start by introducing itself as covering 'New Religions'. In fact, I used to call it 'new religious formations', but this kind of technicalese can appear turgid and opaque to first year students.

The introductory course in institutional context

Although these conceptual lapses, like Freudian parapraxes, seem to undercut everything I have been saying, they only support my argument on the institutionalization of the discourse on 'religions' even in such an avowedly deconstructionist and reflexive teaching programme. In the present case, 'world' has morphed into 'global' and put down roots in comparative area studies. Colleagues are fully aware of the problem, are proactive in attempts to contain, to reform or to subvert it, and discuss these questions regularly with students. No personal blame is therefore implied. My point is precisely that the institutional arrangements which shape the presentation of teaching material are structural rather than personal, and that a superficial rhetoric of agency and self-determination in the humanities and social sciences can disguise a status quo which – in the case of the study of religion – has lasted more than a century. The institutional problem can be seen in miniature in the history of these courses over the last ten years: recently, 'Lived Religions', the first semester pairing, covered Judaism, Islam and Christianity and was thus implicitly an introduction to the so-called 'Abrahamic' or 'Monotheistic' traditions. Because this introduced yet another taxonomic headache, in an earlier presentation it began with 'Hinduism' to challenge the course design by starting with the polytheistic practices of South Asia. This arrangement also fell victim to timetable clashes: no incidental detail, but a real problem for a small teaching unit, as many Study of Religion subject areas or departments are in the UK. It has recently been restructured to include 'Buddhism' as the grit in the oyster. But the master taxon remains frustratingly embedded, however inventively the deckchairs are rearranged, whether it is called a 'world religion', a 'religion of the world', or indeed a 'global religion'. Underlying all sub-types is the core idea of the 'religion entity'.

Why is this concept so entrenched? The reasons are multiple and complex and deserve sustained attention not only within the study of religion, but in the sociology of higher education and in social and political history. The concept is intuitively recognized and indeed expected both by students coming fresh from school, and by colleagues in the wider disciplinary umbrellas of 'Religion' in the US and 'Theology and Religious Studies' in the UK.[8] In the latter, since at least the 1992 Research Assessment Exercise, the concept of 'religions' has served as the institutional framework within which teaching and research is funded and assessed by Higher Education boards and research councils. Most students who matriculate on Religious Studies degree programmes in the UK learn in secondary or high school to divide interesting and ambiguous data about super-powerful agents and discourses – the kind that positively begs for 'training in argument about interpretations' – into bite-sized 'religion entities'. In addition, many colleagues in the university accept this apparently common-sense division of labour, as have civic society institutions such as Inter-Faith councils and government think-tanks, whom academics have been enjoined to embrace as 'stakeholders' since Tony Blair's 1996 'New Labour' manifesto. The self-evidence of this societal consensus about the existence of 'religions' deserves much closer historical and political scrutiny. For my argument it simply means that apparently quite local and particular problems in teaching religion at eleven o'clock on a Monday morning are caught up in a complex and only partially disguised web of interlocking educational and governmental interests and forces designed to regulate debates in civil society. Hence the critique by Fitzgerald (2003) that Religious Studies risks being absorbed into an arm of the liberal (indeed neo-liberal) state as a mechanism of what Althusser called the 'Ideological State Apparatus'. There are powerful 'external' as well as 'internal' forces impinging on classroom teaching in modern societies (Wiegers 2002) in which the widely disseminated idea of a 'world religion', as a subtype of the more general category of a 'religion entity', remains a formative agent.

Pedagogical observations

On the evidence of student feedback forms, essays and exam answers, and my subjective sense of how my teaching goes down in the classroom, I make four pedagogical observations.

First, new categories, and even more so the process of category formation itself, challenge many first year students for whom 'religions' are stubbornly self-evident things. For example, no matter what I say in class, every year many students confuse 'new age' with 'new religions' and write 'new age religions' (*sic*) in exam answers, thus reconstituting under pressure the mysterious 'religion entity' and presenting a kind of regression to the mean. Students also find it difficult to suspend normative judgement. As a result, people, groups and practices are typically assessed as peculiar, deviant or (sometimes) cool. While rarely strongly articulated, this kind of positioning can be gleaned from the way questions are asked in class or certain sentences formed in essays.

This apparent compulsion to evaluation is linked to my second observation: challenging students too much in a brief lecture series can backfire. A 'pendulum swing' can result whereby, swallowing my critique whole, a few students identify with the subaltern self-presentations of Wiccans, Pagans and Findhornians. This inadvertently reinforces the hegemonic subtext, a hangover from secondary school, that the academic study of religion should facilitate students' 'choices' on their own formation, as a kind of 'tertiary Religious Education' (Wiebe 2005). In this way Pagan positions become attractive for some students in light of the currency of environmentalism and 'green' interests. Teaching the cultural history of 'alternative' formations can seem to endorse them by virtue of the teacher (me) simply presenting this material in the classroom. My use of biographical testimonies as evidence for seekership can be another hostage to fortune. Students' exposure to 'eastern' practices through travel is cheaper and more immediate than it was for the baby boom interviewees in my examples and the testimonies of these pioneers may seem to endorse contemporary opportunities. Self-reflexivity can be a helpful pedagogical device when there is enough time to unpack the social formation of self (Jenkins 2014), but in an introductory course, it may invite spectacular identification.

Third, the problem generated by a market economy in higher education is that, interpellated as consumers, some students will not hang around to reap the benefits of a 'challenge' but will migrate to more readily 'enjoyable' courses. In this sense a market oriented to utilitarian and pragmatic outcomes will place a lower premium on comparative theoretical curiosity within the total student experience. This may not be unique to the students themselves but a function of the wider institutional context. In his afterword to a symposium on undergraduate teaching of Religious Studies in North American universities in the early 1990s, J. Z. Smith wrote: 'I can think of no-one in contemporary religious studies who states they chose their particular area of study to solve an issue in the general theoretical construction of religion' (2013c [1995], 72 fn. 12). Smith, of course, is talking about teachers. But if our field tends to lack interest in the 'general theoretical construction of religion', we can hardly fault our students for not responding.

Fourth, my impression of how the cultural history aspect of my teaching goes down is that students are not generally enthused by history and historiography. This is especially the case in the study of 'new' religious formations, which in the methodological design of many textbooks appear literally to have come from nowhere. A disinclination to historicize, and a presentist sensibility, seem to inform this area in paticular. Yet, as I argued in my doctoral dissertation, only a critical historical perspective can fully explain the provenance and durability of the new age 'stuff' I teach – and by extension, other 'stuff' too.

Conclusion: against the grain

> [E]ach thing taught is taught not because it is 'there,' but because it connects in some interesting way with something else, because it is an example, an 'e.g.' of something that is fundamental, something that may serve as a precedent for further acts of interpretation and understanding by providing an arsenal of instances, of paradigmatic events and expressions as resources from which to reason, from which to extend the possibility of intelligibility to that which first appears to be novel or strange.
>
> *(J. Z. Smith 2013a, 13)*

Smith's words describe the rationale through which I try to teach 'new age spiritualities'. On once being asked to speak on the topic 'How I would teach an introductory course in religion', Smith remarks: 'The least interesting term in the title is "religion"' (2013a, 11). I could say the same thing about 'new age/holistic spiritualities'. This makes for a tricky balancing act in a market driven by entities and substances. But it reminds us that category formation in the tradition of Baird and Smith, rather than any particular 'tradition', is key to the study of religion as a disciplinary field. Paradoxically it takes active classroom construction of 'new age spiritualities' as an emergent 'tradition' to reveal this to students. Thus, if nurtured within a theoretical and comparative programme, 'new age stuff' can punch above its weight. But if it remains a holiday from '(world) religions', its marginality will only be confirmed.

Many students struggle with this stuff for reasons I have tried to explain. I struggle with teaching it. But every year a few get it and these students reappear on my advanced courses, 'New Age Beliefs and Practices' and 'Theories of Religion', where we do more of the same. As Mark E. Smith of Manchester band The Fall puts it in their 1977 song 'Repetition': 'We dig repetition … This is the three R's, repetition, repetition, repetition.'

As a postscript, I was chastened to read Kathryn Lofton's (2014) review essay on J. Z. Smith's collection of essays, *Teaching Religion*. As a former student of Smith, Lofton admires his pedagogical theory, but sees it as exactly that: *theory*. Admittedly writing her piece 'with the corruptions of ego and memory' (Lofton 2014, 532), she nevertheless confesses that she found Smith to be 'not a great teacher' and his classes to be 'wan … dull [and] incomplete' (2014, 534). Noting the 'difference between [Smith's] recorded principles and his actual pedagogy', she implies that Smith did not 'walk the talk' (2014, 535). There may be an element of sour grapes here. But in pedagogical terms this is the litmus test, although it depends on a classroom skillset of a different order to the conceptualization of the issues presented here. An ethnography of classroom teaching and learning of 'new age stuff' is the next logical step.

Notes

1 In light of Tiele's *realpolitik* that 'there can be no more than *one* ... world religion' (emphasis added), note that since 1950 a 'World Religion Day' has been promulgated annually in January by the Baha'i movement in the US. Buck (2011) points out the tension between the original purpose of this event – 'a celebration of the need for and the coming of a world religion for mankind, the Baha'i Faith itself' – and its more recent absorption as a common ground for 'interfaith dialogue [and] "spiritual literacy"' (2011, 938). In other words, the Baha'i rationale underpinning 'World Religion Day' confirms the imperialistic logic of Tiele's original formulation of this term.

2 For relevant discussions, see Bocking (2004) and Wiebe (2005). There are several departments of 'religion' in the US at the time of writing: for example, at Harvard, Princeton, Columbia and Dartmouth. In the UK, a mix of 'Theology and Religious Studies' has become the norm but, bucking the trend, Stirling has recently renamed itself a department of 'religion'. For a discussion of webpage departmental self-representations, see Melvær and Stausberg (2013).

3 See for example Menzel *et al.* (2012) on Russia, Horie (2013) on Japan, Chen (2013) on South Korea, Possamai (2006) on Australia, Werczberger and Huss (2014) on Israel, and Maldonado (2009) on Mexico.

4 '"New Age" in Britain: an Ethnographical and Historical Exploration': unpublished Ph.D. dissertation, Religious Studies, The Open University, 1998. A revised version was published as Sutcliffe (2003).

5 Writing in the US, Murphy (2006) is pessimistic about teaching religion to under-graduates at an adequately theorized level; instead, he recommends developing strong postgraduate centres. J. Z. Smith (2013a, 2013b) is more optimistic about the ability of introductory courses to provide *'training in argument about interpretations'* (2013a, 14; emphasis in original). However although for Smith, teaching religion is 'not inherently disciplinary' but 'primarily pedagogical', I would argue that this downplays the economics and politics of higher education institutions. I discuss the impact of the lack of 'second order tradition' in the study of religion on positive classroom learning as an example of the relevance of disciplinary questions to pedagogy in Sutcliffe (2008, 106–109).

6 http://www.docs.hss.ed.ac.uk/divinity/current-students/syllabus/REST08010.pdf (accessed 24/2/15). I have removed tutorial readings here for reasons of space.

7 As introduced by David Robertson when teaching this section in 2012.

8 The conjunction 'and' in this rubric disguises lively contestation between the respective methodologies of 'T' and 'RS'. The names and histories of the two main professional 'TRS' bodies in the UK reflect this: the British Association for the Study of Religions (BASR), founded in 1954 and affiliated to the International Association for the History of Religions (IAHR), and Theology and Religious Studies UK (TRS-UK), formerly the Association of University Departments of Theology and Religious Studies (AUDTRS), founded in the early 1990s. For a brief discussion, see 'BASR, Methodological Diversity and the Politics of Representation' (Sutcliffe 2004, xvii – xxiv).

References

Arweck, Elisabeth and Peter B. Clarke. 1997. *New Religious Movements in Western Europe: An Annotated Bibliography*. Westport, CT: Greenwood Press.

Baird, Robert D. 1971. *Category Formation and the History of Religions*. The Hague: Mouton.

Benavides, Gustavo. 2003. "Review: There Is Data for Religion." *Journal of the American Academy of Religion* 71(4): 895–903.

Beyer, Peter. 2006. *Religions in Global Society*. London: Routledge.

Bocking, Brian. 2004. "Study of Religions: The New Queen of the Sciences?" In *Religion: Empirical Studies*, edited by Steven J. Sutcliffe, 107–119. Aldershot: Ashgate.

Buck, Christopher. 2011. "World Religion Day (January)." In *Religious Celebrations: An Encyclopedia of Holidays, Festivals, Solemn Observances, and Spiritual Commemorations*, edited by J. Gordon Melton, with James A. Beverley, C. Buck and Constance A. Jones, 936–939. Santa Barbara, CA: ABC-CLIO.

Campbell, Colin. 1972. "The Cult, the Cultic Milieu, and Secularization." In *A Sociological Yearbook of Britain 5*, edited by Michael Hill, 119–136. London: SCM Press.

Chen, Shu-Chuan. 2013. "Theorising Emotions in New Age Practices: An Analysis of Feeling Rules in Self-Religion." In *New Age Spirituality: Rethinking Religion*, edited by Steven J. Sutcliffe and Invild Saelid Gilhus, 227–241. Durham: Acumen.

Cox, James L. 2007. *From Primitive to Indigenous: The Academic Study of Indigenous Religions.* Aldershot: Ashgate.

Cusack, Carole. 2010. *Invented Religions: Imagination, Fiction and Faith.* Farnham: Ashgate.

Engler, Steven and Michael Stausberg. 2011. "Introductory Essay. Crisis and Creativity: Opportunities and Threats in the Global Study of Religion\s." *Religion* 41(2): 127–143.

Fitzgerald, Timothy. 2003. "Playing Language Games and Performing Rituals: Religious Studies as Ideological State Apparatus." *Method & Theory in the Study of Religion* 15(3): 209–254.

Fitzgerald, Timothy. 2009. "Review of Contemporary Western Ethnography and the Definition of Religion by Martin Stringer." *Journal of the American Academy of Religion* 77(4): 974–982.

Hacking, Ian. 1999. *The Social Construction of What?* Cambridge, MA: Harvard University Press.

Heelas, Paul and Linda Woodhead, with Benjamin Seel, Bronislaw Szerszynski, and Karen Tusting. 2005. *The Spiritual Revolution: Why Religion Is Giving Way to Spirituality.* Oxford: Basil Blackwell.

Horie, Norichika. 2013. "Narrow New Age and Broad Spirituality: A Comprehensive Schema and Comparative Analysis." In *New Age Spirituality: Rethinking Religion*, edited by Steven J. Sutcliffe and Invild Saelid Gilhus, 99–116. Durham: Acumen.

Jenkins, Richard. 2014 [1996]. *Social Identity* [4th edition]. London: Routledge.

Lofton, Kathryn. 2014. "Review Essay on Teaching Religion: Essays by Jonathan Z. Smith." *Journal of the American Academy of Religion* 82(2): 531–542.

Maldonado, Andrea. 2009–11. "'Una Nueva Forma de Vida.' Seeking 'New Spiritualities' in Urban Mexico – A Note on Research in Progress." *Journal of Alternative Spiritualities and New Age Studies* 5: (no pagination).

McCutcheon, Russell T. 1997. *Manufacturing Religion: The Discourse on Sui Generis Religion and the Politics of Nostalgia.* New York: Oxford University Press.

McCutcheon, Russell T. 2005. "Perils of Having One's Cake and Eating it too." *Religious Studies Review* 31(1–2): 32–36.

Melvær, Knut and Michael Stausberg. 2013. "What Is the Study of Religion\s? Self-Presentations of the Discipline on University Web Pages." *The Religious Studies Project.* http://www.religiousstudiesproject.com/2013/12/06/what-is-the-study-of-religionsself-presentations-of-the-discipline-on-university-web-pages (accessed 28/2/15).

Menzel, Birgit, Michael Hagemeister and Bernice Glatzer Rosenthal, eds. 2012. *The New Age in Russia. Occult and Esoteric Dimensions.* Munich and Berlin: Verlag Otto Sagner.

Murphy, Tim. 2006. "Cultural Understandings of 'Religion': The Hermeneutic Context of Teaching Religious Studies in North America." *Method & Theory in the Study of Religion* 18(3): 197–218.

Possamai, Adam. 2006. *In Search of New Age Spiritualities.* Aldershot: Ashgate.

Smith, Jonathan Z. 1982. *Imagining Religion.* Chicago, IL: University of Chicago Press.

Smith, Jonathan Z. 1998. "Religion, Religions, Religious." In *Critical Terms for Religious Studies*, edited by Mark C. Taylor, 269–284. Chicago, IL: University of Chicago Press.

Smith, Jonathan Z. 2013a [1991]. "The Introductory Course: Less Is Better." In *On Teaching Religion: Essays by Jonathan Z. Smith*, edited by Christopher I. Lehrich, 11–19. New York, NY: Oxford University Press.

Smith, Jonathan Z. 2013b [1973]. "Basic Problems in the Study of Religion." In *On Teaching Religion: Essays by Jonathan Z. Smith*, edited by Christopher I. Lehrich, 20–27. New York, NY: Oxford University Press.

Smith, Jonathan Z. 2013c [1995]. "Religious Studies: Whither (Whither) and Why?" In *On Teaching Religion: Essays by Jonathan Z. Smith*, edited by Christopher I. Lehrich, 64–72. New York, NY: Oxford University Press.

Smith, Wilfred Cantwell. 1991 [1962]. *The Meaning and End of Religion*. Minneapolis, MN: Fortress Press.

Stausberg, Michael. 2010. "Prospects in Theory of Religion." *Method & Theory in the Study of Religion* 22(4): 223–238.

von Stuckrad, Kocku. 2013. "Discursive Study of Religion: Approaches, Definitions, Implications." *Method & Theory in the Study of Religion* 25(1): 5–25.

Sutcliffe, Steven. 2003. *Children of the New Age: A History of Spiritual Practices*. London: Routledge.

Sutcliffe, Steven. 2004. "Introduction: Qualitative Empirical Methodologies: An Inductive Argument." In *Religion: Empirical Studies*, edited by Steven J. Sutcliffe, xvii–xliii. Aldershot: Ashgate.

Sutcliffe, Steven. 2008. "Historiography and Disciplinary Identity: The Case of 'Religious Studies'". In *Theology and Religious Studies: An Exploration of Disciplinary Boundaries*, edited by Maya Warrier and Simon Oliver, 101–118. London: T and T Clark/Continuum.

Sutcliffe, Steven. 2011. "From 'Comparative Mysticism' to 'New Age Spirituality': Teaching New Age as Raw Materials of Religion." In *Teaching Mysticism*, edited by William B. Parsons, 249–267. New York: Oxford University Press.

Sutcliffe, Steven. 2013. "New Age, World Religions and Elementary Forms." In *New Age Spirituality: Rethinking Religion*, edited by Steven J. Sutcliffe and Invild Saelid Gilhus, 17–34. Durham: Acumen.

Tiele, Cornelius P. 1884. "Religions." In *Encyclopaedia Britannica, 9th edition*. General Editor, W. Robertson Smith. Edinburgh: A. and C. Black.

Werczberger, Rachel and Boaz Huss. 2014. "Guest Editors' Introduction: New Age Culture in Israel." *Israel Studies Review* 29(2): 1–16.

Wheeler-Barclay, Marjorie. 2010. *The Science of Religion in Britain, 1860–1915*. Charlottesville, VA: University of Virginia Press.

Wiebe, Donald. 2005. "Religious Studies." In *Routledge Companion to the Study of Religion*, edited by John R. Hinnells, 98–124. London: Routledge.

Wiegers, Gerard A., ed. 2002. *Modern Societies and the Science of Religions*. Leiden: Brill.

3

'NOT A TASK FOR AMATEURS'

Graduate instructors and Critical Theory in the World Religions classroom

Tara Baldrick-Morrone, Michael Graziano and Brad Stoddard

Introduction

Jonathan Z. Smith has written that the task of 'introducing' is 'not a task for amateurs, nor, as is too often the case, should it be assigned casually (or punitively) to neophytes' (1988, 727). As a few of the many graduate students responsible for teaching introductory courses every semester, however, it is clear to us that the task is very often, and very often casually, left to amateurs. This task can be an overwhelming one for young scholars, especially those schooled in Critical Theory. The concept of 'World Religions' remains part of the operating logic for numerous scholars and institutions in the field, even though this is problematic in many respects. Nonetheless, this chapter suggests that critically engaging with World Religions discourse can be professionally productive and methodologically useful for graduate student instructors. In this spirit, we suggest strategies that critically engaged graduate instructors can employ in the archetypal Introduction to World Religions classroom. We argue that choosing to reproduce the conventional World Religions Paradigm (WRP) is a missed opportunity not only for our students but for graduate instructors' scholarship and professional development. Although our role as graduate student instructors lies at the heart of our pedagogical strategies, these approaches can and should be used by any instructors who must teach using a syllabus that works within the WRP.

We are first concerned with the ordeal of teaching a course which is often seen as theoretically unsophisticated. Our goal is to explore the peculiar pressures on graduate instructors – pressures both *practical* and *political*. We will discuss practical approaches we have taken in the classroom which have worked to challenge the dominant WRP, specifically World Religions textbooks and the idea of 'traditions'. This chapter also engages the political challenges of teaching such a class from the peculiar institutional position of a graduate student. This position is inextricably linked with how we approach the methodological concerns that motivate our pedagogy.

Of course, some challenges to this approach lay outside the classroom. Graduate students interested in exposing their students to the critique of the WRP must begin by gauging the overall mood in their respective departments to identify if there are any boundaries within which they must operate. Given the many demands of graduate life as well as the political realities of the academy, we recognize that challenging the status quo is not necessarily a strategic choice for all students. Our experiences have taught us that graduate students should have honest conversations with tenured faculty who might object to the student's methodological proclivities. Assuming there is room in the department for graduate student instructors to incorporate a critique of the WRP, they can then begin the arduous task of building a syllabus, lecture schedule, and reading list.

World Religions is a valuable course for graduate students to teach precisely because its conceptual underpinnings are so problematic. Reckoning with the discourse on world religions serves as a call for graduate students to remain 'relentlessly self-conscious', strategically sharpening their explanatory powers in the classroom and in their own work (J. Z. Smith 1982, xi). In this way, graduate instructors have the opportunity to challenge students' notions that there are these *things* out there in the world called religious traditions, and to explain how 'traditions', 'religions' or even 'world religions' are ideas with particular histories associated with specific institutions, groups and nation-states.

We suggest that even when introductory courses are 'left to neophytes', graduate students can make the best of a difficult situation by taking the opportunity to confront their own classificatory schemes. It is this focus on classification that is at the root of our thinking about the WRP. Instructors who seriously consider this approach must centre their pedagogy around the concept of 'classification' as an organizing principle. Our practical suggestions are rooted in this self-reflexive attention to classification.

By focusing attention on the issue of classification and, more specifically, how the people and groups under study *classify* and *are classified*, graduate instructors can make larger theoretical points about the study of religion more accessible to their students. Such a focus assists instructors in the debate about the worthiness of World Religions classes (or even courses in the humanities in general) by showing that there are, in fact, a variety of useful critical skills that can be taught and developed in our classrooms. Our focus helps students to identify authority structures, trace power dynamics, and become more aware of how ideology and rhetoric operate. As demonstrated later in this chapter, it also provides an easy way to make the content delivery more sophisticated, as it gives our students the tools to follow the textbook while interrogating it at the same time. Similar to other constructed social arrangements, the WRP is neither neutral nor natural, but its social authority derives from appearing as both.

Graduate instructors should also be familiar with the classificatory history of the category of 'religion' in order to teach, and teach against, the WRP. Paying attention to the category's relationship with European Christianity, colonialism, and nation-states can form the backbone of a powerful critique of the WRP on display in most textbooks. Fortunately, graduate instructors now training for degrees have a particularly rich assortment of scholarly work on this topic to guide them in informing their lesson plans.

A class like World Religions all too easily becomes 'death-by-e.g.,' a forced march through a variety of pre-selected 'isms'. By focusing on the issue of classification, we can inject some clarity into the course that simply is not found in most World Religions textbooks when it comes to addressing the all-important question of '*why these traditions and not others?*' A brief survey of any number of the most popular textbooks demonstrates that many authors choose to answer this question by appealing to the difficulty of a comprehensive answer. For example, Willard G. Oxtoby and Alan F. Segal's widely-assigned *A Concise Introduction to World Religions* (2012) suggests that with regard to a definition of religion, 'no single line of definition seems able to trap it, but we can weave a net' (2012, 19). The selection of traditions, all too often, must rest on their presumed self-evidence rather than any conscious attention to classification.

Our goal is to reach a point, early in the semester, where students can begin to understand the fundamentally Durkheimian point that *classification is a social act.*[1] Once the class has this framework in place, we can begin to critically examine things beyond the syllabus – for example, what exactly do nineteenth-century British colonial officials in Nepal have to do with the chapter on Buddhism in the textbook?[2] This also opens up constructive avenues to critique the course itself. Instructors should practise introducing their students to the same choices that they face as instructors: to consider what *is* classified as worthy of inclusion in our syllabus, and what *is not*. For example, students have to wrestle with why their textbook omits any discussion of the Flying Spaghetti Monster, Scientology or Free Market Economics. Students can then begin to hypothesize why we might talk about *some* things rather than others.

As we hope has become clear, focusing on 'classification' in a World Religions class has several benefits for the graduate instructor. By getting our students to think about how the groups of people under study have categorized the world around them – and then how these same groups are classified as 'religious' (or not), we can help to instil practices of critical thinking so needed in the introductory classroom. It allows us to show our students the problems inherent in a conceptual framework that classifies things as a 'world religion'. It gives us the opportunity to address what Smith calls the 'duplicity in the disciplines', specifically the disciplinary lies that make up any introductory course. More importantly, it allows us the chance to turn these potential stumbling blocks into learning opportunities by making object lessons out of the very things that can so easily distract an introductory class. When the semester ends, students leave the classroom not just knowing the content of a so-called 'world religion' but also knowing how to better interrogate the world around them. What follows are two specific examples of how this might be accomplished from the perspective of graduate students teaching World Religions in a critical fashion.

Our approach to the Introduction to World Religions course naturally lends itself to a variety of assignments that allow the students to synthesize the various materials, theories, histories, and methodologies that they learn in class and from assigned readings. By integrating the lectures and supplementary readings, the students also learn that the textbook does not refer to objects or groups that exist in Platonic forms; rather, the students learn that the textbook participates in the construction of the objects it references. To help students understand this, we often ask the students to reflect on World Religions textbooks as primary sources, not as authoritative secondary sources that conveniently correspond to natives' 'religious' identities. We have found several assignments to be particularly useful in this respect.

In practice: the textbook is always right?

In one assignment, the students analyse a particular idea that an individual textbook treats as fact. For example, students might identify an instance when the textbook privileges canon and text in a manner that contradicts the ways that 'natives' or 'practitioners' traditionally approach texts. The study of Buddhism provides an opportunity to explore this. In *The British Discovery of Buddhism*, Philip Almond describes how the middle and upper classes of Victorian era Britain influenced the West's understanding of Buddhism (1988). He argues that in the 1830s, the British acquired new knowledge of the Buddha and the Buddha's teachings. As they gained knowledge about the Buddha via 'Buddhist texts', they came to identify Buddhism as a unique religion, i.e. independent of Hinduism. The British justified their conclusions, Almond argues, by comparing the Buddha with either Martin Luther or Jesus himself. For example, many people in Britain believed that the Buddha was a reformer who protested Hinduism much like Martin Luther protested Catholicism, while others portrayed the Buddha as an Asian Jesus: a reforming prophet who was an object of his followers' devotion.

As Almond describes, the British who were interested in Buddhism located 'authentic Buddhism' in 'Buddhist texts'. This interest stemmed from a desire to demonstrate their new-found literacy, but it also developed out of their Christian belief that texts are sacred, divinely inspired, and authoritative sources of religion. They believed that true or authentic Buddhism would be found in the texts; however, in so doing, they may have over-represented the degree to which the majority of so-called Buddhists privileged texts.

Almond's history of 'Buddhism' and 'Buddhist texts' tends to conflict with the histories of 'Buddhism' presented in most introductory textbooks. When we ask the students to read Almond's book in conjunction with their textbook, they quickly realize that there is a significant discrepancy between the two. The goal of this assignment is not to convince students that the textbook is 'wrong', but rather to expose the students to the idea that the textbook naïvely overlooks or ignores important history that is relevant to the social identity commonly labelled Buddhism. Our goal is to encourage the students to recognize diversity and even contradictions that result from pairing the textbook with critically engaged secondary sources.

In practice: textbooks as data?

While the aforementioned assignment asked students to explore the textbook as a primary source by comparing it with other scholarly writings, another useful assignment asks students to isolate one issue in a textbook and then to compare and contrast the ways that multiple textbooks either address or perhaps even omit that same issue. The topics of Hindu menstruation rituals and prohibitions provide an ideal example. For this assignment, it is important to include a variety of textbooks written throughout the twentieth and twenty-first centuries.[3] John Clark Archer's *Faiths Men Live By* is one such text (1934).

According to Tomoko Masuzawa, *Faiths Men Live By* was the first comparative textbook written for a non-seminarian audience to contain a list of the twelve or so religions that most Introduction to World Religions classes typically study today (2005, 44–45). In Archer's analysis of the individual religions, he meticulously describes what he deems as important beliefs, deities, and sacred texts. He also addresses founding figures and religious institutions, which cultivate and guard the sacred teachings. Archer largely ignores issues of gender, so prohibitions against menstruating Hindus would seem out of place in his narrative.

Another textbook that is often assigned in Introduction to World Religions is Huston Smith's *The Religions of Man*, which similarly ignores this topic (1965 [1958]). This book 'only' addresses seven religions (Buddhism, Hinduism, Confucianism, Taoism, Islam, Judaism, and Christianity) but, contra Archer, Smith discusses the different religions not to compare them, but to *understand* their deeper meanings. 'Religion,' he wrote, 'is not primarily a matter of facts in the historical sense; it is a matter of meanings' (1965, 11). Smith then attempts to provide an insider's view of what makes each religion meaningful to the religion's adherents.

Smith begins most chapters with an analysis of the historical setting of each religion and its founders. He repeatedly stresses that these founders were all fundamentally good people who took seriously their desire to help humanity. Smith is not particularly concerned with religious history, although he does occasionally address it. Instead, he discusses important theologies and sacred rituals, emphasizing those that appeal to a modern, liberal audience. Smith either downplays or ignores theology and rituals that might offend modern audiences; thus he ignores religious prohibitions in general, including prohibitions against menstruating Hindus.

Following the lead of Archer and Smith, the vast majority of textbooks have ignored the prohibitions associated with menstruating Hindus, although this has begun to change in the last decade or so. The move to address Hindu menstruation is part of a larger trend to include the 'lived experiences' of religious people, including women. Beginning in the 1980s, scholars placed a new emphasis on religion outside institutional settings,[4] which coincided with a rise in gender studies more broadly. Collectively, these two impulses motivated scholars to address both 'lived' religion and gender. John Esposito's *World Religions Today* is a textbook that reflects these new emphases (Esposito *et al.* 2006).

World Religions Today addresses the issue of Hindu menstruation rituals and prohibitions within the broader context of Hindu rites of passage. The authors claims that a Hindu woman's first menstrual cycle is an important event, as it ushers her into full womanhood and marks her as eligible for marriage (2006, 354). The young woman is isolated for a week and prohibited from seeing the sun and sometimes men. During this time, older women tell her stories about Hindu deities and provide instruction for adult religious practices. In this textbook, a woman's first menstrual cycle is therefore both restrictive and empowering. It is restrictive in the sense that it confines women; however, it is empowering in the sense that older women comfort the young woman during this transition period.

Another textbook, *A Concise Introduction to World Religions*, also addresses the topic (Oxtoby and Segal 2012). In a section titled 'Women and Pollution', Vasudha Narayanan writes, '[i]n the Hindu tradition menstruation was generally regarded as physically polluting', and therefore menstruating women were not allowed to leave the house (2012, 322). According to Narayanan, modern Hindus have largely abandoned this practice of strict isolation, although women continue to be prohibited from performing rituals and from entering temples. Some women are even unable to cook. Narayanan highlights these practices in such a way as to downplay their importance and prevalence in contemporary Hindu society.

More than any textbook discussed thus far, *Invitation to World Religions* provides the most comprehensive account of Hindu menstruation and relevant prohibitions (Brodd *et al.* 2012). This book acknowledges that regional variations dictate local customs, but it concludes that most Hindu women spend the first three days of their first menstrual cycle in a dimly lit room (2012, 111–112). According to this textbook, the first menstrual cycle is both a private and public event in the sense that the girl is confined to a room during her first period. The community later publicly recognizes her transition into womanhood at a feast that is held in her honour, where the girl often receives a special blessing from an older married woman at a local temple. The girl is now eligible for marriage, and her unsupervised interaction with boys is more restricted.

Collectively, these textbooks do not form a coherent narrative. Instead, they reveal the interests and biases of the scholars who wrote them just as they bear the imprint of the academic climate that produced them. When students learn to treat the textbook as data, they learn much more than 'facts' and history relevant to the so-called religions. They also explore the arbitrary and contested nature of representation itself. They learn that any given source – including textbooks and other academic sources – is not a simple representation of a thing that exists *a priori*; rather, they learn to question the contingent nature of all authenticity claims. This is a far cry from traditional approaches to teaching the Introduction to World Religions course, but it accomplishes much more than simply asking students to memorize names, dates, and places. It teaches them analytical skills that they can apply to their studies more broadly.

In practice: heterogeneity as homogeneity

Another task that instructors must also consider is how best to present the data of the course – the 'world religions' themselves. As graduate student instructors, we have neither the social capital nor the time to overhaul an entire course in order to fully disrupt the WRP; instead, we must find a productive way to work within it. One way to accomplish this is to teach the course using the structure of the conventional model, spending a certain amount of time on each tradition before moving on to the next. In the conventional model, each tradition is presented from the perspective of the dominant group in terms of its historical development and what official voices from within the tradition find to be significant. Because approaching traditions in this way tends 'to portray the many as one and heterogeneity as homogeneity', the focus on each tradition must implement a strategy that deviates from the conventional model at this point (McCutcheon 2001, 27).

We start this process by asking the students to consider how the textbooks present traditions, encouraging them to think about how the particular textbook's narrative recounts the tradition's history, what issues or ideas are portrayed as central to the tradition, and what groups are seen as authoritative. More importantly, though, the students are instructed to pay close attention to the rhetoric that the textbook uses, especially when addressing difference. Once this analysis is complete, we can start to destabilize the homogenizing language of tradition. One way forward is to choose passages from critical scholarship to pair with the textbook reading assignments. Bringing in additional reading introduces other voices into the section, which provide a counter-narrative. It is important to note that the scholarly reading does not need to map onto the textbook exactly. In fact, the exercise proves more fruitful if it does not, for the secondary reading ought to demonstrate that what the textbook presents is merely one rendering of an otherwise contested past. In this sense, then, the ideal choice of scholarly reading addresses an aspect of a tradition that the textbook fails to mention, or that the textbook mentions but in a manner that obscures the 'constructing, legitimizing, and contesting' that goes into the production of that particular social group (McCutcheon 2001, 24). The examples given represent aspects of these specific problems, each paired with a selection from a scholarly reading that demonstrates the strategies discussed.

Changing the emphasis from the presented-as-united traditions to the many social groups that exist within a single 'tradition' brings into view the ways that groups use discourse and force in creating and re-fashioning their identities (Lincoln 1992, 3–5). For example, when considering how early Christian groups distinguished themselves from one another and from other groups (i.e. Romans, Greeks, Jews, etc.), the language of nation or race was often used. This is evident in Origen's *On First Principles*, where he states that 'the present Israelites' could lose their race (*genos*) because they have not lived up to their status as God's chosen people. While this identity can be lost, it can also be gained, as those who exercise their will can 'enter into the church of the Lord' to become Israelites.[5] Although Origen uses the term Israelite here, he does not refer to Jews; instead, he refers to rival groups of

Christians who 'deny the role of free will in favor of a kind of determinism' (Buell 2005, 123). As Denise Kimber Buell shows in *Why This New Race: Ethnic Reasoning in Early Christianity*, Origen understands the term *genos* 'as something that one can change through a better or worse exercise of one's free will' (2005, 125–126).

Rather than continue to tease out the complicated arguments from antiquity on the nature of the soul and will, this example can serve the purpose of illustrating to our students how social groups use discourse to construct and contest their identity internally. As Buell notes, Origen's use of Israelites is 'for the purposes of intra-Christian polemic' (2005, 126). In this way, he links the identity of 'true Christians' to 'true Israelites', deciding who is included and who is excluded from this social group. The discursive strategies that Origen uses here signal the way that language can be manipulated and redefined in order to construct and legitimize one's own position – in this case, Origen's group is defined as the 'true *genos*' of God. The aforementioned assignment that asks the students to look at the ways that different textbooks portray the same topic also communicates this point – the students see not only how groups construct their own traditions through discourse, but how books *about* those traditions do so as well.

In reading Oxtoby and Segal's *A Concise Introduction to World Religions*, before the students even begin the chapter on Hinduism they are presented with the first major heading, ORIGINS. The first sentence states that the 'origins of Hinduism have been much debated'; however, the textbook then proceeds to provide the dominant view of Hinduism's development, which stems from the Harappa Culture (Basham 1991, 4). As the textbook explains, '[t]here is no agreement about what might have brought the [Harappan] civilization to an end. Some scholars think it was destroyed by migrating Indo-European people .... Other theories centre on flooding or epidemics' (Narayanan 2012, 277). From here, the chapter continues to discuss the identity of Indo-Europeans and their 'earliest surviving compositions', which are identified as the Vedas (2012, 278–284). Although these texts are 'considered to be extremely important by all orthodox philosophers and theological treatises, the Vedas are not books that people keep in their homes' (2012, 280). As Narayanan explains:

> For many centuries, acceptance as an orthodox member of society we call Hindu depended on acceptance of the Vedas as authoritative. As custodians of the Vedas, the brahmins reserved for themselves the authority to study and teach these holy words. Though members of two other classes were technically 'allowed' to study the Vedas, in time this privilege was lost or, in some cases, abandoned.
>
> *(2012, 280)*

According to Narayanan, the Vedas provide the first indication of the caste system. In the 'Hymn to the Supreme Person' (*Purusha Sukta*), which details the 'cosmic sacrifice of the primeval man', it states, '[f]rom his mouth came the priestly class / from his arms, the rulers. The producers came from his legs; from his feet came the servant class' (2012, 281–282). These texts are later used as a foundation for the

Upanishads, which address similar topics but emphasize ideas that are said to be fundamental concepts in the tradition's development (2012, 282–284). This leads to the next major heading of the chapter: CRYSTALLIZATION. The production of writings such as the *Ramayana*, the *Mahabharata* and the 'rediscovering' of deities led to the tradition 'as we know it today [becoming] crystallized' (2012, 287). It is in this so-called crystallization of Hinduism that the idea of caste as that which 'set[s] out the roles and duties … that make up Hindu society' emerges, spawning from the writings of the *dharmashastras* (2012, 291).

It is at this point that the scholarly reading can be assigned. For this section, one book to use in order to undermine the textbook's homogenous narrative is Nicholas B. Dirks' *Castes of Mind: Colonialism and the Making of Modern India* (2001). The students read parts of Chapters 1 and 8, which explain the modern idea of caste and the custom of hookswinging.[6] Dirks' main point is that though caste is not quite a modern British invention, it did become 'a single term capable of expressing, organizing, and above all "systematizing" India's diverse forms of social identity, community, and organization' during the colonial period (2001, 5). By using caste in this manner, colonists and Brahmanic groups were able to create a unifying, collective identity for local, heterogeneous groups, which undoubtedly helped to facilitate the British domination of India. While the modern understanding of caste is the central argument in Dirks' book, the chapter on hookswinging proves to be more useful for providing a crucial example of two related issues: (1) how social groups contest for authority over what constitutes 'proper' tradition and practice; and (2) how the many are not one.

As Dirks shows, hookswinging became a point of contention for the British in the 1890s, mainly due to the post-1857 proclamation of noninterference, which stated that colonial officers were no longer allowed to intervene in 'the religious belief or worship of any of [their] subjects' (2001, 149). The proclamation came as a response to the Great Rebellion of 1857, which the British misunderstood as occurring because of 'religious' concerns regarding pollution, not because of British colonization and occupation. However, they eventually redefined the terms of the proclamation so that it excluded customs deemed as either dangerous to British interests in law and order or offensive to various agencies, such as missionaries (2001, 151). The extension of the proclamation included such umbrages as hookswinging due to the 'barbaric' nature of the custom. 'High-caste Hindus', who encouraged the British colonists to ban the practice, condemned hookswinging, arguing that the 'popular practice' had 'no religious sanction' (2001, 161). Dirks illustrates that by denouncing popular practices such as hookswinging, Brahmanic groups were then able to define Hinduism in their own terms, which became the 'measures for authenticity' (2001, 171). The idea of the part (Brahmans) standing in for the whole (the tradition of Hinduism) becomes a teaching moment, particularly in relation to the textbook, as the students are asked to consider its discursive practices. In other words, how does the textbook define the tradition, and in whose terms does it speak? In the words of Bruce Lincoln, 'who wins what, and how much? Who, conversely, loses?' (1996, 226).

Using this approach in our classrooms encourages our students to develop 'critical thinking, debating, and writing skills upon which they will draw long after they have left our classes' (McCutcheon 2001, 217). Moreover, it provides the same opportunities for instructors, who can refine their own analytical skills by finding new and better ways to disrupt the WRP. Teaching traditions critically in the form of the conventional model provides an exit from mere description, especially for those who, like graduate student instructors, are unable to escape the WRP. As we demonstrate, instructors can take the uncritical course given to them and produce a model that takes seriously the discursive practices through which traditions are constructed – by groups themselves and by others (including textbooks).

Conclusion

As graduate students tasked with teaching Introduction to World Religions, we often find ourselves reflecting on a series of questions that form the basis of our pedagogy. Specifically, how do we teach a course that is premised on discredited theory and history? How do we teach a course that assumes that religious systems are discrete entities with identifiable histories and boundaries when recent research has repeatedly demonstrated the opposite? How do we teach Introduction to World Religions without naturalizing 'religious' identities and the category of 'world religions' itself? The short answer is that we do not teach that class. Instead of teaching a traditional World Religions class, we teach the course without naturalizing religious identity. We teach Introduction to World Religions without only teaching world religions.

With this approach, the Introduction to World Religions course is not only salvable, but valuable. It is valuable to the study of religion because students who are exposed to the academic study of religion in this type of classroom and who proceed to major or minor in the department not only possess sophisticated theoretical and methodological tools, but they expect future courses to build on these tools. The department retains the students who are attracted to these types of questions and to this line of academic analysis. Finally, and perhaps most importantly, the course is valuable for the students. For the majority of the students, this will be their only exposure to the academic study of religion. Students can leave Introduction to World Religions with a more thorough understanding of the complex processes that are involved in the construction and representation of group identity.

Notes

1 For more on this point, see Durkheim 1912.
2 On Buddhism, see Lopez 1995.
3 We can put a variety of textbooks on hold in the library, so the students do not have to purchase multiple textbooks to complete one assignment. Such an exercise can also be done using online sources that address similar topics.
4 Robert Orsi is often credited as popularizing this trend. See Orsi 1985.
5 A translation of *On First Principles* appears in Buell 2005.

6 As described by an 1891 news story appearing in the *Madras Mail*, hookswinging 'consists
   in passing iron hooks through the deep muscles of the back, attaching a rope to the
   hooks, and (after the method of a well sweep) swinging the victim to a height several feet
   above the heads of the people. The car on which the pole is placed is then drawn along
   by large ropes' (Dirks 2001, 151).

References

Almond, Philip C. 1988. *The British Discovery of Buddhism*. Cambridge: Cambridge
   University Press.
Archer, John C. 1934. *Faiths Men Live By*. New York: Ronald Press.
Basham, A. L. 1991. *The Origins and Development of Classical Hinduism*. New York: Oxford
   University Press.
Brodd, Jeffrey, Layne Little, Bradley Nystrom, Robert Platzner, Richard Shek and Erin
   Stiles. 2012. *Invitation to World Religions*. Oxford: Oxford University Press.
Buell, Denise Kimber. 2005. *Why This New Race: Ethnic Reasoning in Early Christianity*. New
   York: Columbia University Press.
Dirks, Nicholas B. 2001. *Castes of Mind: Colonialism and the Making of Modern India*. Princeton:
   Princeton University Press.
Durkheim, Emile. 1912. *The Elementary Forms of Religious Life*, edited by Mark S. Cladis.
   Translated by Carol Cosman. Abridged ed. New York: Oxford University Press.
Esposito, John L., Darrell J. Fasching and Todd T. Lewis. 2006. *World Religions Today*. 2nd
   ed. Oxford: Oxford University Press.
Lincoln, Bruce. 1992. *Discourse and the Construction of Society: Studies of Myth, Ritual, and
   Classification*. New York: Oxford University Press.
Lincoln, Bruce. 1996. "Theses on Method." *Method & Theory in the Study of Religion* 8(3):
   225–227.
Lopez, Donald S. 1995. *Curators of the Buddha: The Study of Buddhism under Colonialism*.
   Chicago: University of Chicago Press.
Masuzawa, Tomoko. 2005. *The Invention of World Religions: Or, How European Universalism
   Was Preserved in the Language of Pluralism*. Chicago: University of Chicago Press.
McCutcheon, Russell T. 2001. *Critics Not Caretakers: Redescribing the Public Study of Religion*.
   Albany: State University of New York Press.
Narayanan, Vasudha. 2012. "Hindu Traditions." In *A Concise Introduction to World Religions*,
   edited by Willard G. Oxtoby and Alan F. Segal. 2nd ed., 273–335. Oxford: Oxford
   University Press.
Orsi, Robert. 1985. *The Madonna of 115th Street: Faith and Community in Italian Harlem,
   1880–1950*. New Haven: Yale University Press.
Oxtoby, Willard G. and Alan F. Segal, eds. 2012. *A Concise Introduction to World Religions*.
   2nd ed. Oxford: Oxford University Press.
Smith, Huston. 1965 [1958]. *The Religions of Man*. New York: Harper & Row.
Smith, Jonathan Z. 1982. *Imagining Religion: From Babylon to Jonestown*. Chicago: University
   of Chicago Press.
Smith, Jonathan Z. 1988. "'Narratives into Problems': The College Introductory Course and
   the Study of Religion." *Journal of the American Academy of Religion* 56(4): 727–739.

4

THE CRITICAL EMBRACE

Teaching the World Religions Paradigm as data

Steven W. Ramey

Introduction

News reports about the violence in Myanmar that began around 2012 frequently highlighted the role of monks who incite violence against minority communities identified, typically, as Muslim. Such accounts often reference the violence as 'religious' and the disconnect between nonviolent conceptions of Buddhism and the Buddhist self-identification of the monks perpetrating violence, including labelling the monks involved in the violence in Myanmar as 'extreme' or 'radical' (Fuller 2013). Such accounts illustrate the dominance of the World Religions Paradigm (WRP) in public discourse. Often, we organize the world by defining communities according to broad religious labels (Buddhist and Muslim) and assuming that people who are identified with one of those religions should adhere to particular common traits within that community (Buddhist nonviolence). When those expectations are not met, as in Myanmar, the paradigm necessitates a new explanation (radical monks).

The dominance of such approaches to the world makes the World Religions course challenging. Students often enter the course expecting to understand more about Buddhist nonviolence, for example. They assume the world operates according to the WRP but have limited background in the specifics within that paradigm. This background that our students often bring into our classes is one reason why I advocate teaching the WRP in the introductory courses, but teaching it as a constructed discourse that we critique as we study it.

When I first encountered the critique of the WRP and the idea that descriptions of religions were constructing the object of study rather than simply describing something in the world (during my first semester in the University of North Carolina – Chapel Hill's graduate programme in Religious Studies), it took much of the semester for me to begin to comprehend the ideas and some of their implications.

That experience made me wish that I had encountered these ideas earlier in my academic career (although some of the ideas were not as widely developed and accepted in my undergraduate days as they are today).

My first experience assisting in a World Religions course that displaced the WRP for a thematic approach similarly frustrated students (undergraduates in this case) significantly, as they did not know enough about the discourse to comprehend the alternative organization and the reasons behind it. Common assumptions about undergraduates, especially in introductory courses, fit this experience. Sometimes, faculty see undergraduates as unable to approach theoretical material in a sophisticated manner, leading faculty to de-emphasize the theoretical and fall back on the traditional paradigm, despite the critiques.

These two experiences have had a significant influence on both my research and my pedagogical approaches over the years. I have been surprised how much inertia exists, preventing the reworking of the curriculum in light of the critique of the paradigm. For some, the common explanation that undergraduates are not prepared to understand the critique or a course presenting it justifies the inertia. While at first glance these two experiences, the challenge that I as a graduate student faced and the frustrations that undergraduates experienced, suggest that this critique of the WRP may be too much for an introductory undergraduate course, my experiences have confirmed the need to teach the World Religions course in a different, critical fashion. We should not be teaching undergraduates something that we have to unteach later, particularly because only a few of those in our introductory courses, at least in the US, become majors or graduate students. At the same time, undergraduate students cannot engage a critique of a paradigm about which they possess only very limited knowledge. To face this challenge, I have developed a course that embraces the WRP as a discourse to be taught and critiqued.

Familiarity allows critique

One of the main lessons that I took from my experience of assisting in the thematically designed World Religions course as a graduate student was the need to teach the discourse. Too many of the students had difficulty engaging the alternative approach because they expected a course on the World Religions model but were not familiar enough with the model to comprehend the critique of it. In this sense, starting with where the students are becomes an important principle.[1]

At the University of Alabama (where I teach), the Introduction to Religious Studies course is not designed as a World Religions course. It focuses on an introduction to the field and the issues within it, including questions of the definition of religion and systems of classification along with major theories of religion. When I taught this course, some of the students were disappointed that it was not an actual World Religions course. Hearing similar stories from my colleagues, I proposed that we create a new course, 'Religions of the World', which I would teach in a manner defensible in light of the critique of that paradigm. My hope was that the new course would attract students who might avoid the current introductory course.

The organizing principle for designing this version of a World Religions course was to teach the WRP to students as a discourse rather than a self-evident description.[2] The WRP informs much of the way scholars, journalists, and religious leaders discuss those elements commonly described as religions. Hinduism in textbooks, news accounts and common speech represents to most people a self-evident collection of texts, practices and principles that inform (or should inform) the experiences and choices of people who identify as Hindus. While many of our students do not know much of anything about Hinduism, let alone Daoism or Shinto, they assume that each term references a particular religion that exists out in the world. That assumption becomes the general starting point for a course entitled 'Religions of the World'.

Beyond the issue of what our students understand when they enter a course, the ubiquitous nature of the WRP in society outside academia makes teaching the paradigm imperative. For our students to be educated members of society who function intelligently, they need some familiarity with both the paradigm and its critique. In fact, for our students to do ethnography, whether formally as scholars of religion or informally as social beings who engage others on various topics, including those identified as religious, an understanding of the WRP, which informs the self-perception of so many people who identify as religious adherents, is particularly useful. Despite the history of the paradigm and its roots in European and American constructions of much of the world, many people in places such as India have assimilated many of the conceptions of the paradigm within their own view of the world. Avoiding the paradigm, therefore, fails to educate our students in a significant aspect of how people, including some scholars, construct their worlds.

Critiquing while teaching

The challenge, then, becomes finding ways to decentre the paradigm and critique it while also teaching it. The approach that I advocate uses a World Religions textbook, organized according to specific religions, to accomplish both of these goals. Assigning the textbook provides students with one version of the WRP that they can study. However, the textbook also provides an example of the paradigm to critique. This process requires a shift in focus both for the class session and assessments.

The textbook that I have used is the relatively inexpensive Oxford volume edited by Michael Coogan entitled *The Illustrated Guide to World Religions* (2003). Divided into seven main chapters, the editor selects Judaism, Christianity, Islam, Hinduism, Buddhism, Chinese Religious Traditions and Japanese Religious Traditions to highlight. This selection becomes one of the first critical topics within the course. Juxtaposing this list to the historically shifting list of religions that both Jonathan Z. Smith and Tomoko Masuzawa describe presents doubts about the obvious nature of these lists as straightforward descriptions (Smith 1998, 275–280; Masuzawa 2005, 58–71, 107–120). Instead, these selections become actions that individuals, the editor in this case, employ to construct worlds in particular ways for particular interests. From the very beginning, within the class sessions, the critique of the paradigm, reinforced through the example of the textbook, is central. Adages that systems of classification reflect the interests of their creators and become sites for negotiating competing interests become themes for the entire course.

In my organization of the course, I intentionally highlight the arbitrary selections of the textbook editor and individual chapter authors. I divide the course into four units, focusing generally on several traditionally defined religions within each unit. I organize the course as Judaism and Hinduism (Unit 1), Daoism and Islam (Unit 2), Buddhism and Christianity (Unit 3), and indigenous religions, including Yoruba, Igbo, and Shinto examples (Unit 4). Throughout the semester, I emphasize the role of the textbook editor and myself in selecting how to categorize the religions, what to include and exclude. Pointing out the differences between the textbook's list, which excludes indigenous practices generally and addresses Daoism and Shinto within the broader regional categories of Chinese and Japanese religions respectively, highlights the malleability of the categories and the role of each scholar in determining the different categorizations. Discussing why particular subjects are included, excluded, or organized differently and the assumptions and interests behind those selections and organizing principles helps students employ critical analysis to other examples.

The Coogan volume is particularly helpful in this regard, as Carl S. Ehrlich, the author of the chapter on Judaism, begins with a discussion of why Judaism, despite its size, is included as a world religion. Ehrlich argues that Judaism is a world religion because of the worldwide migration of people who identify as Jews and the influence of Judaism historically (2003, 16). As Judaism is the first world religion that we discuss in the course, these assertions provide another early opportunity to reinforce the analysis of varying lists of world religions. Asking students to consider to whom Judaism has been influential helps them recognize that those collections identified as world religions are important from the perspective of Europeans and North Americans who, as Masuzawa argues, constructed the category of world religions initially (2005). This conception also correlates with the assertion of Jonathan Z. Smith that a world religion 'is, above all, a tradition that has achieved sufficient power and numbers to enter our history to form it, interact with it, or thwart it' (1998, 280). These ideas are particularly useful when we reach the discussion of indigenous religions. Beyond highlighting the problem of assuming commonality across those communities identified as indigenous, the question of influence comes up again. Practices that people commonly place in the indigenous category are not regarded as a world religion for the textbook, at least partially because some people do not identify indigenous communities as particularly influential, a concept students can easily recognize. The focus on Yoruba and Igbo practices further allows a discussion of the label African Traditional Religions and its embedded assumption of commonality across the diverse continent of Africa, and the textbook editor's choice to discuss what he labels Shinto as an aspect of Japanese religions, and the distinction in much discourse between Shinto as a world religion and indigenous traditions further highlights the arbitrary nature of these divisions.

The decision within the Coogan volume to treat some religions (Chinese and Japanese specifically) as regional categories provides further room to critique the larger issues of the WRP. As both of these chapters discuss ways that practices within Chinese and Japanese cultures are neither tightly defined nor exclusive of one another, it becomes possible to illustrate the problems with assuming that religions exist as tightly defined systems. Instead, students can begin to recognize, with guidance, how the categorization of world religions constructs an object of study rather than simply describing elements that exist in the world surrounding us. These examples also enable discussion of alternative ways of viewing and constructing the world. Using the textbook's discussion of practices that do not conform to specific boundaries, since the textbook does not imply that such lack of adherence to specific boundaries is erroneous, suggests other ways that people construct their own worlds. Thus, not only the arbitrariness of specific boundaries becomes clearer but also the assumption that inherent boundaries exist and the process of imposing those boundaries onto reality can be clearly seen.

Beyond understanding that people construct the WRP, determining what counts as important enough to include and where the boundaries separating each religion run, each section of the course also complicates the assumption that everyone who identifies with a particular religion holds elements in common. While the diversity of Hinduism, for example, is a common feature of the WRP, pushing that issue further and connecting it to the broader questions about the paradigm advances student ability to critique the dominant paradigm. Throughout the course, class sessions focusing on particular religions highlight the diversity and contestation within each religion. For example, during the class sessions discussing representations of Judaism, the focus of the sessions highlights differences among those who identify as Jews and contestation surrounding the question, 'who is a Jew?' The first day focuses on the importance of the Torah, discussing both its narrative (very generally) and the ways groups employ it, including its role to establish their community. The discussion of the role of the Torah among some communities who identify as Jewish includes videos of the preparation and installation of scrolls and the study of the Talmud. While these examples connect with standard images within the WRP, comparing different accounts with critical analysis highlights ways people use the Torah and its role in the community to represent themselves in particular ways, as a 'questioning people', as traditional, as both modern and devoted (particularly within the women's study of the Talmud). Thus, the text is more than the story but becomes a means for communities to negotiate status and access to various social and material resources.

The second day continues with the question 'who is a Jew?' through several avenues. I discuss the subdivision along ethnic lines (Sephardim, Ashkenazi, and others) and sectarian lines (Orthodox, Conservative, Reform and others), illustrating in both cases how the particular subdivisions are contested and how the preference of one over another connects with different systems of power, often working to maintain such assumptions of preference. Another conflict over categorization develops in relation to the Israeli Law of Return, which defines a Jew as any grandchild of a Jew for the purposes of immigration, a definition that is more inclusive than many institutional definitions within Israel that recognize Jewish ancestry only through the maternal line. This conflict, arising in part from the concern to provide protection for those who have traditionally been identified as Jews by persecutors, generates contradictions, as people who immigrate as Jews are not considered Jewish within Israel after their migration. Further consideration of the motivations for migration, and efforts of some to police that migration in relation to communities who newly assert a Jewish ancestry, such as the Menashe community in northeastern India, illustrate well the contested nature of identifications and the varied interests that inform the ascription of identities.

Such an emphasis continues through each section of the course, providing discussion of elements commonly included within the WRP and the general issues of identification in ways that illustrate the constructed nature of these categories and the expressions of interests and power that they reflect. The different meanings of the term 'Hindu' and the historical shifts in that category, the overgeneralization of particular theological points in the chapter on Christianity that excludes some who identify as Christian, and the arbitrariness of what is identified separately (Hinduism, Shinto) and what becomes simply an 'indigenous religion' all serve to reinforce the critical analysis of any application of these labels. I further push this point in relation to Buddhism to ask students if the three main branches identified with Buddhism could not be classified as separate religions in the manner that Judaism, Christianity and Islam are identified as separate religions despite often being described as Abrahamic traditions in scholarship. Providing an alternative means of classification, such as this, helps students to look beyond the presumptions embedded within the WRP. In these various ways, class sessions serve not to reinforce what the textbook asserts but to challenge and complicate it, highlighting ways that the textbook and the paradigm more generally are context-specific representations that construct a reality rather than simply describe a reality that exists completely outside the textbook.

Critiquing representations

Beyond the specific critique of the textbook's reproduction of the WRP through its selection and classification of religions, a broader critique of representations becomes central within the class presentations. The textbook is one of a variety of objects for this critique. The consistent emphasis on critiquing representations, including the textbook, reinforces the conception that the textbook and the different representations (as with representations students encounter outside of the classroom) are not unquestionable authorities but sources that present materials in ways that serve a variety of interests.[3]

The assigned readings provide a variety of examples that illustrate the critical analysis that I want my students to embrace. Critiques of overgeneralizations, the evaluation of what topics are included in the main text, what is relegated to sidebars, and what is excluded highlight the hierarchy of importance that authors establish and the effective marginalization of those who are not deemed central, thus downplaying alternative visions of particular religions. Highlighting the assumptions operative in the reading, the various interests that those assertions and assumptions might serve, and alternative ways of presenting the material trains students to think critically about a variety of written sources.

For class sessions discussing a particular world religion, I incorporate a range of sources, often adding clips from documentary videos, motion pictures or news items to the readings to illustrate the selective nature of different types of representations by juxtaposing them to each other, to the textbook, and to the broader representation in the classroom. In the section discussing elements understood to be Daoism, we discuss clips from an English language documentary on the Wudang monasteries that was produced for Chinese television. This documentary discusses aspects of the life of a nun in one of the monasteries, detailing her daily activities that differ considerably from the idealized image of Daoist non-action and harmony. While highlighting that tension with the textbook representations, the students and I also discuss the filmmaker's selection of images and topics and the impressions that they create, which we have linked to particular interests within China about both heritage and tourism, among other interests. The origin tale of Wudang kung fu within the documentary series, which connects it to a Daoist master who moved in unison with the heavenly bodies, further provides opportunity to discuss the use of myth to provide authenticity and authority to one of several forms of martial arts. In a later class, we juxtapose those groups of images to the representation of the Wudang temples in the *Karate Kid III* motion picture, which presents a different, exotic image of the Wudang mountains and the link between martial arts and Daoism. Through extended exercises such as these, the emphasis within class sessions is not conveying information but training students to approach a variety of sources critically, paying particular attention to the discourse surrounding world religions.

This critical analysis of representations extends also to the representation of people who identify with the religion being discussed. As discussions of the problems dividing insiders and outsiders suggest, treating insider assertions differently from presumably outsider assertions is difficult to maintain. The Coogan volume confirms this problem, as at least some scholars identify with the particular religions about which they write. In fact, a full critique of the WRP as a discourse necessitates a critique of the assertions of people who identify with a particular religion, as many times practitioners have adopted the language of the WRP, sometimes because they find it useful for their own construction of community and individual identification as well as a tool with which to negotiate their position within a social hierarchy. With the course emphasis on the competing assertions of people who identify with the same religious label, it becomes impossible to simply accept practitioner statements uncritically, since those assertions contradict or challenge statements of others who self-identify with the same religion. One documentary entitled *Following the Buddha* presents a Thai woman ordained as a Theravada monk who challenges the assertions of other Theravada monks in Thailand. Showing clips from this documentary allows us to critique the selections and exclusions that each participant in the debate is making and the general impression that the filmmaker generates through the selection of quotes and images. Similarly, the analysis of myths and their use within contemporary competitions for resources or power also provides an important opportunity to help students think critically about the assertions of practitioners. Whether it is assertions about the supremacy of Amaterasu through the story of her defeat of Susano-o or assertions through the story of Abram/Abraham that God gave the Israelites the land of Canaan, students can begin to see the ways in which some who identify with each religion can use these narratives that they designate as sacred to promote political interests and arguments.

One particular exercise, however, has been especially useful in helping students to develop these skills. Twice during the semester, students work in groups to present a critical analysis of two news articles. Organized into small groups, students present in ten-minute time slots on the designated day before either myself or a Graduate Teaching Assistant. The emphasis on the critical analysis of a variety of representations throughout the class provides students with examples of the analysis that they should develop and present. As I describe the assignment, referencing those examples and emphasizing repeatedly that group presentations should not summarize the articles but should emphasize critical analysis, helps clarify expectations. Beyond providing examples and explicit instructions, providing opportunities for the groups to work on similar discussion questions, such as a critical analysis of a video clip, during several preceding class sessions facilitates better group cohesion and thus more successful presentations.

Each time I have used this exercise, around twenty per cent of the groups did an excellent job from the beginning, and a similar number did a good job of developing a critical analysis. What appears crucial within this process is for each group to receive explicit feedback immediately and to have another opportunity to present. In the second presentation several weeks later, almost the entire class had improved their performance in this exercise, with a small minority still failing to grasp the concept of a critical analysis in a satisfactory manner. While I wish that I could report that everyone succeeded in understanding what a critical analysis would entail, the improvement that many of the groups showed has suggested that this exercise is vital. In order to get students to think critically about discourses, including the discourse surrounding the WRP, illustrating the analysis then requiring students to develop and express their own analysis and providing immediate, direct feedback to that presentation seems to make a greater difference than the delayed, written feedback on paper assignments.

In practice: comparisons provide alternatives

Another strategy that I employ to help students engage with the critique of the WRP is to encourage them to envision other ways of organizing the world that they observe. Noting the historically shifting list of religions within European understandings (particularly the category Paganism that later subdivides into Hinduism, Buddhism, Daoism, Shinto, etc.) helps students recognize that the currently common list of religions involves decisions about where to draw boundaries that are not inherent in the items which are categorized. The discussion of subdividing those movements identified as Buddhism into multiple religions, as mentioned above, provides another alternative approach to categorization.

I also insert into the course another layer of comparison to provide further opportunities to challenge categories and critique representations, combining portions of W. E. Paden's *Religious Worlds* (1994) and other academic reflections related to each section of the course. Each of the four course sections considers the particular communities in relation to a thematic element. The first unit focuses on myth, narrative, and text, so the different conceptions of canon and textual authority that people commonly attribute to Judaism and Hinduism complicate the conception of a sacred text. Focusing the second unit on ritual facilitates analysis of the different understandings of ritualized action that people associate with Daoism and Islam and the diversity within each community broadly conceived over ritualized practices. Unit three highlights the role of divine and revered figures, developing debates and contestation within and between people who identify as Buddhists and Christians. The final unit, which analyses questions of social structure, morality and discipline, addresses the connections between practices and dictates in Ibo, Yoruba and Shinto communities and various political, material, and social interests that the discourse on world religions often distinguishes from religion.

In the conclusion of each section, after spending time discussing the representation of each religion and the inherent contestations and complications within them, we discuss the specific theme in relation to the selected communities. Beyond contrasting the various ways in which people who identify with each label conceive the specific element, such as the varying conceptions of the Buddha and of Jesus as human or divine, we also discuss different interests that those elements could serve for each community. For example, the discussion of revered figures in relation to the Buddha and Jesus includes the variety of visual images of both figures that illustrate the historical context of each image. This approach easily raises issues of the ethnic and racial assumptions and biases that inform many of those visual images and the interests that intersect with the creation of an image, and subsequent debates over proper visual representations. Discussions of film depictions of such figures, including the controversy surrounding the casting of both Jesus and Satan in the History Channel's 2013 miniseries *The Bible* (where some viewers identified the depiction of Satan as resembling Barack Obama as well as the ethnic/racial overtones of the miniseries' defence that the Moroccan actor had commonly played Satanic figures), illustrate the power of media images to construct impressions of narratives and figures associated with religions. These discussions further challenge the assumption that religion remains obviously separate from other aspects of life.

These comparative sections, though, also provide an opportunity to challenge the assumed distinctiveness of religion in another manner. Discussing each theme allows the comparison of that theme with something not commonly defined as religion, whether the protection of the Declaration of Independence in the Library of Congress as a sacred text or the venerated figures of Bear Bryant and Nick Saban in relation to Alabama football, helping students to recognize that the common system of categorization in relation to world religions that many students enter the class holding (however vaguely) derives from various assumptions and that alternative systems of classification are possible.

In practice: assessment and subversion

Focusing the course on the subversion of the WRP through critical analysis of the discourse surrounding world religions requires a shift in assessment practices. Standard questions about particular terms related to a specific religion or philosophical conception often imply that students are learning the truth about a reality outside of the discourse, which directly contradicts the points that I want to emphasize within the course. However, some understanding of the paradigm, terms associated with it, and specific examples within the paradigm are useful to prepare students to engage with more specialized texts and to analyse them critically. When the World Religions course is one component of a larger curriculum that reflects the WRP, such tension can become even more serious.

One strategy that I have used in assessing student learning is to frame carefully the variety of questions that I put on tests, often multiple choice questions for the larger enrolment courses. Whether emphasizing specific terms or ideas or focusing on the diversity within a religion, I attempt to highlight within the question the issue of perspective and representation. Thus, on quizzes related to assigned readings, a question may begin, 'According to the Coogan volume' to remind students that the defining of a practice comes from that perspective as opposed to being a universally accepted concept. Some questions also shift the focus from the term itself to its representation, asking students to identify the perspective or interest being promoted when a particular source asserts that a practice is standard within a religion. In these ways, students taking the quiz or exam need to understand particular terms and conceptions while also placing them within the context of a specific, critique-able representation.

Questions that emphasize the diversity within a category, such as the diverse meanings of the labels Jew or Hindu, often result in an 'All of the above' answer. Some students have joked that the correct answers range from 'All of the above' to 'It depends on who you ask', and I have noticed some students selecting 'All of the above' even when all answers being correct is logically impossible. While I incorporate a variety of questions on the tests to encourage them to engage with all of the options fully on each question, having students take seriously the idea that answers vary depending on who is making the representation and often simple answers are problematic demonstrates some success in subverting the WRP and student preconceptions that they need to learn the single correct answer for each question.

Moving beyond multiple choice questions also advances the subversion of the WRP even in a large enrolment course. After my first semester teaching this course, I began adding a short paragraph essay question to the exams as an additional tool to require a different level of student engagement. Similarly, throughout the semester I require students to write in class as a measure of their comprehension of the issues that we discuss, particularly surrounding critical analysis, and as a method to improve their engagement with the material. These writing exercises, along with the required group presentations, provide students with the opportunity to apply the critical ideas themselves rather than to observe them passively. For any of these various assessment opportunities, however, the prompts need to reflect the subversion of the paradigm through the acknowledgement of whose representation(s) the question addresses.

The challenges of subverting the paradigm

An obvious challenge within any survey-style course, which this approach often exacerbates, is the challenge of time. When I have taught the course, each segment of the course often feels rushed, as I leave out various significant topics in relation to the selected communities. However, that issue is not unique to this particular approach to the World Religions course, as any survey course, particularly something as broad as world religions, requires significant exclusions to be able to survey the range of material that the course is designed to address. The difficulty, of course, is determining which elements to exclude, as each section can contribute to the overall subversion of the paradigm.

The larger challenge about time, which I touched on in discussing assessment, is the need to learn sufficient vocabulary both to engage other discussions (and hopefully other courses) and to analyse representations of particular religions (whether organized according to the WRP, a regional approach, or a thematic approach). Realizing that many students not only will not take further courses but also will not remember the finer details of terms and their nuances has reduced my concern on this point. Thus, focusing on a few main terms and providing students with the skills both to find information and analyse it when they need further details are particularly effective strategies. However, it becomes important to discuss with colleagues the role of the survey course within the broader departmental curriculum. If faculty assume a certain pool of knowledge in upper level courses because it should be learned in the survey course, then the balance between detailed terminology and critical skills becomes trickier (especially for those in contingent and tenure-track positions). If those teaching advanced courses cannot assume that everyone has taken the survey course, then the lecturer faces fewer obstacles when adopting this approach. It is also possible that some students will recall the shortened list of terms, combined with the skills in critical analysis, better than a broader list and contribute to advanced courses more significantly than students taught in a more traditional World Religions course.

Teaching the course in a fashion as I have outlined brings the additional challenge of an increased divide between student expectations and course content. In my experience, some students are more comfortable with clear and concise facts and want a clear answer about what people do in these other religions that they pre-sume exist outside their personal experiences. Students with such interests may experience some disappointment with my approach. Anxiety often increases around the time of the first test, as some students become concerned about what to study since we spend significant time developing skills. I have compiled brief lists of terms and concepts as study guides, and I have often presented students with the essay question so that they can think through the question ahead of time. Beyond easing the anxiety of some students, it also makes the assessment more of a teaching experience, as the time that they spend preparing for the essay question focuses their attention on the critical analysis that the essay question (and the entire course) emphasizes. The video clips of practices that we analyse as representations of these communities, as well as the textbook, also serve to satisfy some of the curiosity that drives some of the student expectations for the course. While I hope that our analysis mitigates the exoticization that is an element in some of the videos and student expectations, that analysis does not eliminate the interests that many students have about people in other parts of the world. Everyone in these courses does not grasp fully the theory and methods of analysis that I employ, though that was also true in courses that I taught in a more standard form. However, some students have been particularly engaged with the approach and have decided to take additional courses in the academic study of religion. To the extent that later courses also employ a more analytical, less descriptive approach, this style of teaching the World Religions course can result in encouraging those who are open to such approaches to continue with the academic study of religion.

A different type of challenge is the ubiquitous nature of the WRP. The paradigm dominates so much of our language that subverting it is difficult. As soon as you organize the course according to Judaism, Hinduism, Daoism, etc., the course structure already reinforces the paradigm. Using the textbook certainly does not help matters in this regard. However, some simple shifts in language can turn these problems into opportunities to retrain ourselves as well as the students, even though the changes are not easy to maintain consistently. Primarily, the scholar should always identify whose understanding of a religion is being discussed at any moment. Rather than stating, 'Judaism has three main branches', state, 'These three groups are commonly identified as the main branches of Judaism.' The difference is minor, and the first statement is certainly more succinct, but the difference, if used consistently, can become significant. The first statement implies that 'Judaism' is an object that can be factually described, employing a definitive tone. The second statement suggests that everyone might not agree with the designation of three main branches. That kernel of doubt is quite subversive to the declarative nature of the WRP. Moreover, this general statement coordinates well with other assertions within the course concerning the debates over Jewish identity (and the diversity that other community labels represent). Combining that acknowledgement of whose categorization we are presenting at any time with discussions about a particular group's contested claims to be Jewish or the comparison of various post-9/11 statements about Islam constructs a consistent image of the contested nature of the content and meaning of the labels that are assumed within the WRP.

Although I am not always consistent in my acknowledgement of whose application of a religious label is being discussed, some of the students have picked up on this language and have begun using it in their writing assignments, presentations, and exams. Even a few students who continue taking courses in the department have employed the strategy of acknowledging contested labels in other classes and in conversations outside of class. This development, more than any performance on an assessment or group presentation, reflects a successful subversion of the WRP. Teaching the paradigm as discourse, critiquing schemes of classification, and altering our own language, when combined together, can successfully reinforce each other and the challenge to the WRP. Now I have students in my other classes catching my own slips when I fall back on the dominant discourse in a simplified reference to Daoism or Hinduism. For me, that is a cherished sign of success.

Notes

1 See also Corrywright in this volume.
2 For more on discursive approaches, see Taira in this volume.
3 See many other chapters in this volume, particularly Martin, McConeghy, and Taira.

References

Coogan, Michael D., ed. 2003. *The Illustrated Guide to World Religions*. Oxford and New York: Oxford University Press.
Ehrlich, Carl S. 2003. "Judaism." In *The Illustrated Guide to World Religions*, edited by Michael D. Coogan, 14–51. Oxford and New York: Oxford University Press.
Fuller, Thomas. 2013. "Extremism Rises Among Myanmar Buddhists." *New York Times* (20 June). http://www.nytimes.com/2013/06/21/world/asia/extremism-rises-among-myanmar-buddhists-wary-of-muslim-minority.html?pagewanted=all (accessed 17 April 2014).
Masuzawa, Tomoko. 2005. *The Invention of World Religions: Or, How European Universalism Was Preserved in the Language of Pluralism*. Chicago: University of Chicago Press.
Paden, William E. 1994. *Religious Worlds: The Comparative Study of Religion, with a New Preface*. Boston: Beacon Press.
Smith, Jonathan Z. 1998. "Religion, Religions, Religious." In *Critical Terms for Religious Studies*, edited by Mark. C. Taylor, 269–284. Chicago: The University of Chicago Press.

PART II

Alternative pedagogies: power and politics

5

RELIGION AS IDEOLOGY

Recycled culture vs. world religions

Craig Martin

As shown in many chapters in this volume – particularly those in the part on 'subversive pedagogies' (cf. Sutcliffe; Ramey; Baldrick-Morrone *et al.*) – teaching against the World Religions Paradigm (WRP) is made difficult in part by the fact that the WRP is partially hegemonic and, as such, shapes our students' assumptions and preconceptions about the subject-matter of our courses.[1] We risk facing student frustration when they feel they have been a victim of a bait-and-switch: they enrol expecting to be taught the spiritual essentials of the world's religions, only to find such essentialism thwarted at every step and supplanted by, for example, an emphasis on society, classification and authority. Indeed, I'm sometimes challenged by students: 'I thought this class was going to be on religion; why are we talking so much about social structure? When are we getting to Adam and Eve and the Qur'an and stuff?'

Although my courses appear on the surface to be oriented around a specific *content* – I teach 'Religions of the West' and 'Religions of the East' – my courses are actually organized by a *theoretical question* of my choosing, such as how social reproduction takes place, or how gender is constructed and contested. However, I attempt to meet the students' expectations halfway by choosing the data or content from the so-called 'world religions' at hand, to which we will apply the theoretical questions. I typically use a quasi-Marxist, non-essentialist social functionalist theory in my courses, focusing on how the elements of so-called 'religious' traditions are used to advance social agendas. Thus, for instance, I might introduce students to the canonical 'basics' of Christianity, but then go on to show them how those canonical cultural elements are used, reused, and recycled in support of various social agendas in different times and places. In the end, the course turns out not to be about Christianity, but rather about how different groups make functional uses out of their local cultural inheritance. In addition, since such uses are so widely variable, a necessary corollary is that such traditions lack an essence of the sort the

WRP assumes. Contrary to the *sui generis* approach that assumes 'the Sacred' or some other non-empirical, ontologically distinct, transhuman essence is revealed to us through an *axis mundi* or hierophany, I present the contents of the so-called 'world religions' as garden variety, humdrum social rhetorics. On such a view, all religions turn out to be the 'same' in a sense, but the shared elements around which their identity is drawn – discourses, authority claims, power relations, etc. – are, on the one hand, available for empirical investigation and, on the other hand, also the 'same' as those of other social and political formations.

What do I mean when I say I take a 'quasi-Marxist, non-essentialist social functionalist' approach in my courses? I use the phrase 'quasi-Marxist' loosely in order to designate the view that ideologies, discourses, or rhetorics have material effects within a set of power relations – and to recommend that they be analysed as such, using a hermeneutic of suspicion. To take one banal example, in retrospect it is clear that the doctrine of the 'divine right of kings' functioned to protect European kings from encroachments on their power by the Catholic church, and a quasi-Marxist perspective would approach such claims to divine rights as royal justifications for existing powers or legitimations for expanding power. I use the phrase 'non-essentialist' to designate historical investigations – so clearly described in Foucault's reading of Nietzsche (Foucault 1984) – which seek not to document the unfolding of essences over time, but rather to show how such 'essences' are historical accomplishments that are projected backward into the past as legitimations of the present. On such a view, gendered behaviour does not reflect binary sexual essences working themselves out in men and women, and nor do nations reflect the essence of a 'folk' or a people expressing itself in history. From a non-essentialist perspective, 'Islam' is neither intrinsically 'peace', nor 'submission', nor 'jihad', but rather can mean *anything* that contemporary practitioners make of it – although what they make of it often involves the projection of their favourite invented essence into the past and a narrative outlining how it expresses itself in the behaviour of all 'authentic' Muslims over time. Perhaps the best brief description of the non-essentialist approach is provided by Aaron Hughes, who once suggested that 'no such thing [as Islam] can exist. ... Islam, like any other religious tradition, is a series of sites of contestation' (Hughes 2007, 54); on this view, 'Islam' is a floating signifier whose content changes depending on whomever is talking.

When I describe myself as a 'functionalist', I do not mean in the Parsonian sense that every society requires various organs, and 'religion' is a specific organ that serves a central function – such a view is essentialist in assuming that the functions 'religion' can serve are determined in advance and unchanging. By contrast, when I describe myself as a functionalist I mean that the elements of cultural traditions can be used by practitioners or social actors to serve a wide variety of purposes within a social formation. For instance, the discourse on 'inalienable rights', 'liberty' and 'equality' *functioned* in early America to *advance the interests* of white, land-owning men, although this function is by no means essential to the discourse – the terms of the discourse have subsequently been employed to advance the interests of women and ethnic minorities. In addition, the rhetoric of 'fairness' and 'equality' now pervades almost all levels of society, from presidential speeches to children claiming their parents aren't being 'fair' – the rhetoric is extremely plastic and its use is not determined in advance but rather can serve a wide variety of purposes in various social sites. (For a fuller presentation of a quasi-Marxist, non-essentialist social functionalism, see my introductory textbook, Martin 2012 – especially Chapter 1.)

My assumption that authoritative discourses and practices lack an essential social function but can be recycled to serve a variety of purposes – as circumstances change – is in part shaped by Jonathan Z. Smith's essay, 'Sacred Persistence: Toward a Redescription of Canon' (1982). For Smith, culture is like cuisine: ingenious and inventive chefs can turn a very small selection of foods – out of an almost infinite variety available to us in the natural world – into an indefinite number of dishes. Similarly, ingenious and inventive cultural actors can put a very small selection of discourses in a limited canon to an indefinite number of social purposes. The closure or limitation of the canon is reciprocally related to the ingenuity of the interpreters of the canon. Smith writes:

> The process of arbitrary limitation and of overcoming limitation through ingenuity recurs. As the pressure is intensified through extension and through novelty, because of the presupposition of canonical completeness, it will be the task of the hermeneute to develop exegetical procedures that will allow the canon to be applied without alteration or, at least, without admitting to alteration.
>
> *(1982, 50)*

On this view, the 'application' of principles in the discourses at hand 'is not a generalized systematic process, but a homiletic endeavor, a quite specific attempt to make the "text" speak to a quite particular situation' (1982, 51). Consequently, my task as an instructor is to bring the procedures of various hermeneutes into focus, to reveal the rhetorical games continually deployed, with an eye specifically to the social and political stakes at hand.

The phrase, 'my task as an instructor', is of course freighted with normative assumptions about what the academic study of religion should look like. I can make three of these assumptions explicit here. First, I assume that if the academic study of religion – or any subject – wants to retain intersubjective validity (as opposed to objective validity), it should be *historicist* and *naturalist* in spirit, eschewing supernatural claims and ahistorical essentialisms. Second, I assume that we should set ourselves the task of *unmasking* the invisible social functions of, for instance, supernatural claims and strategic essentialisms, and should historicize their appearance. Third, I assume that while social or political agendas related to the world outside academia might direct our gaze as instructors – for instance, familial patriarchy is likely to be of interest as an object of critical academic study not to patriarchs but to academic feminists who desire to expose as social inventions what patriarchy presents as natural – scholarship should avoid imperatives about these matters and restrict itself largely to intersubjectively falsifiable or contestable claims that could, in principle and with evidence, be affirmed by readers whose interests or sympathies are not identical to the author's. Of course, these assumptions set my approach apart from, for instance, that of those phenomenologists or perennialist scholars who see the purpose of scholarship to lie with a nonreductive 'understanding' of the 'meaning' of religion for practitioners; by contrast, my approach is clearly situated within the legacy of the 'hermeneutics of suspicion'.

In what follows I will describe how I use such an approach in two of my courses, while attending to some of the strengths and weaknesses of the approach, as well as what works and what does not in the classroom.

In practice: the evolution of Jesus

The course in which I can most easily use this sort of functionalist approach is one I titled, provocatively, 'The Evolution of Jesus', instead of, for example, 'Christianity'. The description on the syllabus reads as follows:

> Jesus is such an authoritative figure that his legacy is claimed not only by Christians, but also by practitioners in other traditions. The figure of Jesus has not been a constant; his image has evolved radically over time. This course will consider many reinventions of Jesus, as well as the social agendas advanced by those reinventions. A considerable part of the semester will focus on how the reinventions of Jesus changed after the rise of capitalism. Our guiding questions will be the following:
>
> > Who is trying to persuade whom of what with this interpretation of Jesus?
> > In what context is the interpretation situated?
> > What are the consequences should it be received as persuasive?

We begin the course by focusing on first- or second-century texts; students read the canonical gospels Mark, Matthew and John, and one non-canonical gospel, the Apocryphon of John. We of course discuss evidence that the authors of Matthew and Luke copied from Mark and a hypothetical document called Q, while they simultaneously manipulated what they copied over. I offer a historical-critical reading of the texts, situating them in the contexts in which they were written, and showing how Jesus was presented both as an apocalyptic prophet and a teacher with secret knowledge of the 'light' that will enable us to gain eternal life; the figure of Jesus was contested even at the so-called 'origin' of Christianity. The historical-critical reading is intended to denaturalize the Jesus they already know; I take great pains to contrast the Jesus in the gospels with the Jesus of contemporary popular imagination. Whereas the popular version of Jesus is, e.g., all about love or salvation from sins, the author who wrote Mark was clearly more interested in, e.g., abandoning family and friends in preparation for an apocalyptic event expected to arrive in his own lifetime. Such a Jesus is likely of little use for most contemporary readers situated in an industrial or post-industrial society. Consequently, the remainder of the course focuses on how the figure of Jesus is creatively transformed in modern contexts.

I provide students with the critical, theoretical tools we will use by having them read 'Ideology and the Study of Religion' (Martin 2013) and 'How Religion Works: Authority' (in Martin 2012). The first reading introduces students to some of the ways in which Marx talked about 'ideology', specifically focusing on the claims that (1) ideology is produced by the ruling class and in support of the interests of the ruling class, that (2) ideology is part of a superstructure that reinforces a base, and that (3) ideology mystifies reality, and where commodity fetishism is a paradigmatic example. The reading on authority focuses on the concepts of projection and selective privileging; practitioners often project their own voices onto absent authority figures or, where an authoritative canon exists, pick and choose whatever from the canon can most easily be enlisted in support of the social agenda at hand. The chapter concludes,

> [A]uthority is an extremely complicated matter. Although religious practitioners frequently hold particular figures or sacred texts as authoritative, that doesn't mean they follow their authorities in any simple or straightforward manner. On the contrary, authorities are often subjected to projection, selective privileging, partial rejection, … etc. … [For this reason,] understanding Christianity does not require us to understand who Jesus really was, but how the figure of Jesus – as an absent authority – was recreated and recycled over and over in various historical contexts. The reinventions of Jesus are more important than Jesus himself. … Religious traditions are subject to ongoing recreation and evolution, and focusing our studies on their 'origins' is as misguided as trying to measure the height of an oak tree by looking at an acorn.
>
> *(Martin 2012, 142–143)*

Once we've acquired these crucial analytical terms – ideology, ruling class, superstructure and base, mystification, authority, projection, and selective privileging – we move on to focusing not on the New Testament canon but rather on the various uses of that canon.

Since I view the capitalist mode of production – a Marxist term denoting a combination of the means of production (i.e., the materials, tools, assembly lines, factories, technical knowledge and expertise, etc.) and the relations of production (i.e., the relations of property, contracts, profit, capital, wage labour, relations between labourers, business owners, consumers, etc.) – as one of the most important determinants of contemporary culture and behaviour, I focus on how Jesus is (re)imagined after the rise of the capitalist mode of production. We analyse a number of pro-capitalist Jesuses, focusing on Russell Conwell's 'Acres of Diamonds' speech (Conwell 1915), which teaches a gospel of wealth; Laurie Beth Jones' *Jesus, Entrepreneur* (Jones 2001), which presents Jesus as a model businessman and from whom entrepreneurial readers can learn key business insights; and Bill O'Reilly and Martin Dugard's *Killing Jesus* (O'Reilly and Dugard 2013), which presents Jesus as a sort of libertarian icon who opposed taxation and achieved greatness independently of any governmental or institutional support. At that point we turn to a number of socialist or communist Jesuses, focusing on Samuel Zane Batton's social gospel message in 'The Social Nature of Christianity' (1911), Bouck White's *The Call of the Carpenter* (1914), which presents Jesus as a working class hero who agitated against the Romans, who are depicted as capitalists; and Terry Eagleton's revolutionary Jesus in his introduction to *The Gospels* (2007), a book which is part of a series on 'revolutionary figures' from the leftist press Verso.

At every point the students are required to apply the critical concepts introduced earlier in the course to the texts at hand. Do these texts assume, reflect, reinforce or naturalize a particular mode of production? Are these texts designed to advance the interests of a particular class or social group over others? Do the texts arguably distort or mystify how the economy functions? What parts of the New Testament do they privilege in drawing their picture of Jesus? What do they discard or ignore from the New Testament that might be at odds with their agenda? Are their readings of the New Testament anachronistic? To what extent do the authors anachronistically project their own voices onto Jesus?

Sometimes the answers to these questions are remarkably simple. Russell Conwell mystifies the nature of the capitalist economy by advancing a myth of meritocracy according to which *everyone* in America *could* get rich if they wanted to. Bill O'Reilly, in an interview about his book that we watch, anachronistically suggests that Jesus of course hated the USSR. Laurie Beth Jones says that when Jesus told a sick man to 'get up and walk', he meant we should follow our dreams by enrolling in dancing lessons or going to a day spa; she also says that we can know that Jesus had excellent entrepreneurial 'market timing' because he chose to be born right at year one (she seems not to realize that the Christian dating system is *based on* Jesus's presumed year of birth). Bouck White anachronistically portrays the Roman emperors as capitalist pigs and the Israelites as an ancient proletariat. It is clear to all students – even the weakest – that these reinventions of Jesus are tied to competing social or political interests. Because these readings illustrate the social theory at hand so easily, students have very little difficulty historicizing them.

While some students might be inclined to see these Jesuses as departures from an authentic origin, I discourage that simplistic (and self-serving, insofar as it prevents them from interrogating their assumed origin narrative) interpretation by pointing out that the portrayals of Jesus in the first century were already divided. While Bill O'Reilly and Bouck White manipulate the tradition in support of their own (implicit or explicit) political agendas, so did the author of Matthew, for example, manipulate Mark and Q, from whom he copied. The more contemporary authors are therefore doing nothing exceptional: the so-called 'Christian' tradition was from the beginning an ongoing process of recycling inherited cultural materials for new purposes – a fact that of course calls into question the very idea of a 'beginning'.

At the end of the semester, one of my closing lectures points out that the class has never really been about Christianity, and, in fact, nor has it even been about Jesus. On the contrary, the course has actually been about *the processes* or the means by which groups imagine their past in order to advance a particular vision of the present or future. Thus does 'Christianity' as a 'world religion' dissolve; substituted in its place is a cultural process brought into relief by the theoretical apparatus we've deployed on the so-called 'Christian' data. In addition, by pointing out that these processes are utilized in practically all social formations – for instance, the 'founding fathers' trope in American political discourse is a blatant example, or the origins stories attributing the authentic foundation of India to an Aryan race – 'religion' turns out not to be a unique case but just one type of culture alongside other types of culture. Christians are thus interested social actors like any other, employing discursive strategies about the past in order to create a present or future that aligns with their interests.

In practice: religions of the East

This approach to the subject-matter is easy for the 'Evolution of Jesus' course, since I can assign only those readings about Jesus to which the social theory can effort-lessly be applied. When it comes to 'Religions of the West' and 'Religions of the East', the task is made more difficult by the fact that students expect a *survey* of a wider variety of materials, not all of which are as easily interpreted in light of this social theory – in part because I am not an expert in all of the matters that students assume we will cover, and because students often lack any prior familiarity with some of the material and require very basic instruction (that is, we can't historicize claims about karma, samsara, varnas and class dharma until students learn what those terms mean). I can talk about parts of 1 and 2 Kings as royal propaganda, and can show students how the terms of the Bhagavad Gita are tied to the ancient Indian class system, but I'm simply not knowledgeable enough about, e.g., the social contexts in which the Rig Veda or the Talmud were written to apply this form of critique. Of course, it is likely to be impossible that any single instructor could have the in-depth knowledge necessary to historicize all of the texts that students expect to be surveyed in a two-semester 'World Religions' curriculum. However, despite this, it is nevertheless still quite easy to emphasize how cultural tropes are recycled and changed over time, even if the interests served in particular social contexts are not easily discerned.

In 'Religions of the East', we survey Hinduism and Buddhism; here I'll focus on how I cover the former. For Hinduism, I assign selections from ancient texts, including the Vedas, the Upanishads and the Bhagavad Gita, and then we jump all the way to the late nineteenth and twentieth century with a collection of writings by Vivekananda. We discuss the fact that although almost all 'Hindus' write as if the Vedic sources are the most authoritative – as they are the oldest – the Vedas nevertheless show little resemblance to the themes, norms, or cosmology of the Upanishads and the Gita. In fact, the philosophical cosmology that ends up becoming more or less dominant and which is assumed by Vivekananda – involving the characterization of Brahman as a divine substance, the wheel of samsara on which the atman is continually reincarnated, the end goal of escape from samsara, etc. – is derived more from the Upanishads. In addition, we note that while the Upanishads seem to be concerned with the renunciation of action as a means of liberation from samsara, the Gita criticizes that means and emphasizes instead the discipline of acting according to class duty or bhakti worship of the gods. Vivekananda, by contrast, emphasizes duty to some extent but completely empties it of the class connotations found in the Gita. In addition, Vivekananda claims that all 'religious' traditions derive from the same source and are, at bottom, identical in their teachings – we must all get in touch with our inner selves, which are divine in origin; this claim, while arguably consistent with the teachings of the Upanishads, completely glosses over competing claims in the Vedas and the Gita. Later in the course when we talk about the teachings of the Buddha, we can return to this last point; contrary to Vivekananda's assertion, it is clear that many Buddhist teachings are at odds with the claim that we have divine selves with which we must connect.

Thus, much like Jesus, the so-called 'Hindu' tradition is a cultural tradition that has clearly evolved over time. As Olav Hammer writes,

> Diachronic change arises because religions, like 'cultures' more broadly, have no essential components that are inherently stable over time: old doctrines are replaced by new ones, existing rituals die out in favor of ritual innovations, and organizational structures are transformed. Innovations arise when the selection of religious elements from the repertoire changes, when existing elements are discarded or new elements introduced.
>
> *(2009, 11)*

For Christianity, there is a *relative* continuity provided by the canon, which has been more or less stable since the fourth century CE, even if interpretations of that canon are widely varying. However, at this point in 'Religions of the East' we consider: if 'Hinduism' is a cultural tradition in a process of ongoing evolution, but is lacking both a common set of teachings and a stable canon anchoring the tradition, in what sense can we say it is 'a' tradition? If the Vedas and Vivekananda teach completely different things, on what ground can we call them part of the 'same' cultural tradition?

To help answer this question, we read 'Deconstructing Hindu Identity' from D. N. Jha's *Rethinking Hindu Identity*.[2] Jha points out that people have tried to anchor Hindu identity around the subcontinent, Bharata (or Mother India), around a core 'religious' teaching or 'Hindu' identity, around a static, unchanging doctrine, etc. In each case he demonstrates that all involve anachronisms. The use of the term Bharata individuates different geographical regions at different times and the term is completely absent from the Vedas, which are supposed to be the origin of Hinduism. The term 'Hindu' was not used at all by Indians until the fourteenth century and didn't become a dominant term of self-identity for Indians until the nineteenth century. And, as already noted, the doctrines found across the texts that are, only in retrospect, identified as 'Hindu' are clearly variable rather than static. Jha concludes by pointing out that Hinduism as we know it is an invention of the nineteenth century, and that only retrospectively are the Vedas, the Upanishads, etc. identified as 'Hindu'.

It is here that a consideration of British colonialism becomes an important economic and political context for understanding this invention of Hinduism. When the British arrived they began identifying and emphasizing some Indians as Hindu and others as Muslim in a manner out of proportion to prior emic identifications; in addition, they tied those identities to the colonial administration such that it put 'Hindus' and 'Muslims' in an unprecedented zero-sum game. As a result, some 'Hindu' intellectuals invented the myth of an ancient Hindu identity tied to the land, with the corollary that 'Muslims' (and others) could not rightly claim power or perhaps even belong in India. Jha writes, 'indigenous propaganda writings ... demonize[d] Muslims and Christians, and propagate[d] the idea that India and Hinduism are eternal' (2009, 10). From Jha's perspective, 'Hinduism' is not a 'world religion' existing from eternity or even from the creation of the Vedas; on the contrary, it is a nineteenth-century invention as a part of propaganda designed to advance the interests of those who identified as 'Hindus' against those who identified as 'Muslims', a battle that didn't exist as a zero-sum game until the arrival of the British colonizers.

I make it clear to my students that if we had a time-machine and went back to talk to the authors of the Vedas or the Upanishads, they wouldn't identify as Hindus and wouldn't have any idea what Hinduism was. Consequently, one wonders, for what reason am I assigning the Vedas and the Upanishads in a class about Hinduism? The answer, quite simply, is that the framework created by nineteenth-century propagandists has such a hegemony and an inertia that even scholarship on India follows the propagandists' paradigm. It is somewhat odd, of course, that political propaganda has served as the basis for scholarly approaches to the subject-matter; however, for better or for worse, scholars are never able to fully lift themselves to a presumably 'objective' perspective above the fray of the rest of the world's power relations. It is for this reason that for so long histories of Christianity repeated the early Christian narrative of battles of 'orthodoxy' against 'heresy', and parroted the self-proclaimed orthodoxy's construction of a 'gnostic' other. Similarly, histories of the so-called 'relation between church and state' tend to be freighted with the normative assumptions of the Protestant reformers who invented this rhetoric. For reasons clearly documented in Derrida's deconstruction of Hegel's fully realized world spirit, absolute reflexivity about the terms and norms of our discourse is necessarily an asymptotic and always frustrated goal.

One other place in the course where I can explicitly bring up the question of ideology is the creation story about Parusha in the Rig Veda and the prominence of concerns about class duty in the Gita. According to one story in the Rig Veda, the world was created when the gods sacrificed another god, named Parusha, and divided up his body – like play dough – in order to fashion the earth, the animals, and humans. The story claims that the four classes in India were made up of different parts of Parusha: the Vedic priests were created from his mouth, the royal warrior class was made up of his arms, the farmers and commoners were made from his legs, and the servants were made up of his feet. The story thus naturalizes the class hierarchy: while mouths produce intelligent speech, feet are dirty and below every other body part – consequently priests are of course superior to servants (see also Ramey's chapter in this volume). Unless we are to take the story at its word – which none of my students are willing to do, assuming from the outset that the story is fictional – we must assume that the story didn't pre-exist class relations in India. On the contrary, it is almost certainly the case that the four classes *already existed* and someone wrote this story in order to naturalize or legitimate the existing social hierarchy. We revisit the question of class when we get to the Gita, which also legitimates a four-class system, although in a much more complicated manner. To add one last twist to this I point out to students that the Gita remains a popular text in India, but that it is typically read in a way that emphasizes non-political aspects of the text; that is, modern readers for the most part read it as a 'spiritual' text and ignore the emphasis on class.

Of course, the fact that my students typically neither identify as 'Hindu' nor come into the class viewing the Gita as an authoritative text permits some distance from the material that makes a hermeneutic of suspicion easier to engage. As an instructor there is inevitably a tradeoff: on the one hand, when it comes to material students have prior knowledge of they require less remedial and background instruction, but they are more likely to be attached to the material and less likely to be capable of engaging in a hermeneutic of suspicion; on the other hand, when it comes to material with which they lack prior familiarity, they're less likely to resist a hermeneutic of suspicion but more likely to require a great deal of extra time with remedial and basic instruction. Thus, by the end of the section of the course on 'Hinduism', it turns out we haven't been studying 'Hinduism' in itself but rather a number of disparate ideological texts with competing teachings that have no common thread, other than the fact that they were put together by nineteenth-century propagandists who labelled them part of 'Hinduism' in order to disenfranchise Muslims under British colonialism. Two goals have been served at once: on the one hand I've surveyed the literature that students expect the course will cover based on their stereotype of what Hinduism is, yet at the same time we've dismantled that stereotype and shown it to be a creation that was invented to serve a particular set of political interests at a particular juncture in history. The cultural inheritance that is gathered together, retrospectively, as 'Hinduism' is the result of human groups continually recycling their inheritance, always adding some elements and dropping others, and in each case putting their inheritance to new purposes. While as a non-expert I cannot historicize all of the texts and cannot always demonstrate the political purposes to which the texts were put at various times, I can sufficiently historicize certain points and the creation of 'Hinduism' as a whole to undermine the WRP and substitute a theory of culture, ideology, and social formation.

Concluding thoughts

Arguably, a weakness in this approach is that it is extremely one-sided in its myopic focus on texts and their history of interpretation. This approach, one might object, focuses entirely on the elites who produce texts, ideology, and theology, but tells us little about lay practitioners, lay worship, lay practices, or so-called 'lived religion'.[3] Secondly, perhaps it reinforces regnant stereotypes about religion (in part derived from the Protestant tradition), that religion is, in essence, fundamentally about 'belief' and 'doctrine'.

I would argue that the second objection doesn't apply here, because focusing on the situated and political interpretation of texts is squarely at odds with the idea that religion is about timeless belief. In addition, looking at how people radically modify, add to, and discard elements of their cultural inheritance – depending on their local interests rather than pre-existing beliefs – further challenges the Protestant stereotype that beliefs precede and drive behaviour and action.

The former objection is perhaps more serious, but I think it too lands somewhat wide of the mark. The objection that focusing on texts and interpretation mis-represents the religions at hand would make sense, but only if these courses were about 'religion'. However, as I noted in my introductory remarks, at bottom these classes are in fact not at all about 'religions' but about a social theory for which these 'religions' only serve as useful examples. As Jonathan Z. Smith famously claimed, in an introductory course, 'there is nothing that must be taught, there is nothing that cannot be left out' (Smith 2012, 13). The theoretical question I propose – how do people use their cultural inheritance to advance a social agenda – is what drives the selection of the course content, not the emic view of what these religions consist of. 'Religions of the East' is, at the end of the day, not about what modern 'Hindus' think 'Hinduism' is (nor 'Buddhists' and 'Buddhism'), but about how people recycle culture in order to put it to new purposes. I find the theoretical questions far more interesting than the content to which we apply our questions, and I believe students are better served by courses that promote critical thinking as opposed to the accumulation of historical trivia.

Notes

1 It is, of course, not the only paradigm students might have. Increasingly I find my students come into my courses with the 'religion is just bullshit' paradigm. (That's another book – Eds.)
2 It is a rather difficult text for the students given the number of unfamiliar indigenous terms the author uses, but after a lecture on the basic argument of the essay they seem to have little difficulty with the central points, even if they lack an understanding of the details.
3 I place 'lived religion' in scare quotes because I fear its typical use comes close to 'authentic religion', as if 'lived religion' were the *real* thing, the experienced essence of religion, or religion 'fully present' in Jacques Derrida's sense.

References

Batten, Samuel Zane. 1911. "The Social Nature of Christianity." In Samuel Zane Batten, *The Social Task of Christianity: A Summons to the New Crusade*, 64–83. New York: Fleming H. Revell Company.

Conwell, Russell H. 1915. *Acres of Diamonds*. New York: Harper & Brothers.

Eagleton, Terry. 2007. "Introduction." In *The Gospels*. London: Verso.

Foucault, Michel. 1984. "Nietzsche, Genealogy, History." In *The Foucault Reader*, edited by Paul Rabinow, 76–100. New York: Pantheon.

Hammer, Olav. 2009. "Alternative Christs: An Introduction." In *Alternative Christs*, edited by Olav Hammer, 1–15. Oxford: Oxford University Press.

Hughes, Aaron. 2007. *Situating Islam: The Past and Future of an Academic Discipline*. London: Equinox Publishing.

Jha, D. N. 2009. *Rethinking Hindu Identity*. London: Equinox Publishing.

Jones, Laurie Beth. 2001. *Jesus, Entrepreneur: Using Ancient Wisdom to Launch and Live Your Dreams*. New York: Three Rivers Press.

Martin, Craig. 2012. *A Critical Introduction to the Study of Religion*. Sheffield: Equinox Publishing.

Martin, Craig. 2013. "Ideology and the Study of Religion: Marx, Althusser, and Foucault." *Religion Compass* 7(9): 402–411.

O'Reilly, Bill and Martin Dugard. 2013. *Killing Jesus: A History*. New York: Henry Holt and Company.

Smith, Jonathan Z. 1982. "Sacred Persistence: Toward a Redescription of Canon." In Jonathan Z. Smith, *Imagining Religion: From Babylon to Jonestown*, 37–52. Chicago: University of Chicago Press.

Smith, Jonathan Z. 2012. *On Teaching Religion: Essays by Jonathan Z. Smith*, edited by Christopher I. Lehrich. Chicago: University of Chicago Press.

White, Bouck. 1914. *The Call of the Carpenter*. New York: Doubleday, Page & Company.

6

DOING THINGS WITH 'RELIGION'

A discursive approach in rethinking the World Religions Paradigm

Teemu Taira

Introduction

Despite the scholarly criticism presented against the so-called World Religions Paradigm (WRP),[1] it has persistently remained a part of teaching and the disciplinary organization of Religious Studies departments (Taira 2013a, 41–42). In order to find alternatives, this chapter introduces a discursive approach and demonstrates how it can be more generally implemented in existing World Religions modules – if teaching such modules is required – and undergraduate teaching without assuming or maintaining the WRP. This chapter argues (1) that the discursive approach to established 'religious traditions' or 'world religions' should start by exploring how they came to be understood, imagined and classified as a 'religion' and (2) that the approach should include an attempt to explain what kind of classificatory tool such 'religion' (e.g. Shinto as a religion, Hinduism as a religion) has represented at certain times and places, as well as what has been 'done' by the classification. Therefore, special attention will be paid to the question of power relations in the formation of 'religions' and ongoing negotiations on the religiosity of certain groups, practices and traditions.

After clarifying the starting point of a discursive approach and reflecting on my personal experience of teaching a 'Religions in the world' module in Finland, this chapter provides a practical guide for rethinking teaching beyond the WRP in three steps: (1) problematizing, denaturalizing and historicizing the world religions discourse; (2) introducing ethnographic material for the classroom and (3) exploring the category of 'religion' in the classroom.[2] Finally, this chapter offers examples of readings that could be helpful when implementing the suggested aspects in the teaching. The overall impact should, in the long run, mean that students are able to think critically about what kinds of classificatory tools and socially negotiated constructs 'religion' and 'world religion' have been and still are globally.

What is a discursive approach to 'religion'?

There has never been a single and unified discursive approach; indeed, there are many ways to apply a discursive approach as a theoretical framework and method of study. For the purposes of this chapter, I shall distinguish between two approaches that diverge from each other in their consideration of the definition of 'religion'. The first approach focuses on 'religious discourse'. It defines what counts as religion and critically analyses its constituent parts, key distinctions and functions in society at large. An example of this approach is the work of Bruce Lincoln, whose analysis of 'religious discourse' starts by specifying what is distinctive in such discourse. He suggests that religious discourse is unlike all other forms of discourse, because it claims to have 'more-than-human origin, status and authority' (Lincoln 2012, 5). Religion, Lincoln contends, is 'discourse whose defining characteristic is its desire to speak of things eternal and transcendent with an authority equally transcendent and eternal' (2012, 1).

The starting point for the second type of discursive approach to 'religion' is to avoid an analytical definition of 'religion'. Rather, the focus is on studying how something comes to be classified and named as 'religion' and how this is connected to power relations. This type of discursive approach is not simply about studying the historical meanings of a concept or exploring the history of an idea, but about tracing the uses of the word 'religion' – and distinctions typical of the discourse surrounding it, such as statements implying that 'religion' is, or should be, a private, non-political matter – as fundamentally part of changing social formations.

Scholars such as Timothy Fitzgerald and Russell T. McCutcheon can be seen as representatives of the second type. For instance, a recent debate between Bruce Lincoln and Timothy Fitzgerald revolved around the question of whether analytical definitions of 'religion' are useful (Fitzgerald 2006; Lincoln 2007). For the purpose of this chapter's goal to offer tools for rethinking the WRP, the second type is more useful. The differences between the two types of discursive approach should not, however, obscure the fact that they share many aspects, such as the passion for studying what people do with words and which parts of social formation are maintained or challenged by language use. As Russell T. McCutcheon has emphasized, it is relevant to ask what practical interests are involved in discourses on religion and what are the future consequences of including or excluding something from the category in a certain situation and under certain conditions (see McCutcheon 2007, 176). These can be divided into more specific questions, such as: What is done by classifying something as 'religion'? By whom? For what purpose? Who is for it? Who is against it? Or, as Bruce Lincoln puts it, 'Who is trying to persuade whom of what in this text? In what context is the attempt situated, and what are the consequences should it succeed?' (Lincoln 2012, 5).

Some of these questions may give the impression that individuals are mastering discourses, but that is not the case. Different methods highlight different ends of the spectrum – individuals controlling their language use or individuals subjected to discourses – but, in general, discursive approaches assume that language is actively involved in the creation of reality within social contexts in which individual users are not fully in control of meanings and consequences. Discursive approaches reject views that see language as a mirror of reality or as something that describes reality, rather than having an active role in the ways in which societies are organized. Therefore, language is an elementary part of power relations. Aside from the 'repressive state apparatus', such as the army and police, who operate by coercion, force and violence, or the threat of violence, there is also what Louis Althusser called the 'ideological state apparatus', by means of which agents and institutions organize power relations not by brute force, but primarily via language, by persuasion. From the point of view of study of religion, it is interesting that Althusser used the French Catholic Church of his time as one of his primary examples of an ideological state apparatus (Althusser 1971, 85–126).

Even if critical analysis of discourse and power is the focus, the concept of ideology is only one option amongst others. Many Religious Studies scholars use it as their critical concept – Lincoln and Fitzgerald, for example – but other scholars in the debate on discourse are ambivalent about its status. One of the most cited scholars in the analysis of discourse and power is Michel Foucault, who dropped the concept of ideology from his vocabulary. He argued that the standard Marxist understanding of 'ideology' (1) assumes truth by suggesting that some have *false* consciousness; (2) is rooted in the order of the subject (i.e. emphasizing consciousness) and (3) sees language as an epiphenomenon to be explained by references to modes of production and class relations. Foucault pointed out that studying discourse (1) focuses on how something becomes 'true' (i.e. effective) in discourse; (2) foregrounds anonymity of language rather than individual minds and (3) sees language as embedded in institutions and thus functioning as a productive element in a complex articulation of various levels of reality (Foucault 2001, 119).

Later developments in discourse theory and analysis have seen the emergence of versions where ideology has been returned to the vocabulary. One example is advanced by the British linguist Norman Fairclough, who is known as a developer of 'critical discourse analysis' (CDA, as opposed to 'non-critical' linguistic analysis) or 'textually oriented discourse analysis' (TODA, as opposed to Foucauldian analysis, which bypasses detailed textual analysis and linguistic tools designed for such study). Fairclough sees ideology as a particular kind of signifying practice 'generated within power relations as a dimension of the exercise of power and struggle over power' (Fairclough 1992, 67). While meaningful theoretical disagreements can be found between Foucault and Fairclough over the concept of ideology, the practical implications for analysis are minimal. If the concept of ideology is not employed, it appears as if the analysis does not lack anything except rhetorical power in suggesting that whatever is ideological is morally wrong more clearly than if it were simply part of discursive power relations. Thus, my suggestion is that their respective preferences can be explained by social and intellectual context: Foucault wanted to leave an impact on the Marxist intellectual legacy in 1960s France by focusing on discourse and power rather than ideology, whereas Fairclough wanted to be in the cadre of British leftist thinkers in the late 1980s and 1990s by including the concept of ideology in the study of discourse. I see no great practical difference here, as they both share the idea that language use is a key element in understanding and analysing power relations in society, but for someone adopting a discursive approach to religion the more relevant difference is in the type of toolkit that they provide. Foucault's model is useful for analysing large-scale discourses, such as the roles and functions of the category of religion in colonial formations or in the emergence of nation-states. Fairclough's model works well with detailed critical analysis of (1) a particular text and its linguistic and rhetorical features, analysis that extends from textual orientation to the analysis of (2) discursive practices (genre, institutional location, production, distribution and consumption) and (3) social practices (the wider impact in society and ideological dimensions).

This approach may appear to reduce discourses on 'religion' to interests, persuasion and domination. I would rather suggest that while discourses on 'religion' are tied to power relations (broadly conceived), they are not simply about maintaining and legitimating 'ideological formations' whose role is to provide justification for dominant groups in society. Discourses on 'religion' operate at all levels, from everyday life to small groups, even extending further to nation-states and global networks, but their function – what is 'done' with religion – is something that varies from one situation to another and, therefore, needs to be studied empirically.

The idea of doing things with 'religion' includes an allusion to J. L. Austin's famous book *How to Do Things with Words* (1990), originally published in 1962, in which he formulated his theory of performative sentences. He argued that sentences not only report and describe, but that issuing utterances entails performing an action. A typical case would be when a designated person announces 'I name this ship the *Queen Elizabeth*' (Austin 1990, 5) and smashes the bottle against the stern. The idea here is that labelling something as a religion should be considered a performative act. Of course, naming something as a religion is not a typical example of a performative act in an Austinian sense, because it is taken by many as a descriptive sentence. To name something as a religion does make it a religion in certain conditions only – such as in a courtroom, if it is done by a judge. Rather, all claims for religiosity, even when not immediately effective, persuade others to perceive the world in a particular way. While this is obviously not a fully developed analysis of discourses in society, it is the starting idea of the discursive approach. Claims to have a religion and attempts to deny the label to a particular group are the main data for this approach, which focuses on studying how things are done with 'religion', both intentionally and unintentionally.

In practice: teaching 'Religions in the world'

For many scholars, the pressure to adjust their teaching to fit within the WRP comes with an introductory module. For me, however, the introductory course in the Study of Religion at the University of Turku, Finland, has never been about world religions. It has always dealt with theories, concepts and approaches in the study of religion. The material has been taken from anywhere, from any 'religion'.

I have been teaching and, more often, co-teaching another module, entitled 'Religions in the world'. This was not designed by me, and my role was to plan the lectures but not to touch the structure or the required readings. In addition to the Finnish-language *Uskonnot maailmassa* ('Religions in the world'), the required readings have usually included a standard textbook, such as Ninian Smart's *The World Religions* (Smart 1989) and later *Religions in the Modern World*, edited by Linda Woodhead *et al.* (2002). These books have chapters on 'world religions', but also chapters on religion in selected geographical areas. The readings reflect the overall organization of the module. The module has been partly organized according to the WRP, but at the same time it has rarely if ever been limited to a narrow version of it. It has always provided basic knowledge of Christianity, Islam, Judaism, Hinduism and Buddhism, but also extended the list of covered topics to Sikhism, Jainism, Confucianism, Daoism and Shinto. Furthermore, it has included examples of 'indigenous religions' and some geographical areas not otherwise covered (Africa, Arctic areas). Traditions and areas were not given equal attention; the 'world religions' received more hours. The content of a particular topic was usually selected on the basis of a mix between textual, historical and ethnographic approaches.

Practically speaking, we divided the content so that all the teachers would cover different religious traditions or geographical areas. For instance, I started with six hours on Islam and three hours on African indigenous religions (including something about Islam and Christianity in Africa), later adding some hours on Buddhism and an introduction to the various ways of classifying religion. At the moment there is no such module at the University of Turku, but the idea has not been completely abandoned – the module has been rearranged into smaller units, with titles such as 'Asian religions' and 'Religions in the Middle East'.

On the basis of a theoretical rearranging of the module, rooted in the experience I have in teaching and co-teaching it for seven years, my three-step proposal for implementing a new emphasis in modules that assume the WRP includes: (1) that the module should start by introducing, problematizing, denaturalizing and historicizing the concept of world religions; (2) that ethnographic material should be included as a partial (but not sufficient) solution to reified, often text-based and doctrine-based descriptions of 'religions' and (3) that the teaching of established 'religious traditions' – if the module follows a tradition-based approach – should explore when and how a particular formation came to be understood, imagined and classified as a 'religion' and a 'world religion', including attempts to explain what kind of classificatory tool such a religion has represented in certain times and places. This is not to say that all details of the traditional content should be necessarily discarded. For instance, it is useful for students to know what people who consider themselves to be religious think and do, as well as what counts as religious for them. If they rely on certain scriptures in organizing their life and justifying their actions, then the study of such scriptures in relation to people's actual beliefs, practices and identifications is still relevant. However, all this should not be the sole content of the module but should be integrated with the three-step proposal, to which I shall turn next.

Problematizing and historicizing the discourse on world religions

I started my teaching of World Religions by demonstrating that there is something dubious in the category of 'world religions' itself. Through looking at various criteria by which religions have been classified as 'ethnic', 'national', 'indigenous', 'new' or 'world', students came to realize that so-called 'world religions' is not a unified and unproblematic category with neatly justified criteria. For instance, Judaism is practically always included in the category, despite its exceptional nature. If the number of adherents is the defining feature of a 'world religion', Judaism cannot be part of the category. If the attempt to spread its message to the whole world and include potentially everyone is the defining feature, Judaism is not part of the category. Rather, it is often counted as a world religion on the basis of its assumed 'importance', partly because Islam and Christianity have their roots in Judaism and partly because of Judaism's relevance to the (Western) narration of history.

Further problems with the category can be demonstrated by comparing textbooks, namely what they include and what they exclude. Examples can also be taken from society at large, analysing how the list of religions recognized in schools, prisons and the healthcare field may differ even in one country. A good example is Scientology, which was not considered to be a religion by the Charity Commission in England and Wales on the basis that auditing does not count as worship; the Supreme Court decided, however, that a Scientologist church was indeed 'a place of meeting for religious worship' (*R (on the application of Hodkin and another) v Registrar General of Births, Deaths and Marriages* [2013] UKSC 77) and, therefore, qualified for valid marriage ceremonies. Another option is to compare the religions recognized by different states. These lists can also be compared with the religions included in textbooks. For example, pointing out that the Chinese government does not regard Confucianism as a religion, contrary to many World Religions textbooks and modules, is an effective pedagogical move to make students think about the contingent nature of the category of religion and classification systems in various contexts.

If the previously mentioned examples are too far from the core matter of the module, an exploration of the historical development of the category of 'world religion' should at least be a required part of the curriculum. Scholars have differed in their classifications when it comes to how many proper world religions there are and which ones should be included. This brings us to the late nineteenth century and the forefathers of comparative religion, such as Cornelius P. Tiele and Friedrich Max Müller. Tiele suggested in *Encyclopedia Britannica* in 1885 that there are three 'world religions' (or 'universalistic religions'): Christianity, Islam and Buddhism. This list was soon reaffirmed by the Dutch theologian Pierre Daniël Chantepie de la Saussaye, but Müller provided a more extensive list in his *Sacred Books of the East* series, which consisted of eight religions. (See Masuzawa 2005, 107–120; Sun 2013, 61–62.) Müller's list of world religions in 1889 was the following:

(1) the *Vedic*, both ancient and modern; (2) *Buddhism*, Northern and Southern and Gainism; (3) the *Zoroastrian* religion of the Avesta; (4) *Confucianism*; (5) *Taoism*; (6) the *Jewish*; (7) the *Christian*; and (8) *Mohammedan* religions.

(Müller 1907 [1889], 549)

Bringing up these classics of comparative religion can usefully demonstrate how scholarly work that employs 'religion' and other concepts can play an important role in how society at large organizes itself. Scholars are not outside of society and their influence is not limited to academia. Another reason to remember these early texts is to show how arbitrary the original classifications were, driving students to reflect on which categories and concepts are useful and justified. This cannot be the end point, however, because a more detailed examination shows that typologies are not so arbitrary from the normative point of view. After analysing some of the well-known typologies concerning religion, Daniel Dubuisson suggests that classifications agree on one point: 'The positive pole of the opposition or the supreme stage of evolution is in each case occupied by a type of religion identified with Christianity' (2003, 77).

Dubuisson recognizes that many of the nineteenth-century typologies have been abandoned, but he suspects that some of the hierarchies and norms may still be present in thinking about religion: 'it is not at all certain that the influence of this ethnocentric prejudice has disappeared from Western consciousness' (2003, 78). In fact, other studies have argued convincingly that dropping the openly normative preference for Christianity in typologies of religion has not displaced the hierarchy. For instance, in his excellent study on key scholars of the phenomenology of religion, Tim Murphy shows that Christianity has been seen as superior to other formations, explicitly or implicitly, in all significant comparisons and conceptual choices made by phenomenologists of religion working within the Hegelian framework. Take two classic phenomenologists of religion, Gerardus van der Leeuw (1890–1950) and Mircea Eliade (1907–1986), for example. By resisting an explicit evolutionary narrative of religion, Gerardus van der Leeuw claimed that there is no development in religion, yet that did not prevent him from seeing Christianity as superior. By identifying Christianity and Judaism as religions of 'fallen man', doomed to follow linear history – as opposed to peoples who are able to avoid the burden of history by enacting the myth of eternal return to the times of their origin – Mircea Eliade appeared to flip the hierarchy, but Christianity is still nearly always at the higher end of the spectrum of forms that he gives as the basis of a taxonomy of religious phenomena (Murphy 2010).

From the point of view of an approach that foregrounds the beliefs, teachings and practices of particular 'world religions', the suggestions above may look like a withdrawal to theoretical discussion. However, I would propose, following Jonathan Z. Smith, that it is instead a deliberate pedagogical step to help students understand that 'matters are always more complex than they first appear, and that this is liberating rather than paralyzing' (2013, 3).

Partial steps forward: ethnography and 'making the tent bigger'

The next step involves demonstrating the complexity of the situation, this time at the level of particular 'religious traditions'. If standard textbook descriptions of Christianity, Islam, Buddhism and other formations traditionally classified as religious traditions offer relatively homogeneous representations on the basis of institutionalized and established teachings, doctrines and ritualized practices, one way out is to introduce ethnographic studies in the classroom, because they show that actual beliefs and practices are heterogeneous among people who identify with a particular religion and that boundaries are surprisingly fluid between supposedly identifiable 'religious traditions'.

I still remember when Professor Ron Geaves visited a class that I was teaching more than ten years ago. He talked to first-year students about ethnography and fieldwork, suggesting that it is easy even for a beginner to carry out original work: take some descriptions from World Religions textbooks of what people believe and practise and then conduct fieldwork among the people who identify with a particular tradition. Soon it will become clear that people do not match the descriptions given in the textbook, and on the basis of that material one can argue against these texts.

While there is some naïvety in this trick, since authors of textbooks do not necessarily assume that people think and behave according to the canonical teachings of a particular group, I regard it as very valuable pedagogical advice, because it leads students to understand the gap between pristine textbook descriptions and messy practices. It does not solve the problems related to the WRP, but it offers one step forward in assisting students to reflect on the problems that follow when 'religious traditions' are described as relatively stable, homogeneous and identifiable units.

One example is offered by Timothy Fitzgerald (2011, 64), who asked his students in Japan whether visits to shrines were connected with *shūkyō* (a word often translated as religion). Almost all said that they had nothing to do with religion. However, if World Religions textbooks are to be believed, visiting shrines is a typical example of Shinto religion. Observing and interviewing people helps both teachers and students to challenge the existing descriptions given in the textbooks.

The introduction of ethnographic studies in the classroom challenges the understanding of relatively homogeneous and 'artificially-abstracted' (Fitzgerald 2011, 51) 'world religions' and their assumed clear-cut boundaries, but it may leave other aspects of the WRP intact. Therefore, many teachers have tried to solve the problem by including in the module 'other religions', such as 'indigenous' and 'new', thus 'making the tent bigger'. In the module I have been involved in, the solution to the World Religions approach has been exactly this: we have included areas that are not covered in the teaching of major traditions and we have added selections from 'indigenous religions'. In practice, this has meant that the module touched on Arctic or Northern religions, African religions, Native American religions, the Ancient Near East, Ancient Greece and Rome, and, in some cases, Baha'i, Zoroastrianism, Paganism and Western Esotericism. This is a pragmatic solution, but not necessarily intellectually justifiable. It makes it very difficult to draw sensible boundaries when deciding what to include in the module. It is frustrating to attempt to cover almost everything with limited resources. I consider it a better solution than sticking to the usual 'big five' (or six, or seven), but it is exhausting to try to do the impossible.

One study that exemplifies the complex nature of the world religions discourse and its challenges is *Santo Daime: A New World Religion* by Andrew Dawson (2013). The study deals with a movement that emerged in the Brazilian Amazon in the 1930s and whose practices are organized around the consumption of the illegal beverage Daime (ayahuasca). The 'religious' nature of Santo Daime is taken for granted in the study, but Dawson feels the need to explain the pun in the title. He suggests that *A New World Religion* means that Santo Daime is a religion for a new world (*novum mundum*) (i.e. Latin America). Furthermore, it consciously defies inclusion in either 'new' or 'world' religions, hinting that Santo Daime, with its variegated ritual repertoire, challenges such a neat classification (Dawson 2013, 4–5). While it is easy to follow the intention of the author, it does not mean that he – or anyone else – is in control of interpretations of the title. Because he does not challenge the WRP in the study, it is tempting to read the conscious wordplay in the title of the book as an attempt to find legitimation for a small group, as if being regarded as potentially belonging to the family of world religions would make it more interesting and important. For this reason, the wordplay can be somewhat confusing, at least in the context of debating the WRP. In particular, readers who are familiar with earlier attempts to legitimate excluded candidates (such as Paganism) as a world religion (see York 2003) are likely to suspect that something similar is being suggested here. Despite the author's qualifications, the title works as an example of 'making the tent bigger'; leading readers to think that Santo Daime could be interpreted as a new candidate for the family of world religions can be seen as legitimizing the importance of the WRP, rather than challenging it.

One possible way out of this dilemma of an overextended tent is to follow Jonathan Z. Smith, who suggests that '*there is nothing that must be taught*, there is nothing that cannot be left out. A curriculum … becomes an occasion of deliberate, collegial, institutionalized choice' (2013, 13). Accordingly, there is no need to cover every corner of the world, but rather to be precise about the criteria used to decide what is taught and what has been left out. While his solution is to use data as examples of particular theoretical or thematic issues – such as ritual, myth and type of religious specialist – I shall propose a slightly different approach. I do not exclude possible attempts to use Smith's solution in tandem with mine, but I shall leave it to others to integrate the two, since for the purpose of this chapter it is enough to introduce the third part of the solution.

Exploration of the category of 'religion' in the classroom

So far, the reflections and suggestions have followed a quite standard line of critical thought about the problems of the WRP. The next step is presumably less

common than the two previous ones when it comes to modules that follow the
WRP. At least I have not heard of colleagues modelling their courses on it. The
idea here is to instigate an exploration of how something came to be understood and
classified as 'religion' and why. This approach can be extended to recent cases, but at
least units that are conventionally included in the world religions category – and thus
are the least contentious members – should be given special attention.

The intention is not to give a strict list of issues that should be covered when
implementing this third step, but to suggest the following questions as a guide,
because they demonstrate the processes by which religions and world religions have
been constructed for particular purposes: When did 'X' come to be labelled as an
identity and 'religion'? What was the process like? What consequences did it have?
What is the conceptual history of the word that is either translated as 'religion' in a
local language or used to identify the local 'religion' (*dharma* in Sanskrit, *shūkyō* in
Japanese, *uskonto* in Finnish)?

Take Confucianism, for example. Confucianism has been a special or borderline
case in the WRP, because its status as a 'religion' has never been fully established
beyond early constructions in nineteenth-century Western scholarship. For instance,
the earliest formulations of Confucianism in general date back to 1862. It was
named the ancient religion of China by the Sinologist James Legge in 1877, soon
after he was appointed the first professor of Chinese at Oxford University, but even
today the Chinese government does not classify it as a religion (Sun 2013). These
processes have been studied in *Confucianism as a World Religion* by Anna Sun, who
undertook the double task of studying both the historical construction of Confucianism as a religion (and a world religion) and recent Chinese attempts to claim
its status as a religion.

Sun's study focuses on the latter part of the nineteenth century, particularly on
the writings and other actions of James Legge and Friedrich Max Müller. The
study traces the historical formation of Confucianism as a religion in Western
scholarship, particularly at Oxford, where both Legge and Müller taught. Legge
argued that Confucianism was a religion, overcoming his opponents by taking the
controversy from one field (the missionary circle) to another (the science of religion/
comparative religion, which was then in formation). He also received support from
Müller, for whom Legge's argument was useful in promoting his own ideas concerning the science of religion. Confucianism was included in Müller's classification
of eight world religions in 1891. This was followed by the convening of the first
World Parliament of Religions in Chicago in 1893, where Confucianism was
represented among the other 'world religions'. Therefore, the historical formation
of Confucianism as a religion is deeply connected to the history of comparative
religion, whose legitimacy was one of the reasons behind the inclusion of Confucianism in the categories of religion and world religion. This process was not
limited to Europe as it affected China's discourse on religion. Currently the Chinese
word *jiao* (or *zongjiao*) is often translated as 'religion', but this did not start until the
late nineteenth century or the beginning of the twentieth century. Previously *jiao*
meant 'teaching' and *zong* referred to a pictogram of an ancestral altar (Adler 2005,

1580). Before Confucianism became classified as a religion by Western scholars, encounters between Jesuits and Chinese people in the sixteenth and seventeenth centuries solidified Confucian teachings (Jensen 1997). While these can be seen as a precursor to the classification of Confucianism as a religion and a contributing factor to the formation of Confucian identity, they do not yet represent examples of Confucianism as a religion.

Confucianism was later regarded as religion in China, but when the Communists took power in China in 1949, they established the current system in which only Buddhism, Daoism, Catholicism, Protestantism and Islam are considered as religions. This is contrary to the situation in Indonesia and Hong Kong, where Confucianism is part of the official classification of religion. According to Sun (2013), the current situation in China is complex. While many people participate in ancestral worship, only 12 out of 7021 people claimed in a recent survey to be Confucians (Empirical Studies of Religion in China, see Sun 2013, xiii–xiv). Furthermore, Confucian practices are not exclusive; people may also participate in Buddhist or Christian practices, seeing no contradiction there. These examples demonstrate that Confucianism does not fully match what is regarded as typical for a religion – that people identify with it and consider it to be exclusive ('I am Muslim, not a Christian'). However, there have lately been attempts by various actors – from professors to television personalities – to revitalize Confucianism as a religious identity. These include a drive to establish it as a state religion in China, the goal being to provide a backbone of good and just society against the spread of Christianity in a post-socialist China. According to examples given by Sun, the current situation is far from settled: on one hand, claiming Confucianism as a religion may marginalize those who present the claims, but also provide protection and recognition; on the other hand, not classifying Confucianism as a religion opens opportunities for stronger integration in state institutions and protection under the label of 'national heritage' in a relatively antireligious China, but this includes the possibility that it will remain unrecognized.

One of the missed opportunities in Sun's study is that her analysis of recent struggles is not very profound. Another problem is that she focuses on the question of whether it is legitimate to classify Confucianism as a religion, yet she does not use it as a case for exploring and questioning the category of religion as such and reflecting on how various people and groups promote their interests – or 'do things' – by classifying Confucianism. The latter is one reason why Sun's study fits well in the classroom as a useful study and interesting data. She writes, for instance, about Confucianism possibly becoming 'a real religious force' (Sun 2013, xvi), 'the reality of Confucian religious life in China' (2013, xiv), 'China's ritual-rich religious life' (2013, 2) and 'a revival of diverse religious ritual practices' (2013, 2). These are all examples of assuming that there is such a thing as 'religion'. It could have been possible for the work to frame ongoing constructions of the category of religion as part of much wider power relations in China and elsewhere, rather than just exploring whether Confucianism is a religion. Partly because the author does not consistently follow the discursive approach proposed here, her work is very suitable for the classroom. Sometimes studies that are ambivalent in their position are exceptionally good for prompting discussion. Furthermore, Sun's overall narrative can be reread with ease in light of the Foucauldian framework, and some of the examples that she mentions provide relevant data for Faircloughian CDA/TODA. Both Western constructions and Chinese negotiations offer appropriate examples for the question raised above about what people are doing with 'religion'.

To summarize, Confucianism is a good example because its formation as a 'religion' is connected with Western scholarship, but at the same time the classification of Confucianism has deep implications for Chinese society, past and present. The instances where claims have been made for its religiosity and where its classification has been negotiated have varied over time, both in China and elsewhere. Some of these are well documented and are thus easily applicable to classroom use, even by those (like me) whose main area of expertise is not China or Confucianism. Furthermore, there is a term in Chinese language that is translated as religion, but whose historical meaning is not fully compatible with the modern category of religion. Finally, there are recent cases in which the 'religiosity' of Confucianism is negotiated by various actors in order to improve their situation in society, thus demonstrating that the 'religiosity' of Confucianism is not so much a question of whether it really is a religion as what is done with religion. It is an ongoing struggle, rather than a formation that is frozen in one moment in the late nineteenth century.

In practice: resources for the classroom

The brief analysis of Confucianism above outlines the discursive approach that I am proposing here. While there is no space for further detailed examples, I would like to offer a list of useful resources that can be assigned for readings or content that can be integrated into lectures, depending on the length of the texts and the structure of the module. Not all scholars mentioned here can be classified as proponents of some version of discursive approach, and many of them do not use the concept of discourse at all. However, given the previously mentioned guidelines, it is not too complicated to reinterpret available studies from a discursive point of view, even when the authors themselves may be theoretically ambivalent about whether 'religion' is an analytical concept or an element of discourse to be studied.

Wilfred Cantwell Smith's (1991 [1962]) classic study on the category of 'religion' is still a useful resource, despite its much criticized suggestion to replace 'religion' with 'faith' and 'cumulative tradition'. In particular, Chapters 2 and 3 – '"Religion" in the West' and 'Other cultures: the "religions"' – provide a starting point for understanding the emergence of the modern category of 'religion' and the classification of cultural formations as 'religions' outside the Western world. Another classic is Peter Harrison's (1990) study on the emergence of the modern idea of religion in the Enlightenment of England. A more recent work that focuses on the category of world religions is Tomoko Masuzawa's (2005) well-known study, which demonstrates how Western and Christian scholars began classifying cultural formations as world religions while maintaining the privileged and superior position of Christianity.

Masuzawa's study is a step towards a critical approach in which the modern discourse on 'religion' is located in its socio-historical context. This is further foregrounded in studies addressing the emergence of a modern, largely Christianity-related category of 'religion' in connection with colonialism and modern nation-states (Dubuisson 2003; Fitzgerald 2000, 2007, 2007 ed.; see also Arnal and McCutcheon 2013; McCutcheon 2003). These studies do not simply offer a disembedded conceptual history of 'religion', but a more contextualized analysis of the formation (and endurance) of a discourse fully embedded in institutions and the organization of modern societies.

Indian and South Asian examples are especially fruitful, because there are many studies concerning the development of Hinduism as an identity, and later as a 'religion' in a colonial context. Relevant articles for classroom purposes have been written by Richard King (1999, 96–117; 2011) and Peter Beyer (2006, 188–224), but there are many other suitable studies dealing with the topic in various – partly complementary, but not fully compatible – ways (see Balagangadhara 1994; Bloch *et al.* 2010; Lorenzen 2006, 1–36; Sugirtharajah 2003). Sources for Sikhism are scarcer, but perhaps the most substantial study is *Religion and the Specter of the West* by Arvind-Pal S. Mandair (2009). Its third chapter, 'Sikhism and the Politics of Religion-Making', is an overview of the process by which Sikhism came to be consolidated as an identity in general and a 'religious' identity in particular.

Studies on Buddhism that are relevant here have focused on Western inventions. Philip C. Almond's (1988) classic study on nineteenth-century Victorian discourse about Buddhism focuses on it as an independent religious tradition by foregrounding its textual reification and highlighting the historical, rather than mythic, nature of the Buddha. The edited collection by Donald S. Lopez, Jr. (1995) is also a valuable resource, and a chapter-length take on the elevation of the status of Buddhism to the rank of world religion is found in Masuzawa (2005, 121–146).

The Middle East is pedagogically more challenging, because it is so strongly integrated with the modern category of religion. There are some relevant chapters dealing with Islam (W. C. Smith 1991, 80–118; Masuzawa 2005, 179–206; Beyer 2006, 155–185). Furthermore, Brent Nongbri's short comparison of English translations of the Qur'an – and particularly Arabic *dīn* – between 1649 and 2003, showing how *law* has been replaced by *faith* and *religion* (Nongbri 2013, 39–45), is suitable for classroom use. Judaism is an even more complicated issue. Among the few resources I can think of using for classroom purposes are two chapters from Leora Batnitzky's *How Judaism Became a Religion* Batnitzky 2011). However, while they map the invention of modern Judaism as a religion, they are not fully appropriate for the approach proposed here, because the book focuses on the question 'Is Judaism a religion?' (2011, ix). Early Christianity and Ancient Greece and Rome are summarized in Nongbri's *Before Religion* (2013). His work is by no means exhaustive, but the examples from different periods in history and cultures in Europe are chosen well for classroom use. It can be supplemented with Attila Molnár's (2002) article on the construction of religion in Early Modern Europe.

Japan is an extremely relevant area, because discourse on religion has been studied in a rigorous manner in both historical and current contexts. Sarah Thal's (2002) chapter on the construction of modern Shinto in the nineteenth century is short enough for classroom purposes, as is Jun'ichi Isomae's (2007) chapter on the formation of State Shinto; Jason Ānanda Josephson's (2012) *The Invention of Religion in Japan* is more substantial. If some studies limit themselves in terms of the Western constructions of religion, the Japanese case is an excellent example of interaction between local discourses and Western/Christian powers. If there is space for theoretical debates concerning 'religion' in Japan and contemporary case studies, then the three chapters dealing with Japan in Timothy Fitzgerald's (2000) *The Ideology of Religious Studies* can be considered as well.

Confucianism has already been partially covered by the above example of Anna Sun's *Confucianism as a World Religion*. Another resource that can be used in combination with Sun's study is Lionel Jensen's *Manufacturing Confucianism* (1997), because it focuses on the era before Confucianism was classified as a 'religion', particularly on the Jesuits' encounters with Chinese people in the sixteenth and seventeenth centuries. Constructions of 'religion' in Chinese indigenous traditions are not limited to Confucianism; examples of the 'religiosity' of Daoism also provide relevant material for study (see Girardot 1999).

The resources listed above are helpful in describing and explaining how the movements, groups and practices that we call 'religions' in our everyday language have been included in the category in different historical moments for different reasons and, in some cases, excluded from the category in a specific context. In many teaching systems, the list of useful resources is already too long to be integrated in the module. However, they can be used as case studies, because going through one example can sufficiently demonstrate the discursive constructions of 'religion' and the multiple interests and consequences at play in the process. If the list is not lengthy enough, it can be easily extended to cover various examples from the past to the present, from 'indigenous' cultures to Pagans, and even further to include the so-called deliberately 'invented religions' (Cusack 2010) in which 'religiosity' of a group or a specific practice is negotiated by various actors, from colonialists to judges and journalists (see Chidester 1996a, 1996b, 2014; J. Z. Smith 2004, 375–390; Taira 2010, 2013b).

Conclusion

The WRP still casts its shadow on the ways in which Religious Studies departments and modules are organized. This chapter has demonstrated how some of the assumptions and practices maintaining the paradigm, despite its explicit criticism, can be subverted. It is unrealistic to assume that there would be an easy solution to the problems included in the WRP without introducing new challenging questions about the organization of departments and modules. However, an examination of what is and has been done by discourses on 'religion' – particularly in negotiations on the 'religiosity' of this or that group, formation or practice – is an integral and pedagogically effective part of challenging the WRP.

The starting point in this chapter was a version of the discursive approach, which analyses discourses on 'religion' rather than defining 'religion' or 'religious discourse'. There have been recent attempts to rehabilitate monothetic definitions of religion, as opposed to polythetic definitions or positions in which religion is rejected from analytical vocabulary (see Schilbrack 2014). Whatever their value in constructing a fruitful method of research, they do not, in my evaluation, take anything away from the approach proposed here for the simple reason that 'religion' is an interactive kind, rather than an indifferent kind. This means that people who are classified as 'religious' come to know it, on the basis of which their behaviour potentially changes, and 'it loops back to force changes in the classifications and knowledge about them' (Hacking 1999, 105). There are tensions between different approaches, as well as differences in how far the implications of the discursive approach should be extended (i.e. does a discursive approach have a place as one of many complementary approaches or does it have a special role in reorganizing the study of religion?), but no definition of religion can downplay the value and relevance of considering how certain groups have been classified as 'religions' and how the formation of discourse on 'religion' has been intertwined with power relations in various contexts. Studying the history of the category of religion and its part in intercultural relations, David Chidester rightly notes that 'we are gaining greater insight into the complex formations of basic categories in the academic study of religion' (Chidester 2014, 18) and, I would add, insight into the complex social formations in which categories such as 'religion' and 'world religion' have helped to promote interests and organize power relations.

Notes

1 See the editors' introduction to this volume.
2 For further practical examples of approaches that could be labelled 'discursive', see Ramey in this volume.

References

Adler, Joseph A. 2005. "Chinese Religion: An Overview." In *Encyclopedia of Religion*, edited by Lindsay Jones. 2nd ed., Vol. 3, 1580–1613. Detroit: Macmillan.

Almond, Philip C. 1988. *The British Discovery of Buddhism*. Cambridge: Cambridge University Press.

Althusser, Louis. 1971. *Lenin and Philosophy and Other Essays*. New York: Monthly Review Press.

Arnal, William E. and Russell T. McCutcheon. 2013. *The Sacred Is the Profane: The Political Nature of 'Religion'*. Oxford: Oxford University Press.

Austin, J. L. 1990 [1975]. *How to Do Things with Words*. 2nd ed. Oxford: Oxford University Press.

Balagangadhara, S. N. 1994. *The 'Heathen in His Blindness …': Asia, the West and the Dynamic of Religion*. Leiden: Brill.

Batnitzky, Leora. 2011. *How Judaism Became a Religion: An Introduction to Modern Jewish Thought*. Princeton: Princeton University Press.

Beyer, Peter. 2006. *Religions in Global Society*. London: Routledge.

Bloch, Esther, Marianne Keppens and Rajaram Hegde, eds. 2010. *Rethinking Religion in India: The Colonial Construction of Hinduism*. London: Routledge.

Chidester, David. 1996a. "Anchoring Religion in the World: A Southern African History of Comparative Religion." *Religion* 26(2): 141–160.

Chidester, David. 1996b. *Savage Systems: Colonialism and Comparative Religion in Southern Africa*. Charlottesville: The University Press of Virginia.

Chidester, David. 2014. *Empire of Religion: Imperialism and Comparative Religion*. Chicago: The University of Chicago Press.

Cusack, Carole. 2010. *Invented Religions: Imagination, Fiction and Faith*. Aldershot: Ashgate.

Dawson, Andrew. 2013. *Santo Daime: A New World Religion*. London: Bloomsbury.

Dubuisson, Daniel. 2003. *The Western Construction of Religion: Myths, Knowledge, and Ideology*. Translated by William Sayers. Baltimore: The Johns Hopkins University Press.

Fairclough, Norman. 1992. *Discourse and Social Change*. Cambridge: Polity Press.

Fitzgerald, Timothy. 2000. *The Ideology of Religious Studies*. Oxford: Oxford University Press.

Fitzgerald, Timothy. 2006. "Bruce Lincoln's 'Theses on Method': Antitheses." *Method and Theory in the Study of Religion* 18: 392–423.

Fitzgerald, Timothy. 2007. *Discourse on Civility and Barbarity: A Critical History of Religion and Related Categories*. Oxford: Oxford University Press.

Fitzgerald, Timothy. 2011. *Religion and Politics in International Relations: The Modern Myth*. London: Continuum.

Fitzgerald, Timothy, ed. 2007. *Religion and the Secular: Historical and Colonial Formations*. London: Equinox.

Foucault, Michel. 2001. *Power: Essential Works of Foucault 1954–1984, Volume Three*. London: Allen Lane.

Girardot, N. J. 1999. "'Finding the Way': James Legge and the Victorian Invention of Taoism." *Religion* 29: 107–121.

Hacking, Ian. 1999. *The Social Construction of What?* Cambridge, MA: Harvard University Press.

Harrison, Peter. 1990. *'Religion' and the Religions in the English Enlightenment*. Cambridge: Cambridge University Press.

Isomae, Jun'ichi. 2007. "The Formative Process of State Shinto in Relation to the Westernization of Japan: The Concept of 'Religion' and 'Shinto'." In *Religion and the Secular: Historical and Colonial Formations*, edited by Timothy Fitzgerald, 93–102. London: Equinox.

Jensen, Lionel M. 1997. *Manufacturing Confucianism: Chinese Tradition and Universal Civilization*. Durham, NC: Duke University Press.

Josephson, Jason Ānanda. 2012. *The Invention of Religion in Japan*. Chicago: The University of Chicago Press.

King, Richard. 1999. *Orientalism and Religion: Postcolonial Theory, India and 'The Mystic East'*. London: Routledge.

King, Richard. 2011. "Imagining Religions in India: Colonialism and the Mapping of South Asian History and Culture." In *Secularism and Religion-Making*, edited by Markus Dressler and Arvind-Pal S. Mandair, 37–61. Oxford: Oxford University Press.

Lincoln, Bruce. 2007. "Concessions, Confessions, Clarifications, Ripostes: By Way of Response to Tim Fitzgerald." *Method and Theory in the Study of Religion* 19: 163–168.

Lincoln, Bruce. 2012. *Gods and Demons, Priests and Scholars: Critical Explorations in the History of Religions*. Chicago: The University of Chicago Press.

Lopez Jr., Donald S., ed. 1995. *Curators of the Buddha: The Study of Buddhism under Colonialism*. Chicago: The University of Chicago Press.

Lorenzen, David N. 2006. *Who Invented Hinduism?* New Delhi: Yoda Press.

Mandair, Arvind-Pal S. 2009. *Religion and the Specter of the West: Sikhism, India, Postcoloniality, and the Politics of Translation*. New York: Columbia University Press.

Masuzawa, Tomoko. 2005. *The Invention of World Religions: Or, How European Universalism Was Preserved in the Language of Pluralism*. Chicago: The University of Chicago Press.

McCutcheon, Russell T. 2003. *The Discipline of Religion: Structure, Meaning, Rhetoric*. London: Routledge.

McCutcheon, Russell T. 2007. "They Licked the Platter Clean: On the Co-Dependency of the Religious and the Secular." *Method and Theory in the Study of Religion* 19(3–4): 173–199.

Molnár, Attila. 2002. "The Construction of the Notion of Religion in Early Modern Europe." *Method and Theory in the Study of Religion* 14(1): 47–60.

Murphy, Tim. 2010. *The Politics of Spirit: Phenomenology, Genealogy, Religion*. Albany: SUNY Press.

Müller, Friedrich Max. 1907 [1889]. *Natural Religion*. London: Longmans, Green & Co.

Nongbri, Brent. 2013. *Before Religion: A History of a Modern Concept*. New Haven: Yale University Press.

R (on the application of Hodkin and another) v Registrar General of Births, Deaths and Marriages [2013] UKSC 77 (11 Dec. 2013), http://www.bailii.org/uk/cases/UKSC/2013/77.html.

Schilbrack, Kevin. 2014. *Philosophy and the Study of Religions: A Manifesto*. Oxford: Blackwell.

Smart, Ninian. 1989. *The World's Religions: Old Traditions and Modern Transformations*. Cambridge: Cambridge University Press.

Smith, Jonathan Z. 2004. *Relating Religion: Essays in the Study of Religion*. Chicago: The University of Chicago Press.

Smith, Jonathan Z. 2013. *On Teaching Religion*, edited by Christopher I. Lehrich. Oxford: Oxford University Press.

Smith, Wilfred Cantwell. 1991 [1962]. *The Meaning and End of Religion*. Minneapolis: Fortress Press.

Sugirtharajah, Sharada. 2003. *Imagining Hinduism: A Postcolonial Perspective*. London: Routledge.

Sun, Anna. 2013. *Confucianism as a World Religion: Contested Histories and Contemporary Realities*. Princeton: Princeton University Press.

Taira, Teemu. 2010. "Religion as a Discursive Technique: The Politics of Classifying Wicca." *Journal of Contemporary Religion* 25(3): 379–394.

Taira, Teemu. 2013a. "Making Space for Discursive Study in Religious Studies." *Religion* 43(1): 26–45.

Taira, Teemu. 2013b. "The Category of 'Invented Religion': A New Opportunity for Studying Discourses on 'Religion'." *Culture and Religion* 14(4): 477–493.

Thal, Sarah. 2002. "A Religion that Was Not a Religion: The Creation of Modern Shinto in Nineteenth-century Japan." In *The Invention of Religions: Rethinking Belief in Politics and History*, edited by Derek Peterson and Darren Walhof, 100–114. New Brunswick: Rutgers University Press.

Woodhead, Linda, with Paul Fletcher, Hiroko Kawanami and David Smith, eds. 2002. *Religions in the Modern World: Traditions and Transformations*. London: Routledge.

York, Michael. 2003. *Pagan Theology: Paganism as a World Religion*. New York: New York University Press.

7

LOOKING BACK ON THE END OF RELIGION

Opening re Marx

Paul-François Tremlett

Introduction

The traditions of Marxism and Critical Theory stretch from the mid-nineteenth century writings of Marx and Engels through to contemporary thinkers such as Jürgen Habermas and Ernesto Laclau.[1] These traditions have conventionally been understood to be foreign to the concerns of Religious Studies. Nevertheless, impressive and important scholarship by the likes of Talal Asad (1993), Richard King (1999) and Kim Knott (2005) established a series of conversations at the margins of Religious Studies, and introduced the writings of Michel de Certeau, Michel Foucault, Henri Lefebvre, Doreen Massey and Edward Said (among others) to the World Religions Paradigm (WRP). In doing so, they raised a number of questions that could be said to be 'in debt to Marx'. Those questions addressed problems of power and knowledge, of social reproduction, the fabrication of legitimacy, the transmission of knowledge into minds and bodies and indeed the very constitution of minds and bodies as experiencing and thinking things in the first place.

These questions constituted a radical departure from those of the WRP. The WRP had established a cartographic grid of allegedly objectively given, religious facts. This grid provided a base for various lines of scholarly enquiry, particularly historical-descriptive and comparative studies of discrete religious traditions. Central to the WRP was an unflinching if paradoxical faith both in the positivistic grid of really existing religion as if the cartographic method might stand, like its putative objects, forever and always, outside time and the authenticity of the religious insiders' point of view. Little or no attention was paid to the historical inception of Religious Studies in the maelstrom of modernity's violent birth or to what was owed to the Enlightenment in terms of operative methods and assumptions. An orthodoxy reigned over what religion was and there was almost no acknowledgement of the shifting practices of religiosity and spirituality and the hybrid improvisations of technology, magic and healing to be found in spiritualism and mesmerism or the emerging literatures of the urban uncanny which found in the depths of the industrial city intimations of spectres and ghosts but also the marvellous. Religion was changing even as the WRP sought, albeit in contradictory ways, to insulate its object from that change.

Arguments about theories and methods in Religious Studies conducted under the sign of the WRP have typically been reduced to two competing positions. On the one hand, there is the supposed hermeneutics of suspicion exemplified in the writings of Marx, Nietzsche and Freud for which Religious Studies is a form of ideology critique. Religion – conceived as a false explanation of both the natural and social worlds – constitutes an obstacle to reason and as such it has to be unmasked. On the other hand, there is the hermeneutics of restoration exemplified in the writings of Mircea Eliade for which religion possesses a truth on a par with that of art – a truth that cannot be apprehended except by accessing the interiority or the lived experience of the putative insider. This latter approach was dominant under the sign of the WRP. Elsewhere (Tremlett 2008; see also Flood 1999 and Fitzgerald 2000), it has been argued that this binary opposition breaks down quite quickly once a careful analysis of the respective theoretical and methodological terrains are investigated – traces of Eliade's romanticism and the reification of experience are evident in Marx and Foucault just as a critique of industrial-disciplinary society can be found in Eliade.

The objective of this chapter is to think with Marx, or better, to use Marx to enable us to think with greater clarity about reason, how we use it, its implication in power, the nature of its objectivity and the degree to which it is private or public. We will begin with a critique of Marx as a thinker of modernity, of his ascription to modernity of an emancipatory direction and content and to science of an unrivalled power to establish the objective relations of cause and effect between social phenomena and thereby to claim to be able to dissect living society and to expose its workings like a corpse. At the heart of this critique of Marx lies a debate about reason and across this chapter we will develop a complementary pair of practical pedagogical exercises through which to trace a shift in the manner of reason's constitution in the Marxist and Critical traditions from reason as the cool application of scientific method in the writings of Marx, to a critique of reason as a source of political and cultural domination articulated in different ways by Weber, Adorno, Horkheimer and Marcuse before moving on to Habermas's notion of 'communicative rationality' (Habermas 1985). The objective of these lessons is to enable students to see that their own praxis as students of religion is implicated in this history of reason. For example, in the first exercise students will be encouraged to develop a critique of Marx that amounts to a critique of a certain conception of an active, gendered, ocular-centric and paradigmatically modern practice of objectifying reason, yet they will perform reason in exactly these terms upon the 'passive' text fragment in order to make that critique. The insight that reason can enable the formation of (objective) knowledge and yet at the same time be a form of potentially illegitimate power is central to the development of the student's critical faculties and at the same time is a central insight of the Marxist and Critical traditions.

In practice: learning to situate reason

The fragment reproduced below comes from the 'Preface' to *A Critique of Political Economy* (1977), one of the most frequently cited texts in Marx's *oeuvre*. In the first instance this is a lesson in 'close reading', by which we mean an opportunity to get students involved in a reading of a short passage of text in order to learn how to identify key terms, conceptual binary oppositions, use of language and such like. Although the objective is to develop the skill of close reading such that it becomes a routine part of each individual student's critical reading repertoire, in the class-room it works well as a collaborative exercise where students read together in small groups, sharing their observations and insights which can then be brought into a wider discussion. The exercise is developed in two distinct ways: first, student-led collaborative reading and discussion that is rounded off by the lecturer through the collection of student comments and observations, including a lead-back through the fragment to develop their insights and questions; second, students are invited to read a longer extract – in this case an historical case study – where the points developed through the close reading of the fragment can be revisited.

The fragment

Students who have already studied late nineteenth- and/or early twentieth-century theories of religion such as those developed by E. B. Tylor, J. G. Frazer or S. Freud will already be familiar with a certain historical or evolutionary sensibility that permeates those writings where time moves in a straight line and human history is developmental, progressive and defined by a series of stages that without irony confirm the cultural, social, political and economic norms of European society at the time, while religious beliefs are reduced to simple propositional claims. Marx was writing very much from within this same intellectual and cultural milieu. The study of his work complements wider teaching in classical theory and method beyond mere substantive knowledge of key thinkers and key theories to the extent that it helps students to develop a sense of the importance of situating theories and methods historically and culturally. (Maurice Bloch's *Marxism and Anthropology* (1983) is a useful source for demonstrating the extent to which Marx's writings were permeated by the ruling assumptions of the period.)

There are a significant number of elements that we would expect students to be able to identify in this fragment. In it, Marx lays out a theory of societal structuring and societal change and as such it represents an important attempt, in the history not only of Marxism and Critical theory but also of social theory, to model dynamic, fluid and contested processes of transformation. Marx adopts a linear approach to change, and tries to plot – through the empirical specification of pri-mary and secondary relations, causes and effects – specific sets of economic relationships as playing causal roles in both social reproduction and social fracturing. Marx makes strong claims about the relationship between what people think and the structure of the society that they have been born into, and also presumes the existence of a necessary break between what ordinary people say about their experience and the world around them and the knowledge delivered by the 'objective' methods of empirical science:

> In the social production of their existence, men inevitably enter into definite relations, which are independent of their will, namely relations of production appropriate to a given stage in the development of their material forces of production. The totality of these relations of production constitutes the economic structure of society, the real foundation, on which arises a legal and political superstructure and to which correspond definite forms of consciousness. The mode of production of material life conditions the general process of social, political and intellectual life. It is not the consciousness of men that determines their existence, but the social existence that determines their consciousness. At a certain stage of development, the material productive forces of society come into conflict with the existing relations of production or – this merely expresses the same thing in legal terms – with the property relations within the framework of which they have operated hitherto. From forms of development of the productive forces these relations turn into their fetters. Then begins an era of social revolution. The changes in the economic foundation lead sooner or later to the transformation of the whole immense superstructure. In studying such transformations it is always necessary to distinguish between the material transformation of the economic conditions of production, which can be determined with the precision of a natural science, and the legal, political, religious, artistic or philosophic – in short, ideological forms in which men become conscious of this conflict and fight it out.
>
> *(Marx 1977, 389–390)*

When leading students through the fragment they should be encouraged to break it down into its constitutive elements which can be summarized (though not necessarily exhaustively) by a linear reading as follows: (1) 'men' (meaning people in general: students should be encouraged to note the gendered language as a common mark of the time when Marx was writing) are born into pre-existing relationships – what Marx calls 'relations of production' (this means the dominant social relationships through which a society is able to transmit its values and reproduce itself through time) that (2) correspond with a 'stage' in the 'development of their material forces of production' (even though students may not be familiar with what these terms mean, they ought to be able to isolate them as elements; their meaning should ideally be elucidated through the process of collaborative close reading. Of note is Marx's use of the word 'stage' as part of a reference to progressive historical change suggestive of the evolutionary sensibility to be found in other writings of the period while 'material forces of production' refers to the kinds of technology available to a society in the work of social reproduction); (3) taken as a whole, the relations of production and the material forces of production form the 'economic structure' or 'real foundation' (students should be encouraged to remark on the use of the words 'real' and 'foundation' and relevant synonyms and antonyms) and upon this foundation arises a 'superstructure' of 'social', 'political' and 'intellectual' forms. Importantly, and in common with the first point, social existence 'determines … consciousness' or what people think (students should be encouraged to think about the word 'determines' and imagine alternatives such as 'conditions'); (4) 'at a certain stage of development' conflict occurs between the forces of production and the relations of production, leading to a period of 'social revolution' and the transformation of first the economic base of society and then the superstructure – students should be encouraged to think whether this is a convincing account of the causes of social change and should be asked to develop arguments 'for' and 'against' Marx's account; (5) the study of periods of rapid social change should distinguish between the 'material transformation' of the economic base of society which can be 'determined with the precision of a natural science' and the 'ideological forms in which men become conscious of this conflict and fight it out' (students should be encouraged to note the supposition of a radical break between ordinary experience of a period of rapid social change and the kind of knowledge of such a period delivered by scientific study, a break that might correspond with the delineation of 'ideological' or 'ordinary' and 'scientific' or 'objective' forms of knowledge). These five points can be further refined into the following headings which will be integral to the solo-reading exercise to come:

1.   Society vs the individual
2.   Linear time
3.   Base vs superstructure
4.   Centrality of struggle
5.   Scientific/objective knowledge vs ordinary/ideological knowledge.

Those working with advanced students should, at this point, direct them to consult Laclau (1990, 3–85) and Smart (1992, 183–221). Briefly, Smart provides a useful overview of how the Marxist tradition has addressed the epistemological crisis of postmodernism while Laclau develops a close reading of our same fragment but alongside a second from *The Communist Manifesto*. Laclau's reading engages with more or less the same terrain as covered above in points (1) to (5) (see for example Laclau 1990, 21–23).

The reading

Worsley, P. 1968. *The Trumpet Shall Sound: A Study of Cargo Cults in Melanesia*. 2nd ed. London: MacGibbon and Kee Ltd, pp. xxxix–lxix, 11–16 and 221–256.

The reading is intended not merely to build on students' substantive knowledge of a particular religious phenomenon, but also to develop their critical reasoning skills. It was chosen because students will be able to see the five areas that emerged from the text fragment surface again albeit in slightly different ways. Their task is to pinpoint where and how Worsley traverses these areas through addressing the following questions:

1. How does Worsley define cargo cults?
2. How does Worsley explain the emergence of cargo cults?
3. What status does Worsley give to indigenous accounts of the phenomenon in his study?
4. What importance does Worsley ascribe to nationalism in his account?

Worsley's book established 'the cargo cult' as a religious phenomenon and an object of study in its own right. The 'cults' appeared in the Melanesian islands of the South Pacific in the early part of the twentieth century and were understood by Worsley as sharing certain similarities with millenarian movements in other parts of the world and at other points in history. Very much the product of contact with European colonizers, the cults were led by charismatic leaders who emerged from among local populations and who claimed that large quantities of 'cargo' (trade goods that were brought into the islands by sea and by air, by Europeans) would arrive, be delivered to the locals and thereby augur the dawn of a new era of plenty in which the ancestors would return. This, in short, is the cargo cult phenomenon.

According to Worsley, the arrival of Europeans profoundly dislocated local cultural norms and values – 'Melanesians were profoundly disturbed by the impact of the Europeans' economy and its effects on their indigenous economic arrangements' (Worsley 1968, lvii). Indeed, the arrival of Europeans constituted a moment of violent rupture and change that brought local 'relations of production' into conflict with new 'material forces of production' that had arrived, unexpectedly, from the outside (this is apposite for those advanced students also engaging with the Laclau reading – see pp. 43–44). The cults' expectation of the millennium highlighted not merely competing economic arrangements but competing senses of time and competing forms of knowledge. In a sense, the book and our study of it represents the victory of linear, developmental time over its millennial rival and the translation of local knowledge and experience into an 'objective' form through the mediation of a specific form of reason (Worsley worked exclusively from documentary sources, hence the lack of an indigenous voice or perspective to the study; see 1968, lix). The phenomenon of the cargo cult is ultimately explained as an instance of religious enthusiasm caused by a particular social and cultural crisis in Melanesia precipitated by the colonial encounter.

Learning outcomes

The learning arising from the first pedagogical exercise can be summarized in the following terms. Obviously learning is a process so we are not talking about fixed quantifiable outcomes, and efforts to develop forms of assessment that seek to atomize learning by breaking it down into discrete units of cognitive experience should be resisted at every turn. Nevertheless, students were directed, from the start, to think of the exercise as an opportunity to practise skills of close, collaborative and solo reading. Marx provided an account of social change that privileged a particular kind of objectivism typically seen as hostile by the WRP. Worsley likewise presented an account of the cults as an objective result of a particular constellation of certain economic and social conditions, a move that for the WRP would mean disavowing the religious dimension of the phenomenon. The epistemological assumptions of modernity might therefore be said to saturate these readings – an all-powerful (gendered) gaze that sees all, maps all and knows all. But this gaze – problematized by feminist scholarship (Haraway 1991; Harding 1991; Lloyd 1993) – clearly registers the sources it uses and those it does not use. Moreover, the idea that the cargo cults could be discussed without reference to the crisis in the transmission of values and norms that afflicted local cultures as a result of the colonial encounter seems highly problematic. The direction of a Marxist gaze to this site of analysis signals a particular mode of contextualization rather than an attempt to render the cults as epiphenomenal effects of economic or social processes. Moreover, it is worth reflecting on the fact that in the exercise, our classroom methods reproduced precisely the power of this gaze over the passive, decontextualized text fragment in order to make the critique of the knowledge-power nexus.

Students who are interested in reading further about cargo cults should consult Otto (2010), whose overview situates Worsley's study in a scholarly discourse on cargo cults.

In practice: from domination to communicative reason

In our first pedagogical exercise we engaged in a close reading of a fragment of text from Marx's considerable body of writing, and one of the issues that we noted from that close reading was the power of reason to claim to have established the objective relationships of cause and effect in society and to thereby demystify society. In this exercise we will continue our critique of reason. In the writings of Max Weber the power of Enlightenment reason was writ large and indeed partly underpinned the idea of 'disenchantment' which later became an organizing concept within the WRP. According to Weber, instrumental rationality had increasingly come to pervade the cultures and societies of the West in the political-bureaucratic and economic spheres, but also surging beyond these areas and into the realm of everyday life and, in *The Protestant Ethic and the Spirit of Capitalism* (2001 [1930]), Weber set out to investigate the relationship between a specific religious ethic – that of ascetic Protestantism – and the emergence of that rationality.

The central question addressed the cultural and historical peculiarity of capitalism, and Weber argued that ascetic Protestantism generated a new attitude towards labour that was fundamental to its emergence in Western Europe. Importantly, the process of rationalization emerged from within Christianity: impersonal rules and procedures steadily supplanted magical and mystical notions. Moreover, the body became an increasingly important site of rationalization. In a vision that would later be taken up by the writers of the Frankfurt School, Weber argued that history was nothing other than the increasing subordination of the body-disciplined individual to rational-legal norms of authority through which social relations were increasingly instrumentalized and subject to the idea of the rational maximization of personal interest. It was these processes of rationalization and instrumentalization that were central to the idea of disenchantment: disenchantment indicated, according to Weber, 'that there are no mysterious incalculable forces that come into play ... rather ... one can, in principle, master all things by calculation' (Weber 1991 [1948], 139). At the close of *The Protestant Ethic* Weber subsumed this logic within a profoundly pessimistic vision of the future:

> The Puritan wanted to work in a calling; we are forced to do so. For when asceticism was carried out of the monastic cells into everyday life, and began to dominate worldly morality, it did its part in building the tremendous cosmos of the modern economic order. This order is now bound to the technical and economic conditions of machine production which today determine the lives of all the individuals who are born into this mechanism, not only those directly concerned with economic acquisition, with irresistible force. Perhaps it will so determine them until the last ton of fossilized coal is burnt. In Baxter's view the care for external goods should only lie on the shoulders of the 'saint like a light cloak, which can be thrown aside at any moment'. But fate decreed that the cloak should become an iron cage.
>
> *(Weber 2001 [1930], 123)*

This bleak vision of a disenchanted world was mitigated only by Weber's claim that irruptions of charisma – specifically the experience of religio-charismatic power – could disrupt the dominations of instrumental reason (Weber 1978, 1117).

Contemporary debates about religions and spiritualities have been framed precisely in terms of this binary: an all-too-powerful Enlightenment reason responsible for disenchantment, societal rationalization and secularization on the one hand, versus a powerful, religiously inflected potentially Self-shattering experience on the other (see Tremlett 2011). This 'romantic' strand of the WRP is apparent precisely in the theories of vernacular and lived religion which privilege improvised and fluid forms of spiritual practice against a backdrop of the decline in institutionalized forms of religious affiliation. Christopher Partridge's *The Re-enchantment of the West* (2004) and Paul Heelas's more recent *Spiritualities of Life* (2008) are representative of the claim that in the West religion is experiencing a cultured reaction against the 'secularizing forces of rationalization, bureaucratization and technological domination' (Partridge 2004, 43). For Partridge, this relates to the emergence of a 'new subculture of dissent and opposition' and a return 'to a form of magical culture' that Partridge terms 'occulture' (2004, 40). According to Partridge, occulture is not so much a worldview as a reservoir of practices, symbols and ideas that re-invent the archaic and the primitive and the notion of unmediated experience and its allegedly transformative power.

Like Partridge, Heelas foregrounds the social significance of what he calls alternatively 'experiential spirituality' (2008, 5) and 'inner-life spirituality' (2008, 219). This spirituality lies on a 'romantic trajectory' that opposes the instrumentalism of bureaucratic and capitalist modernity and allegedly offers a counter-balance to processes that seem to threaten to suffocate the so-called creative Self. Life in the West is, according to Heelas, 'ever more regulated by legal, quasi-legal or economically justified procedures, rules, [and] systems' (2008, 2). Although Heelas admits to a somewhat partisan approach to new age spiritualities, he also says that he is 'committed to basing ... interpretations and judgements ... on publicly accessible evidence' (2008, 10) and, moreover, to 'ethnographic accuracy' (2008, 12). Heelas appeals to the transparency of facts to speak for themselves and to rational, scholarly discourse that is the product of the very reason he claims is a source of domination by technical and bureaucratic procedures. Yet reason cannot be called upon to be the guarantee of the veracity of his account of contemporary religiosities and spiritualities if, at the same time, it is to be set up as the source of an epoch eviscerated of all values and meaning. The binary of (totalitarian) reason as against (romantic or Self-shattering) experience needs to be overcome through a recalibration of the manner in which we think not only about reason in abstract, theoretical terms but concretely in our daily praxis as practitioners of Religious Studies.

The standard mantra of the WRP was that the Marxist and Critical traditions offered no resources for challenging a too-powerful, all-seeing knowing subject whose hubris had led – inexorably according to some – to Auschwitz and the gulags. Yet, the Critical tradition offers a compelling analysis of reason as capable of enabling individual and social praxis while emphasizing the dominations of Capital, and the subordination of cultural and social life to the technical imperatives of instrumental, means-end rationality. As such, it is precisely these traditions that offer the most persuasive dissection of the violences of reason while offering an alternative conception of reason located in the fragile intersubjectivity of co-enquirers.

In his essay 'Critical and Traditional Theory' (1982 [1937]), Horkheimer drew a contrast between bourgeois, positivist science, which seeks a realm of pure knowledge, and Critical Theory, which rejects the fetishization of objective knowledge and the myth of the disinterested and autonomous scientist – in short, of knowledge without interests. For Horkheimer, Critical Theory is a form of praxis – a kind of creative and self-transforming activity – that emphasizes the active role of thought in unmasking ideology and transforming society. Yet, in *Dialectic of Enlightenment* (1944), Adorno and Horkheimer appeared to preclude the possibility of social change in their analysis and unmasking of mass culture as domination and standardization. Culture turned out to be an industry defined by a calculating means-end rationality that seemed to signal the total eclipse of the autonomous individual:

> The sociological theory that the loss of the support of objectively established religion, the dissolution of the last remnants of precapitalism, together with technological and social differentiation or specialization, have led to cultural

chaos is disproved every day; for culture now impresses the same stamp on everything. Film, radio and magazines make up a system which is uniform as a whole and in every part. Even the aesthetic activities of political opposites are one in their enthusiastic obedience to the rhythm of the iron system. The decorative industrial management buildings and exhibition centres in authoritarian countries are much the same as anywhere else. The huge gleaming towers that shoot up everywhere are outward signs of the ingenious planning of international concerns, toward which the unleashed entrepreneurial system (whose monuments are a mass of gloomy houses and business premises in grimy, spiritless cities) was already hastening. Even now the older houses just outside the concrete city centres look like slums, and the new bungalows on the outskirts are at one with the flimsy structures of world fairs in their praise of technical progress and their built-in demand to be discarded after a short while like empty food-cans. Yet the city housing projects designed to perpetuate the individual as a supposedly independent unit in a small hygienic dwelling make him all the more subservient to his adversary – the absolute power of capitalism.

(*Adorno and Horkheimer 1944, 120*)

Marcuse's *One-Dimensional Man* (1964) similarly envisioned a society dominated by capital and a procedural or formal means-end rationality and, like Adorno and Horkheimer, Marcuse emphasized processes of standardization and homogenization through which individual freedom was steadily asphyxiated:

Domination – in the guise of affluence and liberty – extends to all spheres of private and public existence, integrates all authentic opposition, absorbs all alternatives. Technological rationality reveals its political character as it becomes the great vehicle for better domination, creating a truly totalitarian universe in which society and nature, mind and body are kept in a state of permanent mobilization for the defence of this universe.

(*Marcuse 1964, 31*)

Habermas, in a re-reading of *Dialectic of Enlightenment*, identified the paradox that lay at its heart:

As instrumental, reason assimilated itself to power and thereby relinquished its critical force – that is the *final* disclosure of ideology critique applied to itself. To be sure, this description of the self-destruction of the critical capacity is paradoxical, because in the moment of description it still has to make use of the critique that has been declared dead. It denounces the Enlightenment's becoming totalitarian with its own tools.

(*Habermas 2002, 119*)

In other words, reason cannot on the one hand be shown to have entirely lost its critical function and yet be called upon to perform a critical unmasking.

Habermas's work offers a way through this *impasse* through a conceptualization of reason and objectivity in terms of 'intersubjectivity' (Habermas 2008, 76).

Habermas's work incorporates many of the key concepts and assumptions of Critical Theory: knowledge and interests go hand in hand and the notion of apolitical enquiry depends on an unsustainable separation of facts and values; the goal of Critical Theory is emancipation from technical forms of control and domination; science and technology are increasingly intertwined with the systems of production, consumption and administration and must be shown to be so intertwined; Enlightenment reason is now defined by measures of performativity and efficiency such that its original emancipatory content has been lost – this content must at all costs be recovered; the proceduralization and instrumentalization of decision-making processes by experts – the reduction of social policy issues to technical problems – has resulted in these processes becoming divorced from open society and critical debate. These decision-making processes must therefore be subject to democratic accountability. Indeed, in the appendix to *Knowledge and Human Interests* (1972 [1968]), Habermas referred to Horkheimer's 1937 essay and the distinction drawn by Horkheimer between Critical and traditional theory, and reiterated the claim that Critical Theory cannot be objective, detached and value-free, but rather presupposed an interest in values such as human freedom, autonomy and social responsibility.

However, while Habermas follows the contours of thought established by the thinkers of the Frankfurt School, he has also developed a critical analysis of phenomenological and hermeneutic interpretations of the life-world. If Habermas's aim has been to proffer a diagnosis of structural and systemic problems characteristic of modern societies, in *The Theory of Communicative Action* he elaborates this diagnosis initially through distinguishing between 'system' and 'life-world'. According to Habermas, the life-world is a realm of implicit shared values, norms, symbolic meanings responsible for cultural reproduction, social integration and socialization. This Heideggerian realm of pre-understandings is described as a 'reservoir of taken-for-granteds' (1985, 124) and as an 'intuitively familiar, preinterpreted reality' (1985, 132) and is defined by what Habermas calls 'communicative rationality'.

Habermas defines communicative rationality as form of social action where the actions of agents or actors are calculated not according to criteria of individual success, but rather in terms of reaching agreement with others. Indeed, Habermas claims that implicit in every speech-act or utterance is an orientation towards consensus and agreement. As such, free or un-coerced consensus is the telos of every act of speech: 'the utopian perspective of reconciliation and freedom is ingrained in the conditions for the communicative sociation of individuals; it is built into the linguistic mechanism of the reproduction of the species' (Habermas 1985, 398). The life-world is however threatened by the rational-instrumental form of social action characteristic of the bureaucratic-administrative and economic systems (this is the so-called 'colonization thesis'; for an overview, see Heath 2011). Worse: distortion occurs when the formal imperatives of the system threaten to colonize the life-world:

> Capitalist modernization follows a pattern such that cognitive-instrumental rationality surges beyond the bounds of the economy and state into other, communicatively structured areas of life and achieves dominance there at the expense of moral-political and aesthetic-practical rationality, and this produces disturbances in the symbolic reproduction of the lifeworld.
>
> *(Habermas 1985, 304–305)*

According to Habermas, the colonization of the life-world by a form of rationality alien to it results in the standardization of culture, political passivity and the emergence of new forms of authoritarianism, a situation which can only be addressed through a return to the founding values of the project of modernity, and a re-connecting with the life-world that must be more than the empty celebration of tradition. However, this latter can only be achieved if the process of societal rationalization can be steered onto a different course. Habermas argues that the life-world has to be able to develop its own institutions which can then circumscribe the means-ends technical imperatives of the economic and bureaucratic-administrative system.

According to Habermas, in order to revitalize the project of modernity (and the life-world) we need to find a way out of what he calls 'the philosophy of the subject'. As such, he sketches two positions or two forms of reason. The first is defined by Habermas as subject-centred reason about which we developed a critique through a close reading of a text fragment from Marx's *oeuvre* in the first exercise. The second is communicative reason, where 'the knowledge of objects' is 'replaced by the paradigm of mutual understanding between subjects capable of speech and action' (2002, 295–296). According to Habermas, at the centre of modernity is the notion of a solitary reasoning or knowing subject that measures and classifies objects. This view confines the manner in which human beings can relate to both each other and the world. It is confined ontologically because the world becomes a world of objectively given entities to be measured, named, counted and classified; it is confined epistemologically in our capacity to describe particular states of affairs or to bring them about through purposive and calculating rational action; and it is confined semantically to factual statements. Habermas argues that thinkers such as Nietzsche, Heidegger, Foucault and Derrida have all sought to escape subject-centered reason, but have done so in ways which abandon modernity's original, emancipatory content. On the other hand, a reason that is exercised between subjects – that is enacted in dialogue or communication – is a reason that operates through consensus and which therefore can give or return a moral or ethical content to modernity:

> Fundamental to the paradigm of mutual understanding is … the performative attitude of participants in interaction, who coordinate their plans for action by coming to an understanding about something in the world. When ego carries out a speech act and alter takes up a position with regard to it, the two parties enter into an interpersonal relationship. The latter is structured by the

system of reciprocally interlocked perspectives among speakers, hearers, and non-participants who happen to be present at the time.

(Habermas 2002, 296–297)

Conclusion: why Religious Studies needs Marx

At the heart of Religious Studies and the WRP has been an often inexplicit and poorly articulated critique of modern society. For example, in the 'Preface' and in the various essays that constitute *The Quest* (1969), Eliade talks about the study of religions as a special form of research that operates on behalf of the re-enchantment of the researcher, the sympathetic reader of that research and of modernity itself:

> The hierophanies – i.e., the manifestations of the sacred expressed in symbols, myths, supernatural beings, etc. – are grasped as structures, and constitute a prereflective language that requires a special hermeneutics ... by means of a competent hermeneutics, history of religions ceases to be a museum of fossils, ruins, and obsolete *mirabilia* and becomes what it should have been from the beginning ... a series of 'messages' waiting to be deciphered and understood. The interest in such 'messages' is not exclusively historical. They do not only 'speak' to us about a long-dead past, but they disclose fundamental existential situations that are directly relevant to modern man ... a considerable enrichment of consciousness results from the hermeneutical effort of deciphering the meaning of myths, symbols, and other traditional religious structures; in a certain sense, one can even speak of the inner transformation of the researcher and, hopefully, of the sympathetic reader. What is called the phenomenology and history of religions can be considered among the very few humanistic disciplines that are at the same time propaedeutic and spiritual techniques.
>
> *(Eliade 1969, n.p.)*

Central to this ambitious and politically charged project of restoring authentic meaning to the world is the assertion that only a certain approach – an approach willing to treat its subject-matter in a special way – can accomplish this momentous task:

> It seems to me difficult to believe that, living in a historical moment like ours, the historians of religions will not take account of the creative possibilities of their discipline. How to assimilate *culturally* the spiritual universes that Africa, Oceania, Southeast Asia open to us? All these spiritual universes have a religious origin and structure. If one does not approach them in the perspective of the history of religions, they will disappear as spiritual universes; they will be reduced to *facts* about social organisations, economic regimes, epochs of colonial history, etc. In other words, they will not be grasped as spiritual creations; they will not enrich Western and world culture – they will serve to augment the

number, already terrifying, of *documents* classified in archives, awaiting electronic computers to take them in charge.

(Eliade 1969, 70–71)

This critique is clearly seeking to create a space for forms of knowledge and experience – religious knowledge and experience – in a world increasingly hostile to anything that does not conform to the rationality of the 'archives'. This potentially productive enterprise was, however, fatally undermined by an extremely narrow notion of religion constrained by deference to a disembodied Husserlian positivism and the motif of experience (and, in Eliade's case, a fascination with fascism). These apparently contradictory strands come together through the architecture of the Self. As such, the critique was perhaps particularly notable for what it left out – a whole corpus of writing philosophically, politically and ethically oriented to developing a diagnosis of modern societies and their ills. Now that the WRP is no more, an opportunity exists for scholars and students of Religious Studies to read Marx without shame and to explore questions of knowledge, power and reason and to apply them to their studies, doing so through a conception of reason as a social practice beyond the binary of subject-centred reason and experience.

Note

1 Both Habermas and Laclau trace an intellectual genealogy back to Marx and Engels. However, whereas for Habermas that genealogy is traced through the Frankfurt School and the writings of Adorno, Horkheimer and Marcuse (including the intellectual insights of Freud, Weber and Heidegger), Laclau's can be traced through the writings of Lenin and Gramsci (incorporating the intellectual insights of post-structuralism, particularly the writings of Lacan and Derrida).

References

Adorno, Theodor W. and Max Horkheimer. 1944. *Dialectic of Enlightenment*. Translated by John Cumming. New York: Continuum.

Asad, Talal. 1993. *Genealogies of Religion: Discipline and Reasons of Power in Christianity and Islam*. Baltimore and London: The Johns Hopkins University Press.

Bloch, Maurice. 1983. *Marxism and Anthropology*. Oxford and New York: Oxford University Press.

Eliade, Mircea. 1969. *The Quest: History and Meaning in Religion*. Chicago: University of Chicago.

Fitzgerald, Timothy. 2000. *The Ideology of Religious Studies*. Oxford and New York: Oxford University Press.

Flood, Gavin. 1999. *Beyond Phenomenology: Rethinking the Study of Religion*. London and New York: Cassell.

Habermas, Jürgen. 1972 [1968]. *Knowledge and Human Interests*. London: Heinemann Educational Books.

Habermas, Jürgen. 1985. *The Theory of Communicative Action Vols. I and II*. Translated by Thomas McCarthy. Boston: Beacon Press.

Habermas, Jürgen. 2002. *The Philosophical Discourse of Modernity: Twelve Lectures.* Translated by Frederick Lawrence. Cambridge: Polity Press.

Habermas, Jürgen. 2008. "Communicative Action and the Detranscendentalized 'Use of Reason'." In *Between Naturalism and Religion: Philosophical Essays*, translated by Ciaran Cronin, 24–76. Cambridge: Polity.

Haraway, Donna. 1991. *Simians, Cyborgs and Women: The Reinvention of Nature.* London: Free Association Books.

Harding, Sandra. 1991. *Whose Science? Whose Knowledge? Thinking from Women's Lives.* Ithaca and New York: Cornell University Press.

Heath, Joseph. 2011. "System and Lifeworld." In *Jürgen Habermas: Key Concepts*, edited by Barbara Fultner, 74–90. Durham: Acumen.

Heelas, Paul. 2008. *Spiritualities of Life: New Age Romanticism and Consumptive Capitalism.* Oxford: Blackwell.

Horkheimer, Max. 1982 [1937]. "Critical and Traditional Theory." In *Critical Theory: Selected Essays*, translated by Matthew J. O'Connell, 188–243. New York: Continuum.

King, Richard. 1999. *Orientalism and Religion: Postcolonial Theory, India and 'the Mystic East'.* London and New York: Routledge.

Knott, Kim. 2005. *The Location of Religion: A Spatial Analysis.* London: Equinox.

Laclau, Ernesto. 1990. "New Reflections on the Revolution of Our Time." In *New Reflections on the Revolution of Our Time*, 3–85. London and New York: Verso.

Lloyd, Genevieve. 1993. *The Man of Reason: 'Male' and 'Female' in Western Philosophy.* 2nd ed. London and New York: Routledge.

Marcuse, Herbert. 1964. *One-Dimensional Man.* London: Sphere.

Marx, Karl. 1977. "'Preface' to *A Critique of Political Economy*." In *Karl Marx: Selected Writings*, edited by David McLellan, 209–213. Oxford: Oxford University Press.

Otto, Ton. 2010. "What Happened to Cargo Cults? Material Religions in Melanesia and the West." In *Contemporary Religiosities: Emergent Socialities and the Post-Nation-State*, edited by Bruce Kapferer, Kari Telle and Annelin Eriksen, 81–102. New York and Oxford: Berghahn Books.

Partridge, Christopher. 2004. *The Re-enchantment of the West: Volume 1, Alternative Spiritualities, Sacralization, Popular Culture and Occulture.* London: T and T Clark International.

Smart, Barry. 1992. *Modern Conditions, Postmodern Controversies.* London and New York: Routledge.

Tremlett, Paul-François. 2008. *Religion and the Discourse on Modernity.* London: Continuum.

Tremlett, Paul-François. 2011. "Weber-Foucault-Nietzsche: Uncertain Legacies for the Sociology of Religion." In *Sects and Sectarianism in Jewish History*, edited by Sacha Stern, 287–304. Leiden: Brill.

Weber, Max. 1978. "Charisma and its Transformation." In *Economy and Society: An Outline of Interpretive Sociology*, edited by Guenther Roth and Claus Wittich, 1111–1157. Berkeley: University of California Press.

Weber, Max. 1991 [1948]. "Science as a Vocation." In *From Max Weber: Essays in Sociology*, edited by Hans Heinrich Gerth and Charles Wright Mills, 129–156. London and New York: Routledge.

Weber, Max. 2001 [1930]. *The Protestant Ethic and the Spirit of Capitalism.* Translated by Talcott Parsons. London and New York: Routledge.

Worsley, Peter. 1968. *The Trumpet Shall Sound: A Study of Cargo Cults in Melanesia.* 2nd ed. London: MacGibbon and Kee Ltd.

8

THE SACRED ALTERNATIVE

Suzanne Owen

Introduction

At first glance, employing the category 'sacred' appears to broaden conceptions of religion to include marginalized groups and ritual activity that cuts across boundaries established and maintained by the World Religions Paradigm (WRP). Some studies of religion have favoured this term over 'religion' for these reasons, an example being Ninian Smart's *Dimensions of the Sacred* (1996), which may be applied to some extent to nationalism and other 'non-religious' phenomena. Also, many people reject the term 'religion' to describe what they do, although they may still regard things, places or individuals as 'sacred', which is the case among some indigenous and Pagan groups. The discursive nature of the term 'sacred', as no more *sui generis* than 'religion', will be discussed in relation to the annual Beltane event at Thornborough Henge in Yorkshire.

Both Émile Durkheim and Mircea Eliade employed the binary 'sacred and profane' as an analytical framework for cross-cultural comparisons of social organizations often labelled 'religious', but while Durkheim described them as social constructions, in that 'sacred things' are set apart, Eliade portrayed 'the sacred' as an ontological reality that interrupts ordinary time and space. Eliade's approach is largely phenomenological so it is not surprising that an emic use of 'sacred' often refers to an ontological reality as well. However, some studies appear to import an Eliadian or emic conception of 'sacred' into a Durkheimian or sociological approach, partly because Durkheim himself was ambiguous about what he considered 'real', a term Eliade also used, and partly because of the lack of clarity in scholars' work generally when using the term 'sacred'. Despite this pitfall, I propose that a focus on 'making sacred' as a human activity can be a useful alternative to the 'world religions' approach in Religious Studies.

Approaching 'the sacred'

To begin with, a distinction must be made between uses of the term 'sacred' as a verb or adjective and as a noun. The Latin root of 'sacred' is derived from the verb *sacrare*, 'to sanctify, dedicate', or the related term *sacer*, an adjective. The adjectival use of the term is found in the work of Durkheim and is more sociological or situational (although he occasionally uses it as a noun as well), while Eliade's usage, as a noun, rendering 'the sacred' into an object, is more theological or substantive. Durkheim indicates, in his well-known definition of religion, that it is collective practices that determine what is 'sacred':

> A religion is a unified system of beliefs and practices relative to sacred things, that is to say, things set apart and forbidden – beliefs and practices which unite into one single moral community called a Church, all those who adhere to them.
>
> *(Durkheim 2001, 46)*

At least in this case Durkheim retains an adjectival sense of the term 'sacred'. Putting aside his choice to use the term 'church' generically, which he applies to a group of people who 'share a common conception of the sacred world and its relation to the profane world' (2001, 42–3), it may be unclear who or what is making the sacred–profane distinction, but this is established earlier in the book:

> All known religious beliefs, whether simple or complex, present a common quality: they presuppose a classification of things – the real or ideal things that men represent for themselves – into two classes, two opposite kinds, generally designated by two distinct terms effectively translated by the words profane and sacred.
>
> *(Durkheim 2001, 36)*

He explored this division in the nature of religious prohibitions – for example, certain objects may only be touched by priests. They are sacred and must not be 'profaned' by ordinary people, thus dividing the sociological world into the sacred (set apart) and the profane (ordinary). Although it is 'men' who do the classifying, there may be some ambiguity over the 'real and ideal' in Durkheim, and elsewhere when discussing the distinction made between the sacred soul and profane body; he considers that 'the notion of the soul is not without reality' and that 'there is something of the divine in us' (2001, 193). Nevertheless, the stress is on the human creation of ideas about the soul.

Although Eliade employs the same oppositional terms, he ignores Durkheim's sociological usage and instead takes his cue from Rudolf Otto's *Idea of the Holy* (1923). He extended Otto's work in several ways, including the notion of *homo religiosus*, that humans are fundamentally oriented toward the transcendent and responses to this can be 'expressed' in subjective or cultural forms, but particularly with regard to sacred and profane as two modes of being (Lynch 2012b, 11), with the former more common to pre-modern living and the latter as degenerate and more common to modern living. This understanding, above all an experiential theory of religion, focused on a postulated human response to a transcendent power or being as somehow tapping into a timeless and ahistorical mode of being, where 'the real unveils itself' (Eliade 1959, 63).

Religious 'insiders' might agree with Eliade's analysis of what makes places 'sacred'. He noted in *The Sacred and the Profane* that 'a sacred place constitutes a break in the homogeneity of space', meaning that 'the sacred' interrupts or manifests in places. Further to this, he says, 'this break is symbolized by an opening by which passage from one cosmic region to another is made possible' (1959, 37). Eliade's 'sacred' emerges from a cosmic region that is ontologically real. This is in contrast to a situational approach where 'nothing is inherently sacred', which Chidester and Linenthal relate to Claude Lévi-Strauss's view that the sacred is 'a value of inde- terminate signification, in itself empty of meaning and therefore susceptible to the reception of any meaning whatsoever' (1950, xlix, quoted in Chidester and Linenthal 1995, 6). In the verbal sense of 'making sacred', it is 'a sign of difference that can be assigned to virtually anything through the human labor of consecration' (1995, 6). A situational approach to sacred space is also understood by Moser and Feldman, who state in the introduction to *Locating the Sacred* that: 'Sacred space does not exist a priori but is the outcome of actions, intentions, and recollections – it is the result of past and present interactions among humans, material implements, architecture, and landscape' (2014, 1).

Yet, it is not just any meaning that is ascribed to 'sacred' things or places. Philosopher Don Cupitt describes how traditional cultures are 'created by a series of acts of dis- crimination and discernment' and illustrates this by returning to the root of the term 'culture', which is from the Latin *cernere*, 'to separate', i.e. the wheat from the chaff (2001, 483). As with wheat, one part of a binary pair is of more value than the other:

> Discrimination and discernment evidently involves evaluation, because it does not simply divide the flux of experience into two equal and similar zones: on the contrary, it seems to structure the world, so that two markedly different things or principles or regions appear. One of them is prior, founding, normative, and lucid, and the other is its secondary, darker, and less stable counterpart or 'Other'.
> *(Cupitt 2001, 483)*

He follows this with examples of such distinctions, such as light–dark, male–female. The point, for him, is that these pairs are asymmetrical (2001, 484). Thus, with the sacred–profane distinction, the first term points to that which is considered prior and foundational. Therefore, what is 'sacred' is of higher value to those who designate it as such.

In the study of religion the term 'sacred' is perhaps associated mostly with phenomenological understandings, exemplified by Ninian Smart, specifically his *Dimensions of the Sacred* (1996), in which he aimed to broaden the category of religion to be inclusive of a diversity of worldviews. In his usage, 'the sacred' is more or less interchangeable with 'religion'. In fact, he hardly mentions the term 'sacred' beyond placing it in the book's title. As a phenomenologist, he attempts to replicate an emic perspective oriented toward ontological or theological under-standings of religion. According to Veikko Anttonen, the theological argument for employing the term 'sacred' is that there can be no religion without it as it is the essence of religion, which he says is seen in the work of Otto, van der Leeuw and Eliade, among others (2000, 272). It can be seen in their work that: 'The concept of the sacred has been an inseparable part of the interpretive project in herme-neutically oriented scholarship aimed at "bracketing" the transcendental element as it is experienced by a religious person' (2000, 273). Rather than the more situa-tional interpretation of 'sacred' as 'set apart', reflecting the social values of a group, a theological or ontological interpretation tends to focus on the individual's experience of something numinous.

Without citing Smart, both Gordon Lynch (2007, 135–6; 2012b, 4; 2012c, 10) and Kim Knott (2013, 145) point out that religion and sacred are often conflated in studies of religion. As Lynch puts it:

> People talk about sacred texts, sacred music or sacred space to refer to the texts, music or spaces of mainstream religious traditions. For some people, the sacred might have greater connotations of mystery, a transcendent essence that stands untainted above the vulgar peculiarities and struggles of specific religious lives.
>
> *(2012c, 10)*

Although 'sacred' and 'religion' 'have their own distinctive semantic terrains', used interchangeably, it assumes that 'sacred' 'is essentially a religious matter' (Knott 2013, 145), a problem raised previously by Fitzgerald, who partly blames the influence of Durkheim for defining religion with reference to 'sacred things' (Fitzgerald 2007a, 72). For this reason, Knott has been using the term 'secular sacred' to 'strategically highlight the break with the commonly expressed view that the "sacred" is an exclusively religious category' (Knott 2013, 145). This follows Lynch's view that the binary opposition between sacred and profane ought to be rejected, as it 'is unhelpful because it creates a false distinction between mundane everyday life, and the realm of the transcendent mediated through specific spaces, rituals and personnel' (Lynch 2007, 135–6).

Despite pointing out the differences between sociological and ontological conceptions of 'sacred', Lynch can be just as ambiguous as he finds that:

> Durkheim's own understanding of the sacred is sufficiently complex to allow different, and sometimes competing, readings. His work can, therefore, be reasonably read as supporting a form of (social) ontological theory of the sacred … as well as the cultural sociological approach.
>
> *(Lynch 2012b, 19)*

For a start, 'the sacred' given here is as a noun, which reinforces an ontological reading. Likewise, in choosing 'the sacred' in book titles, Lynch gives the impression of promoting an ontological understanding of 'the sacred' as a noun. In an earlier work, he argues that 'there is something distinctive about religion and the sacred where it appears within fields of human culture, and the study of religion, media and popular culture has the potential to shed more light on its nature and significance' (Lynch 2007, 126). In *On the Sacred*, the meaning of 'sacred' is still ambiguous, such as when he states that:

> sacred forms of communication … typically focus on specific symbols, invite people into powerful forms of emotional identification, and are made real through physical and institutional practices. Sacred forms generate their own visions of 'evil' (the profane), and establish moral boundaries beyond which lie people who are regarded as 'inhuman' or 'animals'.
>
> *(Lynch 2012c, 11)*

'The sacred' appears to have its own agency and it is difficult to determine if he is speaking of a transcendent or socially constructed 'sacred'. Similarly, in 'Public Media and the Sacred', Lynch regards 'the sacred' as 'a communicative structure … which orientates people towards absolute realities that have a normative claim upon the conduct of social life, around which collective forms of thought, feeling and action are formed' (2012a, 245). Although socially generated, 'the sacred' is communicated in some publicly accessible format. In prior times this may have been icons, relics, symbols, architecture, and later texts, but now 'public media are the primary institutional structures in modern societies through which people reproduce and contest sacred forms' (2012a, 246). The problem with Durkheim, and in Lynch to some extent, is that the 'sacred' is top-down, imposed on heterogeneous subject-matter. For Durkheim priests and such figures determine what is sacred, which is replaced in Lynch by 'the media' defining what is sacred, while all others are passive recipients.

Chidester and Linenthal's idea of sacred space as 'contested space' opens up the concept to an analysis of power relations. In this interpretation, 'sacred' is invoked to make a claim of authority over something or some place, reflecting a person's or group's interests. The idea of 'contested space' is already nascent in Gerardus van der Leeuw's *Religion in Essence and Manifestation* (1938), which recognized both the ontological and sociological interpretations of space, which Chidester and Linenthal refer to as the poetics and politics of space (borrowed from Stallybrass and White 1986). An example of the poetics of sacred space is in van der Leeuw's linking of the core of each 'sacred place' with the hearth of a home, the altar of a temple, a shrine of a pilgrimage site and the heart of the body (Chidester and Linenthal 1995, 7), akin to Eliade's view. He also 'recognized that every establishment of sacred place was a conquest of sacred space … appropriated, possessed and owned' and that the 'sanctity of the inside was certified by maintaining and reinforcing boundaries that kept certain persons outside the sacred place' (1995, 8), akin to Durkheim's view.

This is an integral part of making sacred space – regulating who can enter and when. 'The sacred character of a place can be asserted and maintained through claims and counter-claims on its ownership' (1995, 8).

In practice: contested space

To illustrate sacred space as contested space, Chidester and Linenthal give two Hawaiian examples, which I have found useful for teaching this topic in the class-room. One is Pu'uhonua o Hōnaunau, a native Hawaiian place of refuge, and the other is Pearl Harbor. At the place of refuge, now a tourist site maintained by the National Parks Services, native Hawaiians still have access at night to reconsecrate it and thereby reclaim it (Chidester and Linenthal 1995, 2). With the rise of indigenous rights to self-determination, the park becomes a site of political resistance as a contested space with competing interpretations. There was also the question of legitimate ownership as other native Hawaiian sites were marked for development as highways and golf courses. 'Ancient sacred places became modern sites of struggle over nationality, economic empowerment, and basic civil and human rights to freedom of religion and self-determination' (1995, 3). As a 'secular' example, the Second World War battle site of Pearl Harbor has been 'sanctified' and comme-morated in ritualized fashion, thus making it a sacred site for ceremony and pilgrimage performed by 'tourist pilgrims', who buy mementos such as T-shirts and books, demonstrating a 'venerative consumption' (1995, 4). The USS *Arizona* memorial in particular is 'both shrine and tomb', a site for enacting 'ritual relations between the living and the dead' (1995, 4). Bringing more complaints than anything else was the decision by the National Parks Services to include Japanese perspectives and they were criticized for not being an 'appropriate guardian of the sacred memory of those Americans who died in the attack on Pearl Harbor' (1995, 4–5). When we discuss this example in class, students often suggest Ground Zero in New York as a similar space. Such places 'continue to be reproduced as sacred sites through similar spatial practices', which Chidester and Linenthal describe as ritualization, reinterpretation and contestation (1995, 1). To them, 'sacred space' is inherently contested because it is spatial and two objects cannot occupy the same place at the same time, but also, as 'sacred' can signify anything, 'its meaningful contours can become almost infinitely extended through the work of interpretation' (1995, 18).

The triad of ritualization, reinterpretation and contestation of 'sacred space' is apparent at sites such as Thornborough Henge in Yorkshire during the Beltane festival. 'Sacred' is invoked relatively frequently by authors on Paganism, as evidenced by the title of Lynne Hume's article 'Creating Sacred Space: Outer Expressions of Inner Worlds in Contemporary Wicca' (1998) and that of Jenny Blain's and Robert Wallis's *Sacred Sites, Contested Rites/Rights* (2007) about Pagan engagements with archaeological sites in Britain. As Hume points out, the circle is the most prominent symbol in Pagan traditions, represented in the ceremonial spaces they create and, for Wiccans, the constructed sacred space becomes a 'world apart'

(Hume 1998, 309). At the start of a Wiccan ritual a circle is 'cast' with acts of consecration and cleansing. At the end, the circle is 'dismantled' and the space 'is no longer sacred' (1998, 317). 'Sacred space' can be made wherever they wish, but usually in someone's home or a natural environment.

In addition, for many Pagans the land itself is 'sacred'. If a site in the landscape is already in the shape of a circle, like Stonehenge and indeed Thornborough Henge, it becomes a magnet for Pagan ritual activity and reinterpretation. I chose Thornborough Henge as an example because I first heard of it on account of protests by archaeologists and Pagans against nearby quarrying. Shortly after, it became the site of the largest public Beltane event in Yorkshire.

Thornborough Henge

The late Neolithic site of Thornborough Henge (or henges, as the earth embankments there form three rings) in North Yorkshire was described by David Miles of English Heritage as 'the most important prehistoric site between Stonehenge and the Orkneys',[1] but remained virtually unknown in the rest of the United Kingdom until the threat of extensions to quarrying by Tarmac next to the henges was reported in *British Archaeology* in 2004 and publicized at various Pagan events (Blain and Wallis 2007, 146). Several local groups, such as Friends of Thornborough Henge and Yorkshire Archaeological Society, were also concerned about preserving the site and its environs. As an example of a contested site, Blain and Wallis say: 'The case of Thornborough, particularly, has also shown how archaeological emphases have changed even since the mid 1990s, with landscape archaeology coming to the fore, and the adoption of the term "sacred landscape"' (2007, 149):

> [It is] where many groups present their own interest and involvement, where the meanings of Thornborough are intricate and convoluted, and where new relationships of people and landscape, new alliances and identities based in protection and sacredness, are in the forging.
>
> *(Blain and Wallis 2007, 150)*

A few local Pagans had already been holding ceremonies at the site, but not on the scale of the event organized by the Sacred Brigantia Trust, named for the goddess of the Brigantes (the federation of tribes of Britons occupying the area including Yorkshire during Roman times). The trust was set up in 2004 to organize a public Beltane event within the central henge and it has been held annually ever since (apart from 2006, when it was too wet), with several hundred attending each year. An additional event has also been taking place at 'Mabon' (autumn equinox) since 2012. At the bottom of the Sacred Brigantia Trust's website it used to say (at least until 2013) that the Beltane event was supported by Tarmac Nosterfield Quarry, the landowner who gives permission for the festivals, which highlights the nature of the site as a place of conflicting interests between Tarmac, archaeologists, heritage groups and Pagans. Although no mention is made publicly during the Beltane event about the threat of extensions to the quarry, or even the significance of the archaeology itself, the organizers take care to limit damage to the site. However, neither do Christians remark on the architectural importance of their church during a service.

Pagans link the site to a reimagined pre-Roman past, to the time of Thornborough's origins, perhaps, which was roughly 2500 BCE (the Brigante federation existed probably no earlier than 450 BCE). According to the Sacred Brigantia Trust's website, 'Beltane at Thornborough is inspired by the mythology, folklore, ritual traditions and pagan religious deities of the British Isles that form our shared collective heritage. It is open to anyone to attend regardless of their personal beliefs.'[2] They are aware of their contemporary status as Pagans and prefer to see themselves as following in the footsteps of those who have made ritual use of the site in the past. Kelly Cryer, who co-created the ritual ceremony and mystery play in 2007 with Pagan Chaplain Marcus Naylor, was quoted in the *Ripon Gazette* as saying: 'There has been a long tradition of successive cultures re-using ancient sacred sites, of which we are a modern example.'[3] In effect, Sacred Brigantia mixes Bronze Age with Iron Age and post-Roman references to Britain's past and mythology.

The public midday ritual, held on a Sunday close to Beltane in early May, begins with the lighting of a torch on the henge, a processional entry by the performers, a 'hail and welcome' to spirits of the four directions, ancestors and the land, followed by a performance of a seasonal Pagan-themed 'mystery play' (for example, in 2011 they performed part of the *Mabinogion* and in 2013 it was the *Dragons of Dinas Emrys* – tales largely of Welsh origin). For the most part the performance is 'spectacle', with the audience coming and going, visiting stalls where craftwork and other goods may be purchased, or conversing with each other at the margins of the circle. The only audience participation, apart from the occasional pantomime calls, is when the horn of mead is passed around. Handfasting ceremonies may take place by prior arrangement. Very little else of an organized nature goes on for the rest of the day and it resembles a car boot sale rather than a festival.

Why do people attend Beltane at Thornborough, and what does Beltane mean to them? A documentary film on this topic called *Beltane at Thornborough 2012, 'Kinda special …'* and made by Chris Giles and Dave Brunskill has been posted on the Sacred Brigantia Trust website.[4] In it Giles and Brunskill walk around the site during the Beltane festival, asking participants what Beltane means to them and receiving diverse answers, some people expressing what they know about Beltane, others saying they are just looking for a nice day out. I have transcribed three of these conversations:

Transcript 1 (3.10–28 minutes into the film): woman with ivy garland on her head

WOMAN: There's not many places where you can actually openly celebrate Beltane, and be in this wonderful henge. This henge isn't open to the public normally, so it's just the atmosphere and everybody really.

QUESTION: What does Beltane mean to you?

WOMAN: Beltane to me is one of the sacred Pagan festivals and it's about the heralding of the summer and fertility and bringing fertility to the land and without this time of year then we won't have any crops, we won't have food, so it's very important to me to celebrate that.

Transcript 2 (5.10–30 minutes): two men

QUESTION: Would you like to tell me what this event means to you?

BEARDED MAN: Well, it's just a good time, really. It's a way to get out the house and do something different, really.

QUESTION: Have you been here before?

BEARDED MAN: Once before about two years ago.

QUESTION: What about yourself?

SHORN-HEADED MAN: Yes, same thing, really. Yep, yep. Just to come around and see what's happening. I've been here before.

QUESTION: And what does Beltane mean to you?

SHORN-HEADED MAN: (shrugs) Um, not much, really.

QUESTION: You just like dressing up?

SHORN-HEADED MAN: Yeah, yeah, I just like dressing up.

Transcript 3 (6.07–30 minutes): Leeds lads

FIRST LAD: I'm from Leeds, this is my first festival and I'm here supporting my friend, who's a Pagan, so ... seeing what it's all about.

QUESTION TO SECOND LAD: So, you're a Pagan?

SECOND LAD: No. Eh, no, I dabble.

QUESTION: What does Beltane mean to you?

SECOND LAD: Em, I don't really know, it's just a nice way of getting out and celebrating the pagan festival.

What is the purpose of the event? To bring unity and togetherness among Pagans? To entertain the public? The so-called mystery plays are carnivalesque and performed like pantomimes with cross-dressing, villains and so on. As Graham Harvey notes about Pagan festivals, they 'could be seen by passers-by as merely fooling-around or dressing up – no-one hands out leaflets explaining the "serious meaning" of the occasion' (2007, 11), though if they ask they may be told that it is for celebrating the Earth or protesting against some degradation of it.

If preservation of the henges is the focus, how is this aided by these events? This is not entirely clear, nor why they are held within the henge at Thornborough at all except that the earthworks form an arena. At the start of the performance, Oliver Robinson, the Master of Ceremonies, informs the audience about waste and damage control. However, upon entry, vehicles are directed to a field next to the henge and stallholders may drive their vehicles inside. There are concerns about whether the festivals damage the site. More recently the organizers have been telling participants not to climb on the henges because of erosion, yet some performers do at the start and end of the mystery play.

The term 'sacred' is prevalent among those who organize and participate in Beltane at Thornborough. In the film, the woman with the ivy garland referred to 'sacred Pagan Festivals'. The term is also found on the Sacred Brigantia Trust website:

> Is it any wonder that in the digital age we should seek to reconnect with ourselves and to explore the richness of our native traditions: to discover that we are a people and that we have a tribal name and that our goddess can still be found in the sacred rivers and enchanted landscape of our ancestors; to keep the ritual fires burning in this the sacred land of Brigantia.[5]

If 'highly valued' was used instead of 'sacred', the intended meaning would not change (Owen and Taira 2015, 102). Using this word is a rhetorical strategy to assert a claim over a site's use and meaning, privileging those who are self-appointed guardians of 'the sacred'. Arnal and McCutcheon point out that 'social groups use a variety of local devices to navigate decisions about which of the many items of the empirical world get to count as significant and thus memorable' (2013, 119).

Blain and Wallis surmise that '"sacred" lends a reverential and spiritual element to what is otherwise perceived as only an academic resource, a dead past, or a destination on a tourist checklist' (2007, 28). Although they highlight the constructed nature of 'sacred' at such sites, indicating various interest groups' claims, and that '"sacredness" is constituted within discourse and in the interplay between humans and landscape, within time as within place' (2007, 209), they could go further to analyse the implications of what is being stated or claimed in such discourse. To whom is it sacred? It is clear some participants regard the festival, or site, as 'sacred'. Does this mean their perspective is privileged and then rarefied as the Pagan view?

It must be assumed that if something is sacred, then other things are not sacred, implying a secular–sacred opposition, a relatively modern distinction. Archaeologist Cornelius Holtorf's endorsement of *Sacred Sites, Contested Rites/Rights* (inside the cover), states 'Prehistoric sites are sacred sites again' – assuming a sacred–secular distinction was made in pre-modern times. There is a popular idea that 'everything was sacred' before the Enlightenment, re-importing a modern notion into the past. This is a tendency among some Pagans, too, who attempt to apply idealizations about the pre-modern world onto sites using modern categorizations. To be traditionalist, according to *Tyr*, a Pagan journal, is 'to yearn for the small, homogeneous tribal societies that flourished before Christianity – societies in which every aspect of life was integrated into a holistic system', and so they represent the 'Resacralization of the world versus materialism' (quoted in Blain and Wallis 2007, 23). 'Sacred' in these contexts is not an equivalent of the term 'religion' as it operates differently. Rarely do people claim that everything before Christianity was 'religion' or 'religious', mainly because of the popular association between religion and institutions and texts, of which Christianity is the primary model.

In conclusion, the concept 'sacred' essentially points to 'no thing' and is entirely representative of the group's or person's interests. William Arnal and Russell T. McCutcheon chose the title *The Sacred Is the Profane* 'to dispel the notion that these two designators name separate domains that somehow interact with one another' (2013, xi). In recognizing, in Durkheim, that the sacred–profane distinction is not referring to qualities but social categories:

> If there is no fixed content to the distinction between 'sacred' and 'profane,' if the distinction is purely formal and arbitrary, what is the point? ... Durkheim concludes that the point of the sacred-profane distinction is to offer a representation for society as a whole ... that accompanies occasions of communal solidarity. It sets something aside as 'special,' whose special character, defined by the group, turns out to be the group itself.
>
> *(Arnal and McCutcheon 2013, 21)*

Is Beltane at Thornborough 'kinda special', as the film title suggests? 'Special' is certainly closer to what is invoked by the term 'sacred' and does not apply to an ontological reality, even in much of the discourse. If 'sacred' only exists linguistically as an unstable category, like 'religion' (Fitzgerald 2007b, 7), then the term 'sacred' hinders understanding of events like Beltane at Thornborough, where the category 'sacred' signifies, well, nothing much.

Conclusion: making sacred

In my experience students have been able to comprehend the term 'sacred' as a social construction more easily than, say, 'religion'. At Leeds Trinity University, we have two core final year undergraduate modules in Religious Studies that address these two terms: one is 'Religions, Cultures and Complexities', focusing on problems with European terminology and classifications based on the WRP in non-European contexts, such as India, Japan and Korea (co-taught with my colleague Kirsteen Kim) and the other is 'Religions in Leeds and Bradford', which includes a large section on defining 'sacred space'. Several weeks are spent discussing Durkheim, Eliade and other scholars' takes on the term 'sacred' and how it may be combined with the spatial analysis of Henri Lefebvre (1991), such as in the work of Kim Knott (2005), and de Certeau (1984). Apart from the Chidester and Linenthal examples from Hawaii, students also study the *Dedication of a Church and Altar* (Liturgy Office (England and Wales) 1978) in Catholic ritual and 'casting a circle' in Wicca (Hume 1998 and Laura Daligan's *Witch in the City* YouTube video on the topic), both of which highlight human action in the 'making sacred' process and, in the discourse, state ontological interpretations of the spaces they had marked out through ritual. We also examine university spatial practices, discussing expectations and areas 'set apart', but also power relations (e.g. the student union was moved from its own building to the middle of the main building). Students then make their own observations at selected sites (see below).

In the first module, there is still the danger that some students may come to the conclusion that the category 'religion' (or 'world religions', or 'Hinduism', etc.) only needs to be broadened to become more inclusive, referred to as 'big tent' philosophy (from McCutcheon 2003, 184), or that a person or their acts could be Buddhist in some situations and Shinto in others. In the second module, 'Religions in Leeds and Bradford', discourse and practice come to the fore. Two of the most successful site visits for illustrating the social construction of 'sacred' have been Jamyang Buddhist Centre in an office block in Leeds and the Manchester Jewish Museum (not too far from Leeds and Bradford), especially when students asked the members or guides whether they considered the space 'sacred'. In both locations, the guides tended to first deny that the space was sacred and then point out practices they carry out which contradict that assessment, such as taking off shoes before entering the gompa 'out of respect' and, in the Jewish Museum, we were told a visitor had insisted on placing a mezuzah on the doorpost, among other examples.[6]

In the class, the aim is broader than to have students see how 'sacred' is constructed in discourse and practice. By distinguishing situational from ontological definitions of 'sacred space', the topic enables us to bring in identity formation, the nature of representation (and self-representation) and questions about whether 'religion' exists outside discourse. Picking up on the constructed nature of 'religious' space, one group of students chose to test it out at a Pagan 'pub moot', a meeting in a public house. When discussing it afterwards, the students were able to identify the discourse and practice that 'set it apart', such as the lighting of a candle at the start and the change of pattern in conversation afterward, which followed an unstated etiquette and established power relations within the group. The participants were also engaged in identity formation as the conversation revealed what and who was 'Pagan' and the boundary maintenance of that identification. In this way a Religious Studies class that begins with an analysis of the term 'sacred' can open a 'chink in the armour' to lay bare 'religion' itself as a constructed category.

Notes

1 Friends of Thornborough, http://www.friendsofthornborough.org.uk/index.htm
2 Sacred Brigantia Trust, www.celebratebeltane.co.uk/about [accessed 18.11.2013]; this paragraph is no longer found on their website but can still be viewed on another website describing the event at Thornborough: http://www.leodispagancircle.co.uk/events/other-events/ [accessed 19.02.2015].
3 'Colourful Celtic ceremony to be staged at Thornborough Henges,' *Ripon Gazette*, 2 May 2007, http://www.ripongazette.co.uk/news/ripon/colourful-celtic-ceremony-to-be-staged-at-thornborough-henges-1-2630041 [accessed 19.02.2015].
4 Sacred Brigantia Trust website, http://www.celebratebeltane.co.uk/about/ [accessed 19.02.2015].
5 Sacred Brigantia Trust website, http://www.celebratebeltane.co.uk/about/ [accessed 19.02.2015].
6 A gompa is a meditation or prayer hall, while a mezuzah is small box containing a piece of parchment inscribed with the Shema (Deut. 6:4-9; 11: 13–21).

References

Anttonen, Veikko. 2000. "Sacred." In *Guide to the Study of Religion*, edited by Willi E. Braun and Russell T. McCutcheon, 271–282. London and New York: Continuum.

Arnal, William E. and Russell T. McCutcheon. 2013. *The Sacred Is the Profane: The Political Nature of 'Religion'*. Oxford and New York: Oxford University Press.

Blain, Jenny and Robert Wallis. 2007. *Sacred Sites, Contested Rites/Rights*. Eastbourne and Portland: Sussex Academic Press.

de Certeau, Michel. 1984. *The Practice of Everyday Life*. Translated by Steven Rendall. Berkeley: University of California Press.

Chidester, David and Edward T. Linenthal, eds. 1995. *American Sacred Space*. Bloomington and Indianapolis: Indiana University Press.

Cupitt, Don. 2001. "Anti-Discrimination." In *The Blackwell Companion to Postmodern Theology*, edited by Graham Ward, 482–489. Oxford: Blackwell.

Daligan, Laura. 2011. "Casting a Circle." Uploaded to YouTube on 25 August. https://www.youtube.com/watch?v=SCLhwbqv4VU (accessed 7 April 2015).

Durkheim, Émile. 2001. *The Elementary Forms of Religious Life*. Translated by Carol Cosman. Oxford and New York: Oxford University Press.

Eliade, Mircea. 1959 [1957]. *The Sacred and the Profane: The Nature of Religion*. Translated by W. R. Trask. New York: Harcourt, Brace & World.

Fitzgerald, Timothy. 2007a. *Discourse on Civility and Barbarity: A Critical History of Religion and Related Categories*. Oxford and New York: Oxford University Press.

Fitzgerald, Timothy. 2007b. "Introduction." In *Religion and the Secular: Historical and Colonial Formations*, edited by Timothy Fitzgerald, 1–24. London: Equinox.

Giles, Chris and Dave Brunskill. 2012. *Beltane at Thornborough 2012, 'Kinda special ...'* Documentary film. http://www.celebratebeltane.co.uk/about/ (19. 02. 2015).

Harvey, Graham. 2007. *Listening People, Speaking Earth: Contemporary Paganism*. 2nd ed. London: Hurst.

Hume, Lynne. 1998. "Creating Sacred Space: Outer Expressions of Inner Worlds in Contemporary Wicca." *Journal of Contemporary Religion* 13(3): 309–319.

Knott, Kim. 2005. "Spatial Theory and Method for the Study of Religion." *Temenos* 41(2): 153–184.

Knott, Kim. 2013. "The Secular Sacred: In-between or Both/and?" In *Social Identities Between the Sacred and the Secular*, edited by Abby Day, Giselle Vincett and Christopher R. Cotter, 145–160. Farnham: Ashgate.

van der Leeuw, Gerardus. 1938. *Religion in Essence and Manifestation: A Study in Phenomenology*. London: Macmillan.

Lefebvre, Henri. 1991. *The Production of Space*. Translated by Donald Nicholson-Smith. Oxford and Malden: Blackwell.

Lévi-Strauss, Claude. 1950. "Introduction à l'oeuvre de Marcel Mauss." In *Marcel Mauss, Sociologie et anthropologie: précédé d'une introduction à l'oeuvre de Marcel Mauss*. Paris: Presses universitaires de France. Cited in Jonathan Z. Smith. 1978. *To Take Place: Toward Theory in Ritual*. Chicago: University of Chicago Press, 107.

Liturgy Office (England and Wales). 1978. *Dedication of a Church and Altar*. International Committee on English in the Liturgy.

Lynch, Gordon. 2007. "What Is this 'Religion' in the Study of Religion, Media and Popular Culture?" In *Between Sacred and Profane: Researching Religion and Popular Culture*, edited by Gordon Lynch, 125–142. London: I.B. Tauris.

Lynch, Gordon. 2012a. "Public Media and the Sacred: A Critical Perspective." In *Religion, Media and Culture: A Reader*, edited by Gordon Lynch and Jolyon Mitchell, with Anna Strahan, 244–250. Abingdon: Routledge.

Lynch, Gordon. 2012b. *The Sacred in the Modern World*. Oxford: Oxford University Press.

Lynch, Gordon. 2012c. *On the Sacred*. Durham: Acumen.

McCutcheon, Russell T. 2003. *The Discipline of Religion: Structure, Meaning, Rhetoric*. London and New York: Routledge.

Moser, Claudia and Cecelia Feldman. 2014. "Introduction." In *Locating the Sacred: Theoretical Approaches to the Emplacement of Religion*, edited by Claudia Moser and Cecelia Feldman, 1–12. Oxford and Oakville: Oxbow Books.

Otto, Rudolf. 1923. *The Idea of the Holy*. Oxford: Oxford University Press.

Owen, Suzanne and Teemu Taira. 2015. "The Category of 'Religion' in Public Classification: Charity Registration of the Druid Network in England and Wales." In *Religion as a Category of Governance and Sovereignty*, edited by Timothy Fitzgerald, Trevor Stack and Naomi Goldenberg, 90–114. Leiden: Brill.

Smart, Ninian. 1996. *Dimensions of the Sacred: An Anatomy of the World's Beliefs*. Berkeley and Los Angeles: University of California Press.

Stallybrass, Peter and Allon White. 1986. *The Poetics and Politics of Transgression*. London: Methuen.

PART III

Innovative pedagogies: methods and media

9

THE DESJARDINS DIET FOR WORLD RELIGIONS PARADIGM LOSS

Michel Desjardins

Introduction

Over the years I have thought long and hard about ways to structure courses that increase student learning in general and an appreciation for the academic study of religion in particular. My food and religion course best reflects that thinking, and the positive impact that course has had on students encourages me to present it to a wider audience.

This chapter presents a Canadian university course that serves as a thematic introduction to 'world religions' while at the same time deconstructing some established notions of religion. The focus is on pedagogy. The 'diet' I am prescribing is intended for teachers and their students. The analogy is both fitting and cautionary. The vast majority of food diets fail, except by making some of their creators wealthy. Long-term, sustainable health improvement comes about when a person recognizes that change is required, and when the recommended changes are gradual, multi-faceted and consistent with a person's physical and emotional makeup. A key point I make below about course construction and delivery is that students are more apt to reconsider their understanding of religion if those changes help them make better sense of the world. The pedagogical challenge is to help students recognize the complexity of what is typically understood as religion.

'Food and Religion' is a third-year undergraduate course that examines the role that food currently plays in people's lives. For many students it is their sole introduction to religion. The course is grounded in the qualitative research carried out by my wife and me,[1] and influenced by the themes that have emerged from this research that cut across political, ethnic and religious boundaries, underlining common ways in which people engage life, including their imagined worlds. The course structure, the nature of our findings, and food itself as a rich site for examining human nature, allow me to nudge students from thinking about 'Jains and

Muslims', for example, to talking about 'religious individuals' and eventually 'people who generate meaning in particular ways'.

The chapter briefly presents this course then describes at length the thinking that has gone into its design, framed by nine points. My comments derive from experiences I have had teaching this course five times over a period of seven years to students at Wilfrid Laurier University. Laurier, one of Canada's many secular universities, is situated in Waterloo, a mid-sized urban community 100 kilometres west of Toronto. The presence of two universities in Waterloo, also the home of the global phone company BlackBerry, facilitates a vibrant youth, high-tech culture, with increasing ethnic diversity. Laurier students for the most part are from this region of the country, many from smaller towns.

To situate this discussion about pedagogy let me begin with a few autobiographical comments that touch on my journey as a teacher. I taught my first university course at the University of Toronto 30 years ago, having entered graduate school in Religious Studies twelve years earlier at the University of British Columbia, as a secular Canadian student in a programme of biblical studies that would, I then hoped, ground me in Western ways of imagining life. It did, but it was the scholars whose works I read, far more than the texts and traditions I approached through them, who illuminated the ways in which we construct meaningful worlds for ourselves.

Scholars, no less than religious leaders, I came to appreciate, imagine realities that become as concrete to them as the books on their shelves: in my case, their Paul and their Jesus, their Second Temple Judaism, their Q (their Mary Magdalene would come a decade later). All are stimulating when understood as intellectual exercises or personal expressions of hope and healing, just as the spirit worlds they describe. When taken as fact they are quite revealing of human nature – when 'Crossan's Jesus' becomes 'Jesus', 'Segal's Paul' becomes 'Paul' and 'Sanders's Second Temple Judaism' becomes 'Judaism'. The 'religion itself is constructed' discourse had not yet emerged, but in the 1970s and 1980s the transparency of scholarly paradigms was in full sight for those with eyes to see. So too the ideological battles, as scholars vied to inscribe their particular worldviews onto the field alongside (sometimes in the name of) academic objectivity and scientific rigour.

As I developed a passion for teaching, these underlying issues took on added force. I knew, for example, that in exploring 'the historical Jesus' with under-graduate students my data set was both exceedingly limited and over-determined, and the scholarly discourse was riven with theological agendas. I soon came to realize that the students themselves on the whole came to me intellectually violated by their religious training, what little they had, as well as emotionally vulnerable in regards to religion. Like the scholars we studied, and often with little critical self-awareness, they brought substantial baggage to the table. I realized that I too rolled, sometimes dragged, my intellectual luggage into the classroom every time we met. What is *not* to love about that learning cauldron?

Given the typical classroom context in which I taught, and my own predilec-tions, as the number of my students grew into the hundreds in those early years it seemed to me counter-productive to focus on what might be called a hard-edge approach. Yes, I could dwell on showing how we know almost nothing about first-century Judaism, how the scholarly reconstructions are all ideologically biased, how the information students were given growing up is narrow, mostly manipulative and unsubstantiated, and how the very study of that area in the academy inscribes elite forms of knowledge. Just as I could have told them: flee from university before we assimilate you like the Borg in *Star Trek*. But they were there: registered in a university course, ready to trust and to stretch ... a little at first, a bit more later, some of them frightened even to be in the same room with others holding slightly different religious views.

In this context the teaching practice that ended up working for me was student-rather than discipline-centred: meet students where they are, intellectually and emotionally, and do what I can to nurture their growth and curiosity. Taking the backseat in undergraduate courses were those broader ontological and epistemological discussions on the nature of scholarly discourse about religion.

Over the years I perceived an increasing disjunction between academic discussions engaged with method and theory, and teaching Christian origins in the undergraduate classroom.[2] On the one hand, my yearly method and theory graduate classes continued to be nurtured by the academic womb, and I appreciated not only the intellectual rigour of those discussions but also the necessity of ongoing critical thinking about the academic study of religion. My concern, on the other hand, as a facilitator of those critical discussions was that they were disconnected from the realities of the undergraduate classroom, not to mention religious communities and people. To use a war analogy, it felt as if I was in the trenches, occasionally reading government documents or watching movies that presented quite different, and glorified, versions of what actually was happening.

The typical undergraduate student needed many other things to progress along their academic path – especially when confronting supposedly sacred texts or sacred origins – and at times I found myself engaged in Seminary-type discussions about whether Jesus could have performed miracles, or the latest Hollywood blockbuster movie accurately represented the Bible. Although offering productive teaching opportunities, these discussions occurred within the broader context of the primacy of belief, dominated by men, evinced by texts and institutions, with the mainly Christian scholars who studied these topics working within ideological strictures.

Shifting my research focus from Christian origins to the intersection of food and religion helped to resolve some of these tensions. This swing from ancient to modern, texts and archaeological artefacts to interviews and site visits, theology to gastronomy, imagined religion to lived religion, thinking alone to thinking closely with my wife in another discipline, allowed me to bring my teaching more in line with what I know about the complexities of religion and the academic study of religion. Moreover, the broad societal interest in food and food studies has also given me eager and varied audiences, both on and off campus. My interactions with those audiences have nourished my research and the teaching possibilities that emerge from it.

The course

Food and Religion is a twenty-first century variation of the classic thematic, comparative introductory course in Religious Studies.[3] The topic is current, as are the underlying pedagogical and ideological concerns. I embed in it a 'world religions' component that creates a hybrid of the introductory courses that have come to define the field: part thematic, part world religions. We meet for three hours per week over a twelve week term, and our classes include a blend of lectures and group discussions. This coming term I will be 'flipping' the classroom, making my lectures available online, for viewing before each class, allowing class meetings to focus on group discussions and projects. Short readings are required each week, preferably done before class. Course enrolments have averaged 70.

The course is structurally bifurcated. I spend the first, longer, section introducing students to the intersection of food and different religious traditions (Judaism, Zoroastrianism/Parsis, Christianity, Islam, Baha'i, Santeria, Hinduism, Buddhism, Jainism, Sikhism). These sessions are a mix of what people understand by a particular religious tradition (e.g. Judaism) and the standard food-related elements of that tradition (dietary restrictions, fasting, etc.), followed by an extensive selection of examples and stories taken from my own research that both support the standard elements and challenge them. The latter section of the course follows the same blend of lectures and discussions, with the data organized thematically. The themes arise from my research and include food restrictions, fasting and feasting, food offerings and food charity, plus a few others. I make use of this thematic approach to provide mini-summaries of what we have learned up to that point in the course, but the majority of the time is devoted to linking the themes to other interpretive frameworks, such as politics and economics, psychology and sociology, geography and the environment.

Requirements complement the learning objectives. A midterm exam allows me to assess, then tweak, what students are learning from the class material and readings. The main assignment for the students is an extended fieldwork project. It starts with three formal interviews – one done with the student as interviewee, followed by two in which they interview adults who self-identify as religious (different from the student's own religion if the student identifies as religious, and different from one another). The interviews are followed some time later by a first analysis of both the data and the fieldwork experiences themselves, then by a final analysis that integrates their fieldwork data with the course materials. The objective of the cumulative assignments is to reflect continually on how primary experience (interviews) presents varied views of religion, and integrates with theory (readings and lectures).

My basic learning objectives have remained consistent since I first introduced this course in 2007. I expect students who successfully complete the course to be more culturally literate. For example, when someone refers to Buddhists I would hope that they are able to think of examples both locally and abroad, just as I hope that they will be able to position Bali, Goa, Japan and the Punjab on a map. This is a modest goal, to be sure, but before someone can run they first need to walk. No sense, in my view, in introducing students to J. Z. Smith if they think that Muslims are called 'Islams', have never heard of Parsis and Jains, and are disconnected from immigrants to our region. One has to construct before one deconstructs. Increasingly students begin my courses with little or no religious literacy, and that has not substantially changed over the last three decades.

I am keen to have students experience qualitative research. For many of them this is their first and only exposure to this type of research in their undergraduate studies. The thought of interviewing strangers at first terrifies students, and the process of transcribing the interviews of course leaves their fingers numb, but they repeatedly tell me that their fieldwork experiences are their most formative in this course and sometimes in their degree programme itself.

The reasoning behind the course

You might now be asking: what's a nice course like you doing in a book like this? Here is where the details take on significance.

Let me begin by invoking the memory of Marshall McLuhan, a Canadian public intellectual (1911–1980) perhaps best known for his phrase 'the medium is the message' (McLuhan and Fiore 1967). In our case, by understanding 'medium' as 'society at large', and appreciating the ways in which society at large and schools in particular inscribe a particular message,[4] we arrive at the nub of the issue: ways of knowing are socially constructed. So how does one nudge students to understand religion in a different manner when much of what they have been taught before has made religion unique and irreducible? My answer: one proceeds slowly, without being dismissive of previous knowledge, particularly since sustainable paradigm changes need a solid base.

This thought brings to mind a second person, Parker Palmer, whose writings about the profession of teaching over the years have also provided me with valuable points of reflection. One of Palmer's thoughts is: 'the way we diagnose our students' condition will determine the kind of remedy we offer' (1998, 41). This statement comes in the context of his book *The Courage to Teach*, which encourages teachers to reflect on themselves at the same time as they are reaching out to students. Palmer's remark here is applicable to students who have been strongly socialized about religion before they enter our classrooms – so strongly, in fact, that any changes will perforce come slowly and fitfully.

Let me quickly add – both the medium and the malady also affect scholars of religion, even those, dare I say, who critique the World Religions Paradigm (WRP) of teaching. There is as much fear and dualism to be found in journals and books as there is among students in a typical classroom. The challenge for me, every time I teach this course, is to encourage students to open themselves to new ways of understanding people's expressions and actions, while at the same time giving myself permission to do the same.

I would now like to present the core Desjardins diet, i.e. the nine specific factors I built into this course with several goals in mind, one of which is to undermine the WRP by maximizing the possibility that students emerge with a more nuanced view of religion. The box below encapsulates these factors. The course topic may be specific, but the factors are certainly adaptable to fit other types of courses and contexts.

THE DESJARDINS DIET

The Desjardins diet for World Religions Paradigm loss

1. Construct the course at the senior level
2. Refrain from adding course prerequisites
3. Select accessible readings that deconstruct traditional representations of religion
4. Make interviews the core learning component for students
5. Insist that religion is not to be conflated with religious dogma
6. Legitimize narrative data
7. Choose a course topic with current appeal
8. Build personal reflection into each class
9. Draw connections with broad global phenomena late in the course

---

First, I constructed this course for students in their third year of study. Placing a course at this level in a four-year liberal arts programme means that most students entering the course have already had to think critically about politics, social construction, ethnicity, gender, place, and in some cases economics and science. This academic background makes it far easier than it would be in the first year to examine human activity and thought through different lenses, and to appreciate the fact that what passes for religion is also politics, economics, and so forth.

In short, the critical study of religion is best done with some academic maturity, and introductory courses need not always be offered in the first year – all the more so when an undergraduate education is not imagined as primarily preparing students for graduate work in a particular discipline. The vast majority of our graduates, on the contrary, take their degrees into business, government jobs, and the social sector. In that context, an introduction to thinking about religion can, and perhaps should, come in the third and fourth years, complementing (or replacing) those first and second introductions. We are, after all, preparing students to be citizens of the world, and we are addressing a sensitive, complex topic.

Second, this course has no prerequisites. The result has consistently been a wide mix of students who take this course – this past year, ranging from kinesiology and business majors, through almost all the humanities and social sciences specializations. This academic diversity, especially among senior students, can lead to spirited, productive discussions, and the generation of new ideas. The years when I have had a preponderance of religion majors have created the most difficult setting in which to teach because these students arrive thinking that they know 'Buddhism' and 'Islam'. The year when half the students came from global studies was the most exhilarating; our conversations about 'charity', for example, led to sophisticated discussions about development and the mobility of capital across the globe. This past year the business majors continually reminded the rest of us of the marketing implications of food restrictions and charity.

Interdisciplinary exchanges, in my experience, are more apt to elicit paradigm-challenging occasions. The Boyer Commission (1998, 23) recommended that America's universities remove barriers to interdisciplinary research and teaching, as part of their mandate to promote effective undergraduate education, with full awareness of the difficulties:

> The principal barrier to interdisciplinary research and study has been the pattern of university organization that creates vested interests in traditionally defined departments. Administratively, all educational activity needs to 'belong' somewhere in order to be accounted for and supported .... Courses must be offered under some kind of sponsorship; students are asked to place themselves in one discipline or another.

Commission members extended their thoughts to teaching:

> undergraduate education should also be cast in interdisciplinary formats. Departmental confines and reward structures have discouraged young faculty interested in interdisciplinary teaching from engaging in it. But because all work will require mental flexibility, students need to view their studies through many lenses.
>
> (1998, 23)

In our institution most academic units offer second and third year courses that require at least one disciplinary prerequisite. Sixteen years after the Boyer Commission the academic silos are as rigid as ever. Removing prerequisites from this upper year course has been a simple way to break through this barrier, creating classroom and online contexts that elicit fruitful interdisciplinary and multidisciplinary interactions.

Third, I select accessible readings that (subversively) deconstruct traditional representations of religion. These are not method and theory type readings; rather, they are short, easily accessible pieces that challenge students to imagine religion within broader frameworks. Among them is the classic article about religious New York Jews in the early twentieth century who socialized into American culture by eating regularly at Chinese restaurants, despite the presence of pork and non-kosher beef in those dishes (Tuckman and Levine 1993). There are excerpts from *The Halal Frontier* that present religion as business and global politics (Fischer 2011, 1–30, 137–157), and a discussion about fasting that puts body image to the forefront (Griffith 2001). I also have students read Marvin Harris's functionalist ruminations about religious pork and beef taboos that look to environmental change and health as the main drivers for a particular group's decision to ban a food item (Harris 1987). As a result of the readings, midway through the course the more astute and engaged students begin to appreciate that issues normally placed in one silo (e.g. religious food restriction) can as easily be put in another (business marketing opportunities).

Appropriate readings continue to form an important part of most Canadian university courses these days.[5] For a variety of reasons students, as bright and keen as they have ever been, are not reading much outside social media, and they typically understand little of what they read from course reading lists. Complex articles by scholars of religion are incomprehensible to most of them – yet they are better able to find information on their own than students were thirty years ago. Changing undergraduate perceptions of religion, in my institution at least, will not come by assigning long reading lists of books and articles typically found on doctoral comprehensive exam lists – or assuming that students have understood their core message.

Fourth, I make interviews the core learning component for students. These interviews are done by the students. I consider this student process a vital form of experiential learning, done outside the university walls, which increases the likelihood that students will not only learn better but also think outside the box.[6] A course requirement is that they seek out people who are not like them, and not like one another, at least when it comes to religious affiliation. If students are to transform the way they imagine religion, I find it helps to place them in a situation outside the classroom where they are forced to speak about important matters with people they do not (always) know. An added bonus occurs when these interviewees are ethnically different, including recent immigrants who bring with them a wide range of experiences that are less common for the majority of our students.

As Paulo Freire (1921–1997) noted long ago, learning is relational and knowledge is increased through interactions with others. Insisting that my students learn through interviewing others, and then reflect intensely on those experiences, is a deliberate attempt on my part to bring a Freirean flavour to the course. As I have said elsewhere:

> what are many of us doing wrong when we teach? We *still* typically practice the 'act of depositing,' or 'banking' as Freire calls it, imagining students as containers and expecting them to reproduce facts and frames of thinking – even though we know, or at least we should know, that 'knowledge emerges only through invention and re-invention, through the restless, impatient, continuing, hopeful inquiry' we pursue 'with the world, and with each other' (Freire 1970, 58). Freire long ago encouraged educators to abandon deposit-making and replace it with 'problem-posing education' that embodies communication, respect and humility, where the teacher 'is no longer merely the-one-who-teaches, but one who is ... taught in dialogue with the students' (66-67).
>
> *(Desjardins 2013, 223)*

For a few of my students, doing interviews leads to heightened global consciousness; others experience lesser but nevertheless significant transformations as they come to appreciate how perspectives and practices are historically and culturally contingent.[7]

Some of the most powerful moments in the course, each time I teach it, come just after students have completed their interviews, when they share their thoughts with their peers in class. It might be just two interviews they have each conducted independently, but their ownership of the process, and the mixture of fear going into the interviews and exhilaration coming out of them invariably results in comments indicating that something important, something out of their ordinary experience, has taken place.

The same type of exhilaration comes when students complete their first analysis and have the opportunity to reflect more deeply on what they have learned about themselves and others through the interview process. A significantly larger percentage of students than usual in third year courses take the time to do this assignment carefully, and express the degree of learning they have experienced.

My students of course love learning new facts – 'I hadn't even heard about Zoroastrians before, cool!' – just as they enjoy having their own experiences confirmed and challenged – 'I've been attending Baha'i firesides this past year and liked that you mentioned them.' ... 'I've been a lifelong Christian and never imagined the Lord's Supper as a food event.' In my experience, though, their interviews are where they start questioning more fundamental assumptions about themselves and others. In this context they are not just listening and absorbing, but making themselves vulnerable and encountering different voices.

Returning to McLuhan, I am increasingly convinced that the medium of instruction and assessment is crucial to the message I am trying to convey. If my students are to become independent learners, pushing the boundaries of their experiences, they need to become engaged and open to new ways of learning that offer possibilities for different types of knowledge.

Fifth, religion is not to be conflated with religious dogma. I tell students that they cannot choose a religious leader or expert as an interviewee. A guiding motif in the course is that individuals who self-identify as belonging to a religious group each have reasons for acting and thinking as they do, and their thoughts and actions are sometimes widely divergent. The result: interview questions posed by students invariably elicit answers that do not fall within standard paradigms. Adherents themselves are more apt to break down the silos when they are encouraged to tell their stories, and my students arrive at that insight as they are listening to these stories, and reflecting on them later. Vatican dogma about Lenten fasting is 'Catholic', and so too are the millions of Catholic variations.

I tell stories to each class about individuals I have interviewed who do not fall within standard categories – for example, self-professed meat-eating Jains, vegetarian Jews, and the Indonesian Muslim community in Pangandaran, Java, that holds an annual ceremony dedicated to the sea goddess. As I have said elsewhere concerning this point:

> this type of evidence suggests that the data with which the scholar works constantly challenge standardized categories, including the coherence of religious traditions themselves. To be sure, such an appreciation of categories is (or

should be) understood by all scholars of religion, but the functional rather than ontological nature of academic categories, such as Jew and Christian (and religion), is more quickly ignored in an established area of study like Christian origins, with its centuries-long academic tradition and its ongoing links with religious authority. When it comes to the study of food and religion, however, it is more difficult to ignore the fluidity and functionality of categories – and the role that the interpreter plays in determining and interpreting information.

(Desjardins 2012, 154)

Moreover, I encourage students to tell food stories about their own upbringing. These invariably underline the importance of geography, migration, gender, and family traditions. For those who self-identify as religious, religion quickly becomes multi-layered as the stories are told. The students' own stories allow me to move seamlessly to discussions concerning aboriginal cultures across the world whose food myths are stories told in similar ways. Telling stories and listening to them, appreciating how stories change every time they are told, quite naturally adds layers of complexity to how religion is understood. Students 'get it' much better through these stories than by theoretical discussions.

Sixth, narrative data is legitimized. I encourage students to consider the data they have collected in their interviews as fully legitimate in their own right. What most students come to see once again is that the religion that many of their interviewees practise is not always consistent with the textbook variety. Focusing on food rather than ideology, on lived religion rather than textbook-constructed religion, allows students to appreciate, on their own, from their own data rather than from the classroom lectern, that religious food customs sometimes have more to do with ethnicity and immigration than they do with religion, and that some Muslims can have more in common with some Sikhs than they do with other Muslims. Letting the students discover this truth on their own makes it more likely that the knowledge will stick. Indeed, I know this to be the case, based on what graduates continue to tell me years after taking the course.

In addition, learning grounded in the data generated by students themselves helps to legitimize their learning, and increases the chance that they will take that data seriously. When their interview transcriptions deconstruct the traditional notions of religions, as they often do, it becomes easier for me to generate broader discussions about the nature of religion and culture.

This is why I built the final assignment into the course. Their first analysis asks them to describe the data they have gathered in their interviews, and to unpack their fieldwork experiences. Their capstone analysis asks them to compare their interview data with the information gathered from classroom information and readings. It is at this point in the course where a significant number of students come to appreciate the contextual and constructed nature of all knowledge.[8]

Seventh, the course topic must have current appeal. I introduced Food and Religion in our departmental curriculum because I know that our choice of what we study, when we study 'religion', affects students' notions of religion. I noted this point in the introductory section to this chapter, and argued it at some length in my contribution to the 2012 Wiebe Festschrift (Desjardins 2012). Change the object of study, and you change the study of religion. Moreover, when the object of study is popular, it is far more effective in attracting students, and teaching them in ways that challenge their expectations while at the same time introducing them to critical topics in the study of religion.[9]

Eighth, I build personal reflection into each class session. Throughout the course I dedicate the final 15 minutes of each class to asking the 'So what?' question: 'So what was most transformative to you about this evening's class?' To be sure, there are sound pedagogical reasons for asking a question like this; in this case I built this closing question into the course in order to create another opportunity for students to go beyond the surface level of learning that merely summarizes, or compares in traditional ways (e.g. Christians typically engage in a great deal of food charity, while Buddhists place more attention on the type of food that goes into their bodies). Students have been taught to place information into societally supported silos, but when forced to think about knowledge that matters *to them*, the silos sometimes start to break down – not always, and not as often as I would like, but the cracks do appear. 'That's how the light gets in', to quote a Leonard Cohen song lyric (1992). Making time for self-generated knowledge is never a waste of time in this course.

This form of teaching is a variation of the Socratic method grounded in the belief that asking the right question is bound to elicit the right sort of answer because individuals already know those (right) answers. A Christian variation of this view is the Quaker principle that there is a part of the divine spirit in everyone. I am not convinced that those universally-true answers exist, and I think that good answers can vary depending on the person, but I am convinced that, given enough safe space in which to reflect, people will recognize the shortcomings of a particular way of thinking, even when better options are not immediately apparent.

Ninth, late in the course I draw connections with broad global phenomena. By week ten I explain to students that my decision, almost a decade ago, to shift from a traditional area of Religious Studies (Christian origins) to an emerging area (Food and Religion) in part came from a deeply-felt need to address some of the biases in the field, including sexism and colonialism. The focus on traditional ways of presenting religions – including the WRP – reinforces those biases. Women all but disappear (or at times are introduced and praised in ways that distort the evidence), and the imperialistic and colonial components of the 'world' religions are barely mentioned and rarely taken seriously. All missionary-based religions are colonizing forces, after all, and our field, even as it resisted the Christian theological constraints of late nineteenth-century Europe and mid-twentieth century America, was born within a colonizing mind-set that has perdured.[10] With a snap of the fingers, and a change in focus to food in lived religion, women reappear, sacred texts move into the shadows,[11] social and economic elites become less important, and the complexities surrounding 'world' religions multiply, including the importance of culture, geography and ethnicity in resisting the hegemony of those world religions. Teaching then becomes transgressive.[12]

When I raise these issues with students at this moment in the course it becomes clear that many have had similar thoughts, and at that point those ideas start to tumble out of them into open and group discussions. The intellectual energy and critical thinking in those discussions emerge, I think, from the fact that students have developed, or at least feel they have developed, these thoughts on their own, as a consequence of making their way through the course. When I talk about these issues openly, and personalize the conversation – presenting it as part of my intellectual journey rather than as something they need to learn – they are comfortable raising their own reflections as part of their intellectual journeys. Significant student responses like this remind me, throughout the course but especially in the second half when students are integrating their learning and breaking some of the paradigms with which they entered the course two months earlier, that each time I engage students I need to be as grounded as possible – in my course learning objectives, current academic discussions in the field, the confidence that I can nudge each student along their own learning path, and my own self-awareness.

Conclusion

The Desjardins diet, like sustainable weight-loss diets, recognizes that reducing adherence to a WRP will be successful to the extent that it is part of a broader pedagogical equation. At Weight Watchers, for example, activity, healthy habits, support and smart food choices are the keys that can lead to lasting success. In my case, I have modelled a course that has the potential to lead to more nuanced views of religion. I would not want to push the analogy with effective weight-loss diets too far, but what is fitting in both cases is the recognition that effective change is most often built step by step, slowly and patiently, and not through radical means imported from outside.

I have argued for a course structure that honours active and engaged learning,[13] and requires students to generate their own information about religion, culture, and food practices. This type of learning is reflected especially through the fieldwork project that extends throughout the course, and puts students in direct contact with self-professed religious individuals. Many of the questions that we as professionals would like our students to raise, about the nature of religion and their own role in understanding it, arise organically from these interviews and from the conversations that students have with one another about their fieldwork data, particularly in the context of a course that reinforces the complexities of religion and its construction.

I have also increased the likelihood that deep learning will happen by placing this introductory course in the third year,[14] and removing all disciplinary prerequisites. As a result, the students who enrol in the course arrive with broad and sometimes deep knowledge from a wide range of disciplines, and they have the confidence that comes with being senior students. In this context, discussions both inside and outside class allow for the real possibility that paradigms will be challenged.

Add to this the readings and classroom presentations that acknowledge traditional religious frameworks and also tease out the many ways in which people can, for example, identify as 'Muslim', my ongoing encouragement that students reflect openly about their own learning and priorities, and the modelling that I do for them by talking about my research experiences, and students *do* lose some of that WRP baggage. Many keep it off.

Notes

1 Ellen Desjardins has a quarter of a century of experience as a community nutritionist in Ontario, and earned a PhD in Human Geography. We have conducted most of the research together, have a jointly-authored book forthcoming, and have also co-published articles, including M. Desjardins and E. Desjardins (2009) and (2012).
2 Scholars of religion deal with this disjunction in various ways. In Canada, Christian origins has generated some of the most engaged scholars of method and theory in the study of religion; I think in particular of William Arnal and Willi Braun, e.g. Arnal and McCutcheon (2012); Arnal, Braun and McCutcheon (2012); and Braun and McCutcheon (2000).
3 For an influential overview of these types of courses, with examples and some critical engagement, see Carman and Hopkins (1991). Their book is 'a product of the Berkeley-Chicago-Harvard Program, a five-year series of institutes, workshops and related projects aimed at enlarging the role and scope of religious studies in the undergraduate liberal arts curriculum' (ii). Themes exemplified include pilgrimage, healing, sacrifice and mysticism.
4 A point famously made by Postman and Weingartner (1969, 16–24). Their book makes good reading for those wanting to explore different teaching strategies for deconstructing the World Religions Paradigm. Postman and Weingartner advocate for a new type of education that, in their words, reinforces the 'crap-detecting and relevance business' (1969, 82).
5 There are alternatives. In 2013 I framed my Master's Method and Theory course around audio clips from the UK-based *Religious Studies Project* (http://www.religiousstudies-project.com/) rather than readings. Students selected and discussed issues from these podcasts that interested them the most. For my students at least, these podcasts were more effective as starting points than the traditional collections of readings.
6 There is nothing new here. One thinks of the American education theorist, John Dewey, and his plea for educators to move students outside the classroom (Dewey 1938), and the Brazilian educator Paulo Freire's project-based approach to learning (Freire 1970).
7 For more information on types of education that lead to transformations in perspective see Mezirow (2000).
8 If only I had another four weeks, or an additional term, in which to make meaning with them after they do that assignment. The constraints within which I teach in 12-week terms are most glaring in situations like this.
9 For example, our department offered 40 undergraduate courses in 2013–14. The Food and Religion course was the first course to fill after registration opened, and soon after it had a waiting list equal in number (75). The course had not been taught for three years; it is not as if students enrolled because their friends told them to do so. They enrolled because food matters culturally in 2014.
10 This is a well-known point, which Tomoko Masuzawa examined in some depth (2005). See 'Introduction' in this volume for more details.
11 See Sullivan (1990). His point that 'religious studies has many ways of coming at culture' (58) supports a focus on food as an entry point into people's relationships with 'religion.'
12 See especially hooks (1994), who builds on Paulo Freire's insistence that education can be the practice of freedom-making, and ought not to be about 'banking' data imparted by the professor exercising their control.

13 For a review of assessment methods that complement active learning see Gillett and Hammond (2009). Their reference list is particularly helpful.
14 Roughly a quarter of the students are in their fourth and final year, and since I deliberately offer the course in the second term and make the final analysis due after classes end, their analysis for them becomes a degree capstone learning experience.

References

Arnal, William E. and Russell T. McCutcheon. 2012. *The Sacred Is the Profane: The 'Political' Nature of Religion*. New York: Oxford University Press.

Arnal, William E., Willi Braun and Russell T. McCutcheon, eds. 2012. *Failure and Nerve in the Study of Religion*. London: Equinox.

Boyer Commission on Educating Undergraduates in the Research University. 1998. *Reinventing Undergraduate Education: A Blueprint for America's Research Universities*. Stony Brook, NY: State University of New York at Stony Brook for the Carnegie Foundation for the Advancement of Teaching.

Braun, Willi and Russell T. McCutcheon, eds. 2000. *Guide to the Study of Religion*. London and New York: Cassell.

Carman, John B. and Steven P. Hopkins. 1991. *Tracing Common Themes: Comparative Courses in the Study of Religion*. Atlanta: Scholars Press.

Cohen, Leonard. 1992. "Anthem." In *The Future*, by Leonard Cohen. New York: Columbia Records.

Desjardins, Michel. 2012. "Religious Studies that *Really* Schmecks: Introducing Food to the Academic Study of Religion." In *Failure and Nerve in the Study of Religion*, edited by William E. Arnal, Willi Braun and Russell T. McCutcheon, 147–156. London: Equinox.

Desjardins, Michel. 2013. "Practicalities and Pedagogies: Implementing International Learning Opportunities for Students." In *The World Is my Classroom: Priorities for Globalizing Canadian Higher Education*, edited by Joanne Benham Rennick and Michel Desjardins, 215–235. Toronto: University of Toronto Press.

Desjardins, Michel and Ellen Desjardins. 2009. "Food that Builds Community: The Sikh *Langar* in Canada." *Cuizine: The Journal of Canadian Food Cultures/Revue des cultures culinaires au Canada* 1(2), http://www.erudit.org/revue/cuizine/2009/v1/n2/037851ar.html (April 2, 2014).

Desjardins, Michel and Ellen Desjardins. 2012. "The Role of Food in Canadian Forms of Christianity: Continuity and Change." In *Edible Histories, Cultural Politics: Towards a Canadian Food History*, edited by Franca Iacovetta, Valerie J. Korinek and Marlene Epp, 116–132. Toronto: University of Toronto Press

Dewey, John. 1938. *Experience and Education*. New York: Simon and Schuster.

Fischer, Johan. 2011. *The Halal Frontier: Muslim Consumers in a Globalized Market*. New York: Palgrave Macmillan.

Freire, Paulo. 1970 [1968]. *Pedagogy of the Oppressed*. Trans. M. B. Ramos. New York: Continuum.

Gillett, A. and A. Hammond. 2009. "Mapping the Maze of Assessment: An Investigation into Practice." *Active Learning in Higher Education* 10(2): 120–137.

Griffith, R. Marie. 2001. "'Don't Eat That': The Erotics of Abstinence in American Christianity." *Gastronomica* 1(4): 36–47.

Harris, Marvin. 1987 [1985]. 'The Abominable Pig.' In *The Sacred Cow and the Abominable Pig: Riddles of Food and Culture*, edited by Marvin Harris, 67–87. New York: Simon and Schuster.

hooks, bell. 1994. *Teaching to Transgress: Education as the Practice of Freedom*. New York: Routledge.

Masuzawa, Tomoko. 2005. *The Invention of World Religions: Or, How European Universalism Was Preserved in the Language of Pluralism.* Chicago: University of Chicago Press.

McLuhan, Marshall and Quentin Fiore. 1967. *The Medium Is the Massage.* New York: Bantam.

Mezirow, Jack. 2000. "Learning to Think Like an Adult: Core Concepts of Transformation Theory." In *Learning as Transformation,* edited by Jacl Mezirow & Associates, 3–33. San Francisco: Jossey-Bass.

Palmer, Parker J. 1998. *The Courage to Teach: Exploring the Inner Landscape of a Teacher's Life.* San Francisco: Jossey-Bass.

Postman, Neil and Charles Weingartner. 1969. *Teaching as a Subversive Activity.* New York: Delacorte Press.

Sullivan, Lawrence E. 1990. "'Seeking an End to the Primary Text' or 'Putting an End to the Text as Primary'." In *Beyond the Classics? Essays in Religious Studies and Liberal Education,* edited by Frank E. Reynolds and Sheryl L. Burkhalter, 41–59. Atlanta: Scholars Press.

Tuckman, Gaye and Harry G. Levine. 1993. "New York Jews and Chinese Food: The Social Construction of an Ethnic Pattern." *Journal of Contemporary Ethnography* 22(3): 382–407.

10

NARRATING THE USA'S RELIGIOUS PLURALISM

Escaping world religions through media

David W. McConeghy

Introduction

As the second episode of the 2010 PBS (Public Broadcasting Service) documentary *God in America* begins, the camera pans over a lushly wooded valley while Lauren F. Winner's voice describes the late eighteenth-century USA. 'OK, you've created this nation,' she says. 'What's the story? What's the story of this nation? What does it mean to be an American?' Alert viewers might have remembered the programme's answer, given in the opening moments of the premier episode aired the previous night. Stephen Prothero, the series' Principal Editorial Advisor, called it 'a story of [Americans] in relationship to God'. From colony to nation, through slavery to Civil War and past the Scopes trial to the rise of the Religious Right, in the USA history walks hand in hand with religion. It is a powerful union that lets Americans inscribe their nation's brief history with divine significance. As Randall Balmer tells viewers in the series' final episode, 'Americans have a sense of their destiny as a nation. They have a sense that America occupies a unique niche in the divine economy' (Belton 2010: 'A New Eden', 'A New Adam' and 'Of God and Caesar'). So it has been no coincidence that the American self-narrative draws meaning through religious themes. In its populist form it expresses the idea 'that God held the New World in abeyance until after the Protestant Reformation, lest it be populated by the ungodly' (Prothero 2006, 2). And though it is important to acknowledge this kind of manifest destiny as a historical artefact of the early nation, it is also necessary to ask how that idea has changed in response to the growing religious diversity of the USA in the twentieth century. What does *God in America* do with the many gods of the USA's contemporary religious pluralism?

God in America aired its six hour-long episodes in primetime over three days in October of 2010. The documentary's presentation of religious pluralism followed Diana Eck's lead in labelling the USA the 'most religiously diverse nation on earth'

(2001). Yet this claim seemed incongruous with the documentary's narrative preferences. Its episodes had been filled with the experience and perspective of Protestants. Was the story of the relationship of Christians to their God the same story as the emergence of a multi-religious landscape that today includes a wide representation of global faiths? As the series argued, it was the ideal of religious liberty championed and contested by Christians that held the tensions inherent in a voluntary religious marketplace. Perhaps it is the fullest expression of the nation's debt to its Christian roots: even as immigration changed the country's demographics, religious liberty could always be traced to sources that revealed particularly Christian features. For example, the evangelical understanding of individuals as voluntary participants in their salvation fostered competition among denominations and, later, among religions. From this perspective, *God in America* tells the paradoxical story of how a nation whose emblem declares *E Pluribus Unum* – out of many, one – preserved itself by becoming the pluralist nation whose official motto is 'In God We Trust'.

For undergraduates I taught at the University of California, Santa Barbara in 'Introduction to Religion in America' courses from 2010–2012, *God in America* was introduced as a somewhat duplicitous object. On the one hand, its triumphalist narrative of the perfection of religious liberty is a familiar and even comfortable presentation of religion in American history. It has become the prevailing model not only for cultural histories but also a key element of US foreign policy (Preston 2012). As an object that builds consensus out of interviews with preeminent scholars, *God in America* cultivates academic credibility for its version of that history. Yet interrogating the historical accuracy of the series would be missing the forest for the trees. It might serve to clarify minor details, but the overall structure and message of the narrative would remain intact. What can and should be questioned, on the other hand, is the privilege the series gave to certain perspectives that collectively produced its contentions about religious liberty. As I showed my students, it is the *story* being told – how the USA became not just *diverse* but *pluralist* – that should generate reservations. David Sehat, for instance, while not responding specifically to *God in America*, dismissed the entire narrative of religious liberty as fantasy in his 2011 book *The Myth of American Religious Freedom*. If students or audiences are unaware of such profoundly dissenting views, then the casual normativity presented by the documentary and its experts reinforces consensus by omission. In other words, religious liberty may help audiences appreciate some elements of the framework of modern pluralism, but it gives them few tools for critique, no perspective on alternatives, and little sense of the baggage it bears.

God in America is therefore an opportunity for teachers to help their students recognize and respond to the ongoing fight for control over the meaning of American history and identity as expressed in the ideals of religious liberty and pluralism. Seeing this as a story built with a highly selective range of historical elements makes it possible to challenge ideals that are so often presented as facts about the modern USA. This can also make the challenge of interpretation and criticism somewhat easier: show how the narrative changes with different pieces. Such substitution is often straightforward. What if Catholic New Spain is emphasized instead of Puritan New England? What if the pre-Civil War era was filled not with Methodist circuit riders but Mormons and Spiritualists? What if the emergence of the Pentecostals replaced the Scopes trial as the key religious development of the first third of the twentieth century? How might the Civil Rights movement look if the focus is placed on Malcolm X instead of Martin Luther King, Jr.? In fact, these are the very conversations that have emerged among scholars who specialize in the study of American religious history (Tweed 1997; Prothero 2006; Brekus and Gilpin 2011). And yet none of these are the choices made by *God in America* in its presentation of religion's role in American history. These are sincere alternatives that challenge the status quo and its consensus presentation of religious liberty, but they are absent from the series. While they could be seen as mere variations in historical emphasis, I believe they are instead the leverage necessary to move students from being passive content viewers to critics and even, where a course permits, authors of their own counter-narratives.

To show the logic that supports this process, in this chapter I survey the major works for undergraduates and popular audiences that preceded *God in America*. The textbooks common in American religious history classrooms reveal the struggle to overcome Protestant biases. The victors – especially those successors to Sydney Ahlstrom – settled on pluralism as a way to expand the canon of religion in the USA to include the nascent and growing body of world religions. As textbooks shifted from implicitly Christian perspectives to explicitly comparative and relativist approaches, pluralism was lauded as a neutral playing field for discussing world religions. Moreover, the tacit approval for the World Religions Paradigm (WRP), especially embodied in Eck's code phrase the 'world's most religiously diverse nation', left those teaching with a choice between embracing the pluralist model and finding themselves without textbooks. Students came to survey courses to learn about Hinduism, Buddhism, Islam, and other new additions to the nation's religious landscape. They left courses having had these traditions presented primarily using 'universal' features such as ritual, belief and institutions. It seemed a necessary tradeoff in classrooms where the majority of students still identified as Christian, but it was dependent almost entirely on the WRP to support its broad model of religion.

In my classes, I have preferred to present religion not as a pre-established definition to be found in culture or history, but rather as a tool that shapes the narratives available to scholars. For me, the question is not 'what is religion?', it is 'what is the utility in labelling this thing or that experience religious?' I believe this makes it possible to defer the thorny questions of essentialism, definition and taxonomy that plague many comparative approaches. Must we decide whether the New Age is a capital-R Religion? No. We ask students to compare the portrait of the religious climate expressed in the film versions of *Hair* (1979) and *Godspell* (1973). What do these films say about what it meant to be 'religious' in 1970s USA? This implicitly generates (but does not necessarily resolve) discussions about boundaries and definitions. When similar methods are applied to *God in America* through topic substitution, students can see the cohesive and deliberate efforts to show the USA's religious history as the inexorable march to religious pluralism rather than other plausible alternatives.

Here I do not dwell on the criticisms that surround the integration of pluralism and the WRP. Others have raised them in the context of critiques of religion's *sui generis* discourse, the ideology of the discipline of Religious Studies and the creation of the category of world religions (McCutcheon 1997; Fitzgerald 2000; Masuzawa 2005; Introduction to this volume). I believe these criticisms should be discussed with undergraduates, but I also hesitate to begin with them. I solved this problem by attempting to make them arise more organically as necessary elements in the construction of counter-narratives. If the widely used perspective of religious pluralism as the state of religion in the USA today operates as a proxy for an incipient allegiance to the WRP, then my narrative emphasis has the secondary effect of making space where these criticisms can be appropriately deployed. This is the reward we can offer to students who have made the effort to see the contingency of the stories they might otherwise accept. If this appears so much like having one's cake and eating it, too, then this may be the price scholars must pay to critique a paradigm that they might otherwise use without much ado.

From American religious history to world religions in the USA

Contemporary presentations of religion in the USA owe a considerable debt to Sydney Ahlstrom's *Religious History of the American People* (1972). More than any other work, this volume encouraged scholars to think twice about the value of the legacy of Puritans and their descendants as lynchpins to the nation's religious history. Winner of the 1973 National Book Award in Philosophy and Religion, Ahlstrom's seminal text redefined the academic study of American religious history. For nearly a century the field had been the purview of church historians. Now it became the domain of Religious Studies. Church historians had seen the USA's religious history as the progression of Protestant denominations out of the Puritans. This required doctrinal and confessional metrics to assess and catalogue lineages. This was not so much history as it was a genealogy of the increasing perfection of God's Kingdom on earth embodied in USA-born denominations. Ahlstrom was one of the first to use the nation's growing diversity as an alternative organizational principle. This made the story independent of explicitly Christian theological judgements and returned it to the scrutiny of more objective historical methods.

In hindsight the change seems inevitable, but it had been daring to challenge the claim that Puritans and their descendants were the keys that unlocked the secrets of the present. Ahlstrom's provocative claim was that 'only a minority of Americans have ever believed that Christianity holds the central ruling position in history' (1972, xiii). It lay so far off the path set by previous historians that twenty years later, historian Jon Butler was still being incendiary when he similarly proposed in his work *Awash in a Sea of Faith* to 'open up the discussion of the first three centuries of the American religious experience by reconstructing a more complex religious past … far removed from a traditional "Puritan" interpretation' (1990, 2). Even another decade after that Eck could argue that though Americans are more conscious than ever of the demographic shifts due to a new immigration law in 1965, 'we are surprised to discover the religious changes America has been undergoing' (2001, 2). Eck, Butler, and Ahlstrom all represented a new strain of historical revisionism that was emerging from Religious Studies as it scoured the ground covered by church historians. What would have formerly been a heresy that diminished Christianity's power to explain all of the nation's religious history was now becoming the dominant paradigm. To see this as an inevitable change was as simple as recognizing that the field's approach to the past was changing in response to the present. Where earlier authors had to account for the plurality of Protestant denominations, historians of religion in the second half of the twentieth century felt compelled to explain the diversity of non-Christians as essential to the story's latest chapters.

Consider one of the earliest works on American religious history published just prior to the Civil War. For decades after its appearance, Robert Baird's *Religion in America* (1970 [1844]) stood as the model for the presentation of religion in American history. Baird was an insider, a life-long missionary whose work 'embodied most of the leading Protestant assumptions about what constituted evangelical Christianity and how such religion ought, legally and theologically, to function in the lively experiment of American democracy' (Bowden 1970, xiv). He spoke for and helped solidify a consensus where the USA stood as the model of the successful implementation of Christian voluntarism. As historians would still argue over a century later, the genius of religious innovation in the nineteenth century was the nation's democratization of religious affiliation (Hatch 1989). It was up to every individual to find his or her place in the religious landscape. Birth did not bind a person to a faith. They could, in the popular evangelical model, always be reborn as a member of a new religious group.

Yet the world did not understand the religious revolution. Was the explosion of denominations not a diffusion of authority that suggested American Christians had lost their way? *Religion in America* was inspired by 'a patriot's desire to answer European claims of increasing pluralism' that denigrated the American experiment (Bowden 1970, xvii). A plurality of denominations belied an underlying confessional unity, Baird contended. Illustrative examples appeared in his efforts to present a more agreeable image of the nation on the verge of its Civil War. He dismissed reports of dissent, as in the anti-abolitionist riots of 1834, as 'greatly exaggerated' and the products of 'newsmongers, in their eagerness to concoct a piquant article' (Baird 1970, 296). The USA was being misrepresented and unfairly portrayed as a political, moral and institutional failure. Despite a plethora of evidence to the contrary, he argued that it was untrue that there were churches that approved of slavery. 'In some parts of the country', he admitted, 'they think they are compelled to *tolerate* it as an evil from which circumstances do not at present allow them to extricate themselves'. Anything stronger, however, was 'going beyond the bounds of Christian charity' (1970, 303). Since history was subject to such limits, this left Baird unable to discuss much of what was happening simply because it was uncharitable or would have presented American Christians in an unflattering light.

When Ahlstrom published his text in 1972, he felt compelled to distinguish clearly his own approach from that of church historians (especially with reference to Baird and his peer Philip Schaff's *America* [1855]). After all, his move to explain American history beyond the limits of Puritanism was not particularly charitable to the Christian consensus. Four points emerged. First, religious history, he maintained, was a part of 'world history' and could not therefore call upon 'divinely inspired sources of insight' or other scriptural or doctrinal authorities. Second, and presaging many contemporary discussions of non-religion, he claimed, 'agnosticism does not preclude religiosity'. Third, though 'white Anglo-Saxon Protestantism enjoyed a long hegemony', this did not mean there had not been dissenters, opponents or outsiders. They all belonged in the story. Finally, even as 'the search for a trans-cendent reference above and beyond mundane considerations' set religion apart from other human concerns, he argued that analysts must never forget the social context of religion (xiv). Religion was not just what but also why, where, when and for whom.

Ahlstrom's methods were innovative, and his work set a demanding standard for his colleagues to follow as they attempted to include its perspectives in shorter introductory textbooks. At over a thousand pages in length, *A Religious History of America* would have been an unwelcome addition to undergraduate reading lists. Instead, many instructors turned to a work initially written by church historian Winthrop S. Hudson in 1965 but edited and reissued in 1973, 1981, and 1987. Early editions of Hudson's *Religion in America* (the first through the fourth) now read like the last hurrah of the church history model. He began with the Protestant New England corridor. Then pre-Revolutionary America was portrayed in the denominational rubric. Religion in the nineteenth century included the panoply of Christian groups, but it was evident that he agreed with the Second Great Awa-kening's Charles Finney that the newest arrivals primarily embodied a 'spirit of sectarianism'. Like Baird, Hudson's work held competition among congregations to an unspoken confessional standard of ecumenism. Unlike Baird, however, he was willing to say that everything had not been agreeable during this period. This meant utopian and communitarian Christians were introduced as divergent and 'discordant notes ... in the midst of [evangelical] harmony' (Hudson 1965, 158). Although he acknowledged the heterogeneity of the religious scene after the Civil War as 'Post-Puritan', he also emphasized that it collectively represented a trend toward ecumenical and interfaith unity. 'Americans of all faiths', he wrote in the conclusion, 'in the presence of diversity, were learning to live together in a way that was mutually enriching rather than impoverishing' (425). It was − at best − a timid embrace of the country's pre-existing and swiftly growing pluralism.

Beginning with its fifth edition in 1992, Hudson's textbook gained a co-author − John Corrigan − trained in the post-Ahlstrom era. In the subsequent editions of *Religion in America* (1992, 1999 and 2004), Corrigan's influence was palpable as the narrative shifted away from church history's orbit. The seventh edition of 2004, for instance, contained an entire chapter of material that prefaced what used to be the first chapter of Hudson's text. Corrigan had made room for the views of native peoples as well as the Catholic colonies of New France and New Spain. Denomi-nationalism still reigned in the treatment of colonial America, but another new chapter appeared to discuss religious views such as deism that could be seen in the nation's political birth amid interactions with Enlightenment philosophies. Utopians got their own say in a chapter on the 'Visions of Religious Community' rather than being simply sectarian obstacles to mainstream Protestants. Moreover, there was space to introduce Judaism, Eastern Orthodoxy, Catholicism and Pentecostalism. Some of these had been discussed in previous texts, but they were now presented as legitimate alternatives to Protestantism and not simply cultural baggage carried by immigrants who were ready to convert and assimilate. For the first time in any of the editions, the 'world religions' of Islam, Buddhism and Hinduism appeared as the 'new' parts of the USA's 'Old and New Centers'.

To a considerable degree the differences between the first and seventh editions of *Religion in America* (1965 and 2004) are the wages of time. For Corrigan and most other observers at the end of the millennium, the changes in the religious landscape were no secret. But even with only a handful of years of hindsight over Hudson's first edition, Ahlstrom saw further. His work began the nation's story not with Puritans but with Catholics in New Spain and New France. In a section on 'democratic evangelicalism' he found room for positive portraits of spiritualists, Shakers and an assortment of other utopians and communitarians. His discussion of rising diversity included Jews, Eastern Orthodox, the new age and even the positive thinking of Norman Vincent Peale. The final section of his work, 'Toward Post-Puritan America', was a warning shot for those who had not yet grasped the full scope of the nation's religious diversity or its effects. If the name of the section had not been plain enough to indicate his opinion, his conclusion was forceful. The days when everyone in the USA 'had in some way, negatively or positive, to relate themselves' to colonial era Puritans or their Protestant successors were over. In the 1960s, 'the age of the WASP, the age of the melting pot, drew to a close' (1079). Later the 1979 ninth printing would declare on its back cover, this text was 'no survey, but a saga'. In other words, this was an epic story for Protestants that announced to them the end of their time at the center of the country's religious history.

Though the co-authored editions of *Religion in America* (1992, 1999 and 2004) broke new ground for the extension of Ahlstrom's paradigm into the undergraduate curriculum, Corrigan's changes were limited by the underlying structure of Hudson's original work. One alternative was the textbook written by my mentor at the University of California, Santa Barbara and which I used in the classroom in my courses. Throughout its now five editions, Catherine L. Albanese's *America: Religions and Religion* took many more risks in following through on the implications of Ahlstrom's reconfiguration of American religious history. The first edition, published in 1981, began with an introduction that famously defined religion 'as a system of symbols (creed, code, cultus) by means of which people (a community) orient themselves with reference to both ordinary and extraordinary meanings and values' (9). One of the most fascinating sections of Albanese's first edition was a discussion of forms of civil and cultural religions. The observations about the primary trope of US television and cinema – that a stranger will end trouble in paradise with righteous violence – continue to describe films at box offices thirty years later

(316–317). More than any textbook that came before it, *America: Religions and Religion* took the USA not merely as a stage for the evolution of European faiths, but rather as a social and cultural context capable of producing extra-denominational religious systems. It diminished the lineage obsession that Protestant influences on American religious history had generated, and instead took religion to be the fullest measure one can make of the forms produced by religious persons, even if those measures meant considering unconventional data. 'From this perspective', she insisted, 'while many people live without Gods, nobody lives without a religion' (9). It seemed impossible to avoid the influence of religion. After all, who could dis-orient themselves from an experience as pervasive as the USA's civil religion or ignore the products of its media empires?

This was a different kind of discourse about religion as an object for study. Fitzgerald has argued that broad definitions of religion (such as orientation) may make it impossible to distinguish religions from secular ideologies (2000). Albanese avoided this problem by looking at the legal, cultural, social, and other spheres wherein religion becomes defined and used by individuals and groups. Religion operates not merely as orientation but as a complex system to support the creation and maintenance of orientation. If one asks, 'what is religion?', no context has been set for the limits of answers. It begs ahistorical comparisons that ignore significant culture differences. As an alternative, this system-based definition is always qualified. Instead there are questions about how or why a specific group of people might see themselves or their concerns as religious in relation to the context in which they find themselves. While this is significantly relativistic, it offers a basis for creating references that are rooted in data demarcated by or with the subjects and less so by potential interpretative fictions. This leaves the force of comparison dependent on careful study of subjects and less reliant on the prowess of gifted scholars. The effect of Albanese's definition is that students are left with no resort but to let subjects speak for themselves about what they find meaningful. For whom is the designation religious valuable? Is it a self-identification? If so, how is that orientating that person or group within society or history? Analytically, an interpreter's goal is then to explain that speech and how it signifies in a given context. This mirrors Fitzgerald's ethnographic model, but not only preserves the use of the term religion but also welcomes a diversity of methods for identifying significance from history, sociology, and other allied fields.

Among popular works on the world's religions this relativism was largely absent until very recently. For decades, Huston Smith's bestselling work, *The World's Religions* (originally published as *The Religions of Man* in 1958), was the exemplar. Smith wanted to introduce readers to the timeless, essential truths of Hinduism, Buddhism, Confucianism, Taoism, Islam, Judaism, Christianity and 'Primal Religions'. He was surprisingly open about his biases. He would show 'the world's religions at their best', even as he acknowledged it was possible to do otherwise. He made no secret of his belief that the 'empowering theological and metaphysical truths of the world's religions are … inspired'. Those truths were worth presenting with as few institutional trappings as possible, because, as he quipped, 'the biggest mistake religion ever made was to get mixed up with people' (1991, 5). In tones that Albanese and Ahlstrom would both echo, Smith saw all religions as the product of 'people who were struggling to see something that would give help and meaning to their lives' (11). Despite the wide survey of faiths, readers were left to make their own comparisons of their merits. If Smith offered meaning by orientation, it was to a trans-historical, trans-national truth that lay beyond the grasp of humble historians. This was not Religious Studies or even religious history; this was Smith's search for the truth behind power that had been distributed across the world throughout human history. In other words, it was the comparative magic that made pluralism attractive as a force to allow a diversity of faiths to co-exist (see J. Z. Smith 1982).

A recent work by Stephen Prothero was a notable departure from this model. *God Is Not One* argued that though 'the world's religions do converge when it comes to ethics … they diverge sharply on doctrine, ritual mythology, experience, and law' (2010, 3). These differences matter not only because it becomes unsustainable to make universal claims about capital-R religion, but also because it may fundamentally change what religion is. Prothero, however, does not take Albanese's cultural relativism very far. His discussion of the world's eight 'rival' religions models the heart of the WRP's control over the presentation of global religion as a set of traditions. This continued the work that Smith had undertaken half a century earlier – even if now religion itself was the trans-historical object and religions were no longer presented as limited instances of a shared truth.

Smith's method for selecting traditions to appear in his volume seemed to privilege an undisclosed mixture of population and influence. Remarkably, his portrait of the world's religions remains reasonably accurate, even after the fiftieth anniversary of the publication of his bestselling book. As the latest data on religious affiliation around the world from the Pew Research Center's Religion and Public Life Project's report on 'The Global Religious Landscape' suggest, Christians (31.5%), Muslims (23.2%), Hindus (15%), Buddhists (7.1%) and the Pew's equivalent of primal religions, 'Folk Religionists', (5.9%) make up more than eighty per cent of the global religious population (2012). According to its report, sixteen per cent of the world was unaffiliated with a specific tradition, while those who claim to be Jewish, Shinto or Tao together would make up less than a single per cent of the world's peoples. The unarticulated motives for the inclusion of these latter faiths on Smith's list of world religions appear likely to follow the arguments identified by others including Tomoko Masuzawa (2005) and J. M. Blaut (1993), who have seen such categories as examples of Eurocentric colonial models. Smith's decision to include Judaism, Taoism or Confucianism was undoubtedly not based solely on a simple measure of adherents, but instead on an impression of their 'truth' and pervasive influence on a particular geographic region. Could you explain Chinese history, for example, without referring to the works of Confucius or Lao Tzu? How would one explain Christianity or Islam as Abrahamic traditions without discussing the faith of Abraham? As Ahlstrom might have said, these were decisions that saw religious history's place as part of world history. Even if Smith believed he was showing his readers a higher truth, he was reluctant to ignore the basic elements of history as he saw them. Just as Albanese later argued for a full measure of religious content, Smith implied that there was much more to say in the story of world religions than a simple list of those religions with the greatest number of adherents might suggest. Prothero surely agreed, as his list was identical apart from replacing 'primal religions' with the specific example of Yoruba and adding atheism.

This approach, which condensed faiths to a series of globally significant or populous traditions, was also adopted in textbooks that presented religious diversity after 1965 as pluralism. Ahlstrom had argued this change meant re-considering all the old consensuses. Albanese likewise shifted away from older models that emphasized Protestant denominations to this new paradigm where a plurality of world religions coexisted. The very idea of pluralism became a form of post-Puritan rebellion. In her *America* (1981), Native Americans, Jews, and Roman Catholics preceded any discussion of Anglo-Saxon Protestants in New England. Afro-American religion merited its own chapter, as did Utopians and metaphysical movements of the nineteenth century. There was an entire chapter devoted to 'Eastern Peoples and Eastern Religions'. The diversity now appearing in textbooks was a far cry from the denominational roll call of Protestant groups in Baird. Pluralism obviously meant something more. It was a climate of significant diversity and competition that described the inability of the mainstream and margin to be insulated from the impact of a free marketplace. Voluntary affiliation encouraged adaptation but forced interaction. If a religious group sought to protect itself from assimilation into the melting pot, it had to do so over and against its competitors. By seeing religion as the orientation people had concerning these affiliations and boundaries (i.e. their fashioned beliefs, morals, ritual and community), Albanese could point to pluralism as that feature of religion that championed and challenged religious communities. 'America', she said, 'has been beset with the serious *religious* problem of crossing the human boundaries that hinder community' (370). Pluralism became the climate where world religions vied with each other because before the law, if not in practice, they were supposedly equal. Beyond the voluntary character of religious adherence in the USA, religious liberty affirmed the heart of the equality of the truth of all religions.

The universal claims about religions notwithstanding, the parity of faiths in survey courses often meant ignoring basic demographic realities in the face of more ideological motivations for content distribution. In introductory courses or textbooks on religion in the USA, especially those arranged chronologically, Christianity has naturally taken centre stage. As so many authors appear to argue implicitly, is it not impossible to tell the story without discussing the pivotal influence of Americans who were devout Christians? Baird could not have foreseen the explosion of faiths that accompanied multiple waves of immigration in the twentieth century. Hudson was likewise unable to account for changes that took place just as his first edition was published. Today, by self-declaration of affiliation, the USA is perhaps more Christian than it has ever been in the past. The Pew report cited above estimated that in 2010, seventy-eight out of 100 Americans would identify as Christian. This did not make it the most Christian nation in the world, but it did make it the nation where the largest population of the world's Christians live. Muslims, Hindus, Buddhists, Jews and members of folk religions combined – everyone who is considered today part of the USA's pluralist landscape – amount to just sixteen million people or a scant 5.3 per cent of the population. For contrast, Pew estimated that there were more than fifty million Americans who would decline to identify themselves with any religious tradition. While Albanese's orientative definition of religion has a place for these unaffiliated people in the country's religious tapestry, not all textbooks do. (Where, for instance, would they fit in Hudson and Corrigan?)

If the survey data sets a substantial gap between claims of diversity and what appear to be the on-the-ground realities, what is to be made of the nation's pluralism? If *God in America* was a normative or mainstream representation of the consensus, then it also showed the compromise between accurate data and a story that reflects the climate of pluralism. Explaining the dynamics and limits of religious liberty, for instance, took precedence over other developments. As Eck wrote in 2001, 'We must embrace the religious diversity that comes with our commitment to religious freedom' (25). Tolerance for difference – even when it contradicted one's own faith – was the inevitable consequence of the legal contracts that ensured religious freedom. As a model of influence and assimilation, pluralism was the outcome of the dual posture of significant diversity amid substantial liberty. Even if there were a substantial majority, it was necessary for consent to be granted for the minority to open the narrative (Prothero 2006).

In the final minutes of episode six of *God in America*, Purdue University historian Frank Lambert described the limits of this acceptance:

> American religion operates in this great sphere of freedom, in this great marketplace of religion. I mean, 90 percent of Americans say, 'I believe in God.' But they also reserve for themselves the right to say exactly how they believe in God, and what they mean by God. With religious liberty there is no official church. This is no official religion. There are hundreds, and it is a matter of fact, if we count mega-churches as individual religious groups, there are thousands of religious groups in America.
>
> *(Belton 2010: 'Of God and Caesar')*

Diversity, yes, but much of that diversity remained attached to conventional understandings of what it meant to be religious. As Stephen Prothero reiterated the search for the meaning of American identity during the series, he argued that it was the effort of coming together despite the limitations of religion that was representative of the present. 'What's happened over time', he said, 'is more and more and more people have been included'. It was pluralism that defined the relationship Americans had to God today. 'We just keep making the space bigger', he continued, 'extending the sacred canopy over more and more people' (in Belton 2010: 'Of God and Caesar'). Whether the nation would remain united by its effort to bring more people and groups under the sacred canopy, Prothero could not say.

For the moment at least, the integration of the multi-religious USA was not only the defining characteristic of the present, it was also that willingness to let the canopy extend, thereby altering the way it understood what it meant to be religious. This was a post-Puritan ideal that most scholars of American religious history seemed willing to support.

In practice: *God in America* in the classroom

If *God in America* embodies the WRP in its embrace of pluralism and religious liberty, then I believe the challenge for classrooms is to provide minority and anti-consensus access to the narrative. The documentary series is so much the straw person in this effort, but only because it articulates the lingering consensus views so clearly. As I noted at the outset, substitution is one approach that gives students reasonable boundaries within which to work on particularly historical or religious issues. When we lead students to destabilizing materials we can always ask, 'what happens if this instead of that?' Since the courses I taught were distinct from available courses in the department on specific traditions or theoretical elements of Religious Studies, I was disinclined to tackle certain topics. In my own seminar-sized classes, using the fourth edition of Albanese's *America* alongside required viewings of episodes of *God in America*, I settled on tasks organized around terms from *Critical Terms for Religious Studies* including 'conflict', 'performance', 'territory', and 'time' (Taylor 1998). These focused the questions I posed about *God in America*'s narrative preferences, giving students a way to discuss the construction of the documentary in light of competing content.

Here is an example of how this process worked for episode five, 'The Soul of a Nation', which deals primarily with the relationship between religion and politics in the years after the Second World War. Martin Luther King, Jr. played a key role as the leader of the Civil Rights movement that ended racial restrictions in the US. As Frank Lambert says in the episode, 'King saw America's founding documents as … giving expression to fundamental biblical principles of justice and peace and equality.' Civil Rights became a *religious* issue as King deftly used biblical themes to articulate the deficiencies in the application of the nation's founding principles. 'Be true to what you said on paper', King said in his famous 'I've Been to the Mountaintop' speech in Montgomery, Alabama. What *God in America* does not explain very well, however, is that King's rhetoric was only part of the story. Yes, his nonviolent civil disobedience was instrumental in the changes the country saw in the 1960s, but there were also other radical voices that called for violence and other solutions to the Jim Crow-era of limited civil rights for black Americans. So I asked students to tell the story of the Civil Rights movement from the perspective of Malcolm X instead. Immediately, this changes the discussion. Instead of King and his dream that called upon Judaeo-Christian narratives of Exodus, we get Malcolm X, who became an all-too-outspoken leader in the Nation of Islam. How did the man born as Malcolm Little find his way to Elijah Muhammad? Why did he choose a new surname? Why was X so unsatisfied with King's efforts? And so on. Shifting the narrative in this way encourages students to consider, as Malcolm X did, that legal equality for African-Americans was insufficient to end the kind of systematic oppression he believed they faced. If X was right, does this help to explain more or different things about the experiences of people of colour in the subsequent decades leading up to the election of Barack Obama in 2008?

While the use of Malcolm X to tell a very different story about the Civil Rights movement definitely upends the consensual narrative of God in America, I also believe it works against some of the WRP's influence. King's biblical rhetoric is a popular example of a moment when the nation made progress in more fully applying the spirit of its founding values. The Declaration of Independence's proposition that all men were created equal, for instance, described American experiences after the Civil Rights era better than it had before. This downplayed the racial conflicts that persisted and reduced a highly complex narrative to a series of sound bites. By questioning the documentary's perspective we can practise how to avoid reducing the Civil Rights movement's religious elements to a particular brand of Protestant discourse about freedom. We need not reject the persuasiveness or ubiquity of that discourse. We need only to work on developing a story that reflects the import of religious voices beyond King's. Since the episode emphasizes the consensus narrative, we do ourselves few favours by avoiding obvious alternatives. In the classroom, every step away into these muddy waters makes religion's role in the Civil Rights movement increasingly variegated and dynamic. Ultimately, this works with the argument made in God in America that religion is essential to understanding American history. Even those that were marginalized by more successful narratives have something to contribute that creates a more vibrant picture of how religion has functioned in this country.

I do not wish to overstate the case against universalism or generalization. Both appear necessary tools to tell the story of more than 400 years of religious lives and traditions and beliefs. With just six hours to complete this task, God in America required a kind of ruthless reductionism. When students have a chance to realize the limitations of the format, they are one step closer to identifying the biases and editorial choices made by its creators. They need not become masters of all content relevant to every chapter of American religious history. Instead they are presented with the opportunity to think critically about the way any content is presented. It is a structural pedagogical goal that encourages interrogation from discrete standpoints. What were the other religious models besides nonviolent, civil disobedience to resolve the issues of the Civil Rights era, I might ask as I broaden their understanding of conflict as a controlling factor for this topic.

I see the challenge of destabilizing the WRP in introductory classrooms – especially those that may implicitly use that construction in supplementary materials – as one of recognizing the opportunity to work through topics that avoid the generic presentations that have been perpetuated by that model. Huston Smith's meaningful 'inspired truths' give way to Albanese's system of symbols that reveal complex systems of orientation to mundane and extraordinary objects. Students have found that the episodes of God in America, for example, seemed to present the Exodus-based narratives in ways that diminished the differences in the uses of those biblical stories. Early Puritan use of Exodus themes, such as John Winthrop on the *Arbella*, was nothing like that of the African-American slave spiritual 'Go Down, Moses'. Nor were these the same as Martin Luther King, Jr.'s powerful integration of them alongside political rhetoric from the USA's founding fathers. Bruce Feiler's *America's Prophet* (2009) has helped students parse these differences, but at the cost of wedding students to that consensus interpretation. Using the critical term of 'time' has side-stepped the latent Judaeo-Christian elements of these examples and encouraged a more practical and detail-oriented approach to understanding the use of Exodus narrative across American history.

Other items on pedagogy in introductory survey courses in religion have grappled with the challenges of definition and time management for the presentation of world religions (Walvoord 2007; Juergensmeyer 1991). As scholars begin to confront the WRP as an outdated model for undergraduate instruction, I hope they also find the presentation in these terms of the problem of designing courses inadequate. Perhaps by using materials like *God in America*, instructors might be persuaded to avoid relying on universal constructions of both our object of study (capital-R religion) and its examples (world religions). I was fortunate to be bounded not only by American history and culture, but also by my commitment to a thematic and methodological approach. Seeing *God in America* as a narrative and then breaking that narrative into discrete, contestable units moved the discussions toward defining religion and religions. It did not, however, presume to hand students a ready-made model of religion to seek somewhere out there in the ether. This made all the difference, I believe, because it asked students to do that work themselves. They were given explicit permission to question the way the story had been presented to them, and then they were expected to use that opportunity to see if they could not find alternatives that brought greater detail, complexity and life to religion in the USA. I never encouraged them to answer the question 'what is religion?' because I found it more productive and engaging to see them articulate why it mattered that a group identified itself or its actions as religious. For challenging the presentation of the WRP in *God in America*'s use of pluralism, this made all the difference between accepting and rehearsing the consensus and becoming authors of powerful, alternative narratives about America's religious history.

References

Ahlstrom, Sydney E. 1972. *A Religious History of the American People*. New Haven, CT: Yale University Press.

Albanese, Catherine L. 1981. *America: Religions and Religion*. Belmont, CA: Wadsworth.

Baird, Robert. 1970 [1844]. *Religion in America*, edited by Henry Warner Bowden. New York: Harper & Row.

Belton, David, dir. 2010. *God in America*. Boston: WGBH. Transcripts available at http://www.pbs.org/godinamerica/transcripts/ (accessed March 2014).

Blaut, J. M. 1993. *The Colonizer's Model of the World: Geographical Diffusionism and Eurocentric History*. New York: The Guilford Press.

Bowden, Henry Warner. 1970. "Introduction" to *Religion in America*, by Robert Baird, xi–xxxvii. New York: Harper & Row.

Brekus, Catherine A. and W. Clark Gilpin, eds. 2011. *American Christianities: A History of Dominance and Diversity*. Chapel Hill: University of North Carolina Press.

Butler, Jon. 1990. *Awash in a Sea of Faith: Christianizing the American People*. Cambridge, MA: Harvard University Press.

Corrigan, John and Winthrop S. Hudson. 2004. *Religion in America*, 7th edn. Upper Saddle River, NJ: Pearson.

Eck, Diana L. 2001. *A New Religious America: How a 'Christian Country' Has Become the World's Most Religiously Diverse Nation*. New York: HarperCollins.

Feiler, Bruce. 2009. *America's Prophet: How the Story of Moses Shaped America*. New York: Harper Perennial.

Fitzgerald, Timothy. 2000. *The Ideology of Religious Studies*. New York: Oxford University Press.

Hatch, Nathan O. 1989. *The Democratization of American Christianity*. New Haven, CT: Yale University Press.

Hudson, Winthrop S. 1965. *Religion in America*. New York: Charles Scribner's Sons.

Juergensmeyer, Mark, ed. 1991. *Teaching the Introductory Course in Religious Studies: A Sourcebook*. Atlanta: Scholar's Press.

Masuzawa, Tomoko. 2005. *The Invention of World Religions*. Chicago: The University of Chicago Press.

McCutcheon, Russell T. 1997. *Manufacturing Religion: The Discourse on Sui Generis Religion and the Politics of Nostalgia*. Oxford: Oxford University Press.

Pew Forum on Religion and Public Life. 2012. *The Global Religious Landscape*. Washington, DC: Pew Research Center. Available at http://www.pewforum.org/files/2014/01/global-religion-full.pdf

Preston, Andrew. 2012. *Sword of the Spirit, Shield of Faith: Religion in American War and Diplomacy*. New York: Anchor.

Prothero, Stephen R., ed. 2006. *A Nation of Religions: The Politics of Pluralism in Multireligious America*. Chapel Hill: University of North Carolina Press.

Prothero, Stephen R. 2010. *God Is Not One: The Eight Rival Religions That Run the World*. New York: HarperOne.

Schaff, Philip. 1855. *America: A Sketch of the Political, Social and Religious Character of the United States, in Two Lectures*. New York: C. Scribner.

Sehat, David. 2011. *The Myth of American Religious Freedom*. Oxford: Oxford University Press.

Smith, Huston. 1991 [1958]. *The World's Religions*. New York: HarperOne.

Smith, Jonathan Z. 1982. *Imagining Religion: From Babylon to Jonestown*. Chicago: The University of Chicago Press.

Taylor, Mark C., ed. 1998. *Critical Terms for Religious Studies*. Chicago: The University of Chicago Press.

Tweed, Thomas, ed. 1997. *Retelling U.S. Religious History*. Berkeley: University of California Press.

Walvoord, Barbara E. 2007. *Teaching and Learning in College Introductory Religion Courses*. Malden, MA: Blackwell.

11

ARCHAEOLOGY AND THE WORLD RELIGIONS PARADIGM

The European Neolithic, religion and cultural imperialism

Carole M. Cusack

Introduction[1]

'World religions' are typically characterized by written scriptures, systematic theology, missions and proselytization, other-worldliness, professional clergy, exclusivism and universalism, and have been linked to expansionist economies and global under-standings of warfare. This model is the polar opposite of that of indigenous religions, which are typically characterized as this – worldly, orally transmitted, non-proselytizing, folk-oriented, generally expressed in myths and traditional law, pluralist, and linked to subsistence economies and local notions of warfare. This chapter interrogates a major thematic of the World Religions Paradigm (WRP): the spread of particular, self-contained, boundaried and systematized 'world religions' across geographical and temporal locations (via mission, imperialism, colonialism and so on) and the concomitant destruction of the forms of indigenous religion existing in the societies so dominated. Rather than affirming this thematic, the chapter argues that by utilizing the archaeological data left by the Northern European Neolithic peoples (including the Stones of Stenness and the Ness of Brodgar in the Orkneys, and Stonehenge and Durrington Walls on Salisbury Plain), the emergence, prosperity and decline of a variety of human enterprises (and not only religions) can be demonstrated to be a perennial and inevitable aspect of human history. By directly examining archaeological evidence rather than employing *a priori* religious categories, it is possible to focus Religious Studies away from the WRP and towards other models that are non-elitist, fluid, and non-normative.

Mission, expansion and colonialism as tropes of 'world religions'

During the eighteenth century, European colonialism expanded and was con-solidated throughout the inhabitable regions of the world, and the rational, intellectual Enlightenment and its affective concomitant, Romanticism, both developed explanatory discourses as to why the colonized were advantaged by the domination of their colonial overlords. The Romantics understood the indigenous peoples of colonized lands as both 'noble savages' possessed of wisdom, yet also as childlike compared to mature Europeans (Liebersohn 1994), and the Enlightenment rationalists saw colonialism as inevitable and European culture as superior. Beth Fowkes Tobin notes that the latter view was evidenced in 'the customs-and-manners sections of natural histories, a kind of proto-anthropology that described native peoples in the same terms that natural historians used to describe botanical or zoological specimens' and in the desire of Europeans to classify and categorize every new phenomenon they encountered (Tobin 1999, 145). Those behaviours and attitudes that were included in the writings of missionaries and explorers – which tended to be 'exotic' and sensationalist, and to emphasize differences rather than similarities – and that fitted the Western notion of 'religion' were classified accordingly.

The medieval and early modern West understood 'religion' primarily to mean Christianity and the related monotheisms, Judaism and Islam, which were regarded as inferior to Christianity. This perception was held by the devout (who claimed the Christian faith as the sole path to salvation) and the irreligious (who nonetheless thought Christianity exemplified the highest morality and the most perfect institutional forms) alike (Cusack 2013). Traditions that are now termed 'indigenous religions' were generally not recognized as 'religions' due to their lack of resemblance to European Christianity. Thus, it was not until the publication of Edward Burnett Tylor's *Primitive Culture* (1871) that the existence of indigenous Australian religions, previously classified as merely 'traditions' and 'customs', was recognized (Swain 1985, 30). Because Aboriginal people had no written texts, formal priesthood, religious buildings or supreme deity, Whites assumed they had no religion. Tylor's definition of religion, 'belief in spirit beings', birthed a changed understanding of religion that enabled Whites to see that the Ancestors of indigenous culture were religious, after almost a century of ignorance and denigration of Aboriginal culture (Swain and Trompf 1997, 11). It follows that those traditions that were recognized as 'religions' resembled Christianity in certain crucial ways. These included: written scriptures; formal doctrines and a developed theological or philosophical worldview; dedicated clergy or other religious functionaries; formalized ritual practices; and a revered founder or an origin in remote history (MacWilliams *et al.* 2005, 2). Thus the WRP replicates and reinforces a model of religion that reflects the high value that (Protestant) Christianity accords to doctrines, texts and institutions (King 1999, 66).[2]

'Indigenous religions' do not fit the WRP because they are typically this-worldly, orally transmitted, non-proselytizing, folk-oriented, expressed in myths and traditional law, and pluralist. The WRP also excludes religions that are deemed to be unconventional or otherwise suspect, such as 'new religious movements' (Owen 2011, 258). In short, the WRP promotes an essentialist idea of religion, that each religion is a unified whole of which all adherents will be exclusively and uncomplicatedly members, and also suggests that it is relatively easy to identify a 'world religion'. Suzanne Owen notes that many academics continue to teach the WRP even when they object to it; 'after presenting the World Religions paradigm, they spend another several sessions trying to dismantle it' (2011, 258). There is a certain amount of sense in this, in that the WRP represents the largest and most powerful examples of what is generally understood to be 'religion', and the smaller and less well-known religions are subsequently introduced to students as variations of, extensions of, or exceptions to the 'world religions' model. In fact, this is a respected pedagogic strategy in other disciplines, particularly the 'hard' sciences, like Mathematics and Physics, in which the more complex study is preceded by students becoming familiar with a substantially simplified version of the disciplines, to which higher concepts are introduced as exceptions or separate, incompatible systems (Kirsch 2000). Further, a pedagogic move from simple to complex forms characterizes student learning in virtually all domains from languages to music.[3] It may be that the WRP attracts more criticism than science education paradigms because the study of religion involves human actors and not abstract concepts or a seemingly remote and uncaring universe.

There are other manifest inadequacies that merit comment. One feature of the WRP that is less frequently observed is its unreflective Darwinianism; the 'world religions' are those that have spread across the world, obliterating other smaller, local, non-imperialist and non-colonialist religions, and now dominate indigenous peoples (who have gratefully adopted them) due to their innate superiority. A second, equally disturbing aspect of the WRP is its unreflective presumption that the protagonists of its narrative are masculine; like 'world history' and the majority of academic fields that traverse the *longue durée*, female activity within religions is virtually absent, or is presented as a 'special case'. Judith Zinsser has argued that, rather than writing a history that includes both sexes, even the work of gender-inclusive scholars results in 'the creation of a separate women's history within articles or monographs that are otherwise about men' (Zinsser 2013, 310). Owen has observed that the WRP makes particular demands on teachers, in that it is unfeasible to expect high school or even university teachers to be expert across such a wide range of traditions (Owen 2011, 263), and Zinsser reinforces this by noting that 'world history' is rarely an academic's research area, but rather is a phenomenon encountered when teaching, along with the concrete matters of textbooks, constrained notions of curriculum, and external examinations (Zinsser 2013, 312). Thus, one answer as to why the WRP is resilient in pedagogical contexts is that it is externally driven, by governments and other educational authorities, which prescribe national curricula, academic standards, quality assurance and other metrics.

It remains for me to state that the WRP offers a remarkably homogeneous and 'clean' model of religions, one that is an ideal type rather than a model congruent with embodied, material, contingent, messy religious reality of the majority of 'real' people. Further, it is a model in which there are no internal differences of note in any religion (though phenomena such as Christian denominations or the Sunni–Shi'a divide in Islam may be mentioned); no human individuals or communities may have dual, mixed or ambiguous religious allegiance or identity; an identical set of markers are identifiable in all religions (rites of passage, scriptures, priests or religious functionaries, a 'universal' system of ethics and morals, dedicated buildings, and exclusive membership); and where difference is erased in favour of sameness. Those groups that are excluded from or marginalized by the WRP, such as 'indigenous religions' or 'new religious movements', may be added to the list of 'valid' religions by means of a catch-all category (Tafjord 2013, 225). It is easy to see the advantages as well as disadvantages of teaching using the WRP. Virtually all religious studies textbooks employ the WRP, it offers a clear and simple description of religions that students recognize, and it is reproduced in governmental exercises such as the five-yearly censuses that collect data on religious affiliation in Australia, for example (Zwartz 2012). The type of learning fostered by the WRP tends to be a 'knowledge transfer' model based on simplified descriptions of religions, which is less challenging and interesting than what Owen calls a 'knowledge questioning' model, in which students are taught to critique, question and evaluate the apparently value-free descriptions with which they are confronted (Owen 2011, 257–258).

When confronted by the difficulties of teaching a WRP-based course, academics have a range of viable alternatives available to them for use in the classroom. It is possible to retain the WRP framework (which may be mandated by external examinations and prescribed textbooks) and teach it in ways that negate its effectiveness as a replicable 'meme'. The WRP may be dismantled from within, for example, focusing on radical difference and deviation from textbook descriptions. Thus, it is possible to teach Buddhism with regard to heterodoxy and heteropraxy, emphasizing women's experiences and popular and folk rituals and beliefs, rather than reifying the texts, doctrines, and practices of male elites (Kawahashi 2003). Another strategy is to focus on religious deviance, as in descriptive expositions of religions being both positive and uncontroversial is paramount, and issues of violence, repression, racism and criminality are never evaluated frankly and critically (Cobb 2006; Selengut 2008). It is also possible, if not constrained by the WRP, to provide students with entirely different entry points into the study of 'religion' through using non-normative case studies and evidence other than the usual texts, doctrines, rites of passage, and so on. Archaeological case studies can be used pedagogically either within the WRP or as an alternative to it. This chapter is focused on the use of an archaeological case study, the Neolithic monuments of the United Kingdom, to interrogate one theme of the WRP: the spread of those traditions identified as 'world religions' and the destruction of the 'indigenous' religions of the peoples conquered and colonized by the dominant, thus more 'evolved' or 'sophisticated' culture.

Monuments and the development of complex societies in the Neolithic

Despite the recent popularity of 'material religion' and 'lived religion' as new paradigms through which more holistic and nuanced ideas of religious traditions might be reached, archaeological data is rarely used to teach Religious Studies.

It usually appears only in the introductory chapters of WRP textbooks to illustrate the 'origins' of religion. In these chapters archaeological case studies are often linked to contemporary indigenous religions in questionable ways. One example will suffice: in the thirteenth edition of the venerable textbook *A History of the World's Religions* (attributed to Blake R. Grangaard and David S. Noss, the son of the original author John B. Noss), the first chapter, which is regrettably titled 'Some Primal and Bygone Religions', covers the Dieri in Australia, the BaVenda of South Africa and the Cherokee of the United States along with Neanderthals, Cro-Magnons and Neolithic humans of remote and more recent prehistory. Prehistoric religion is described in fairly vague terms as involving goddess worship, shamanism and ceremonial inhumation, and modern 'primal' religion is described in terms of apprehension of the sacred, myth, and ritual (Noss and Grangaard 2011). This misleading use of archaeological evidence perpetuates the nineteenth-century evolutionary schema in which modern indigenous peoples were viewed as 'survivals' of the prehistoric era, because they had 'failed' to invent certain technologies (like the wheel) or adopt 'civilized' habits (like living in permanent stone or brick dwellings).

In contrast, this section will consider the monumental complexes of Neolithic Orkney and southern England. Prehistoric cultures pose great challenges for students, but also great opportunities, due to their lack of corroborating textual evidence. Here the focus is on two interrelated questions: first, what can we know of the initial development and geographical spread of the classic Neolithic monumental structures (stone circles, henges, chambered tombs, and so on) which involved engineering innovation and massive social change; and second, to what extent was this architecture 'religious' and the spread of Neolithic material culture thus linked to religious, as well as technological, political and aesthetic, dominance? To put it slightly differently, is it possible to conceive of the monumental culture of the Neolithic as a prehistoric 'world religion', in that it dominated and eliminated the previous religious and material cultures of those lands into which it spread? And if Neolithic culture fulfils the majority of apparent criteria of a 'world religion', what does its lack of inclusion tell us about the politics of the category? These questions can be unpacked successfully only because of very recent discoveries that have transformed our perception of the Neolithic in the United Kingdom.

The Neolithic ('new stone') era is characterized by a revolution from gatherer-hunter societies to agricultural societies, and the development of urbanization. This trend is first observed around 9000 BC and resulted in a pastoral and agricultural farming economy with people living in settled villages in the Fertile Crescent by approximately 7000 BC (Fuller and Grandjean 2001, 373–374). The spread of Neolithic culture is a controversial topic, as it is categorically the case that the technological and scientific innovations it depended on and the external markers that define it (agriculture, villages, cities, monuments, and so on) spread rapidly and quickly eradicated the cultural patterns of the earlier Mesolithic ('middle stone') age. As Mike Parker Pearson notes, the issue is whether the indigenous Mesolithic hunter-gatherers of Britain took up farming by getting hold of the 'package' through cross-Channel trading with farmers on the Continent, or whether domesticates were introduced by Neolithic colonizers who brought animals and crops to Britain in their small boats, perhaps wiping out the indigenous people in the process.

(Parker Pearson 2012, 18)

This question may be resolved via DNA analysis that suggests contemporary British communities have only a tiny smattering of Middle Eastern ancestors, but that there are more substantial traces of genes 'from a large-scale movement of people along the Atlantic seaboard from Spain and Portugal' around the time that agriculture was introduced to Britain (Parker Pearson 2012, 19). This type of explanation is familiar to students, as they know that Christianity spread to Africa, Asia, the Americas and the Pacific through mission and colonialism, not through the displacement of the African or Asian populations by Europeans.

Before considering the British Neolithic specifically, it is important to consider what other types of transitions might have been facilitated by agriculture and urbanization. Jill Fuller and Burke Grandjean have noted that the change from subsistence to the accumulation of surplus food can be linked to wide-ranging religious changes that are archaeologically observable in the Neolithic era. These include the proliferation of buildings 'with no sign of mundane habitation' (no hearths and food residues for example), human and animal figurines that are presumed to be used representationally in rituals, and adornment of the dead and ceremonial burial with grave goods, possibly in 'response to a rising death rate if the sanitation problems, risk of communicable disease, and high fertility in fixed settlements reduced the life expectancy of Neolithic villagers compared to their low-fertility nomadic ancestors' (Fuller and Grandjean 2001, 375). These changes are generally linked to the rise of social inequality, as scholars posit that the massive monuments are evidence of centralized leadership and the direction of group labour and effort towards the realization of goals (religious or scientific, generally) that are set by elites. This may not have been the whole story, and Wason and Baldia have suggested that 'it may be that people were inspired to build them at least as much to satisfy ritual needs as the leaders' desire to enhance or show off their power' (Wason and Baldia 2000, 222).

Explanations of the Neolithic cultural shift tend to be of two kinds: materialist explanations emphasize the accumulation of wealth and display to dominate the less affluent, whereas the 'culturalist' narrative emphasizes that goods being required for burials 'could create anxiety about accumulating enough to meet those needs ... [and] anxiety could drive a "spirit of accumulation" that would be a powerful motivator to human ingenuity' (Fuller and Grandjean 2001, 378–379), rather in the way of Max Weber's thesis concerning the Protestant ethic fuelling the development of capitalism in the early modern era. It is hypothesized that mythologies and explanatory narratives regarding the meaning of life, death, and the afterlife developed in tandem with these social transformations. There is also evidence that Neolithic people were deeply interested in calendrical calculations which allowed the accurate identification of the equinoxes and the solstices, as many Neolithic monuments are aligned to the sunrise or sunset on the midsummer or midwinter solstice, which might most accurately be termed 'scientific'. Examples of this phenomenon are the chambered cairn, Maes Howe, in the Orkneys, which was completed by 2700 BC but begun as early as 3000 BC (Wickham-Jones 2012, 46–47) and the contemporaneous Irish passage tomb of Newgrange, in the Boyne Valley (O'Sullivan 2012, 21). Therefore, both the materialist and culturalist narratives of the Neolithic revolution go some way towards answering the two questions that are the focus of this chapter, regarding the origin and spread of Neolithic monuments to cover a vast geographical area, and whether these structures were 'religious'. The evidence points towards a qualified 'yes' to both questions.

The Neolithic period began in the Orkneys and Ireland c. 4000 BC, and from approximately 3500 BC the construction of vast stone monuments was widespread. Across Britain, apart from the great stone circles, avenues, passage graves, and chambered cairns, the remains of Neolithic communities are rare, as most domestic buildings were made of timber and are no longer extant; 'Orkney, however, has few trees, so more, though not all … buildings were made of stone' (Ravilious 2013, 40). The well-preserved village of Skara Brae, dating from c. 3000 BC and thus older than Stonehenge, has beds, cupboards and other domestic features all made from local 'stone that would split into flat slabs' in a collection of closely located houses (Daniel 1962, 11). In addition to Skara Brae, domestic dwellings have been uncovered at the Barnhouse site, excavated by Colin Richards, who (with Nick Card, excavator of the Ness of Brodgar, discussed below) is an expert on the Neolithic in the Orkneys. At Barnhouse the excavation uncovered houses that lacked the linking passageways of Skara Brae, but were otherwise quite similar. Richards also uncovered two anomalous buildings, House 2 (which 'is larger than the rest and seems to have two rooms') and Structure 8, which is a totally 'different construction, comprising a circular clay platform, on which stood a large rectangular building … [enclosed by a] circular drystone wall' (Wickham-Jones 2012, 32). Structure 8 has been related to the nearby stone circle of the Stones of Stenness, and Richards (1996a) has argued that the monumental complex of Stenness and the nearby Ring of Brodgar (the third largest stone circle in Britain after Avebury and Stanton Drew) are informed by cosmological ideas.

Richards contends that Neolithic people were aware that they were erecting structures that would long outlast them, and that these were intended to endure and to permanently *order* the landscape. He states that,

> it should be noted that concepts of order are inevitably cosmologically based: cosmologies allow a particular cultural understanding and categorization of the lived and experienced world; they represent a way of 'thinking about' the multiplicity of images and experiences of individuals. In this sense they are not merely abstractions but structure daily practices and perceptions of space and

time: they are as real as people's lives. Cosmology is therefore embedded in natural topography and the environment.

(Richards 1996a, 193)

The deep connection that archaeologists draw between the monuments of the Neolithic and cosmology is very important for the argument of this chapter, because the unstable and complicated designator 'religion' has been traditionally associated with the cosmic order, and Daniel Dubuisson (a scholar who has called for the abandonment of the term 'religion') has proposed 'cosmographical formations' as a more viable alternative (Dubuisson 2003, 49, 89, 204). Richards boldly speculated that the key to the puzzle of the central Orkney complex of monuments is the relationship between the places of the living (Barnhouse) and the dead (Maes Howe), and nearly twenty years later that link has been strengthened by Card's excavations at the Ness of Brodgar and arguably confirmed by the findings of Parker Pearson's Stonehenge Riverside Project (2004–2009).

The final piece of the social, and arguably religious, picture that emerges from Orkney's Neolithic sites is the massive dig that Nick Card has directed since 2003 at the Ness of Brodgar, a site that sits on a natural land bridge between the Stenness/Barnhouse complex and the Ring of Brodgar. What has been uncovered is a huge site, with multiple buildings with no sign of everyday use, enclosed by 'a massive stone wall – 13 feet wide – with a ditch running along the outside of it' (Ravilious 2013, 41). There is also a huge assemblage of the pottery known as Grooved Ware, in many different styles, and this is one factor that has led Richards and Card to hypothesize that the Ness was an enormous ritual site in which each Orcadian community had its own building, and that these communities gathered at times of significance for ritual (Card 2013, 17). A religious reading of this would suggest that the Ness was a temple site, but in the pre-modern era 'ritual' and 'religion' may also encompass meetings about matters of government and other activities (astronomical observations and suchlike) that are regarded as 'secular' in the modern world. Wason and Baldia, discussing the Neolithic monument complex centred on Avebury in southern England, asserted that 'leadership and acceptance of social inequality may well have developed in the process of accomplishing what were originally religious ends, the building of monuments to accomplish religious purposes' (Wason and Baldia 2000, 226). In a similar vein, Joshua Pollard notes that ritual and religion are embodied practices, and that they 'will be worked through and given dimension by material forms … [including] shrines, temples, and other archaeological foci … and ceremony itself as embodied within architectural forms' (Pollard 2009, 332). Two problematics emerge from these archaeological interpretations regarding the place of 'religion' in Neolithic culture: asking what is 'science' and what is 'religion' leads students to investigate the important debates within religious studies regarding the secularization thesis; and archaeological hypotheses challenge them to identify the different ways in which the term 'religion' may be used (as naïve realism, rhetorical strategy, and so on).

What did Neolithic cosmology comprise, and how can twenty-first century scholars and students access that cosmology through the material evidence of archaeological remains and the shaped and manipulated landscapes that these distant ancestors left behind? In addition to places of the dead and the living, and what may be termed mundane sites (houses and farmsteads) as well as those sites more accurately termed 'sacred' due to burials, the erection of structures that are clearly not domestic, and so on (Cooney 1994, 34–35), Richards contends that water is a core element in Neolithic ritual complexes. For example, the Stones of Stenness and the Ring of Brodgar are set on promontories separating the lochs of Harray and Stenness. Thus, 'both monuments take on the appearance of being surrounded by water that is encircled by hills' (Richards 1996b, 324). Human settlement began on the Wiltshire plain around 4000 BCE, contemporaneous with Orkney, and recent excavations led by Parker Pearson demonstrate that Stonehenge was from the outset a place of burial, the first monument being 'a cremation cemetery demarcated by a bluestone circle, later dismantled to leave the Aubrey Holes' (Parker Pearson et al. 2009, 34). These excavations confirm that the sarsen building phase (the massive sandstone trilithons that modern people think of as 'Stone-henge') was finished by c. 2400 BCE. Two miles from Stonehenge lies Durrington Walls, an enormous henge monument that is almost five hundred metres in diameter. The relationship between the two structures, according to Parker Pearson, is complementary (and parallels the Barnhouse and Maes Howe relationship hypothesized earlier by Richards); Durrington Walls is the site of the living and the recently deceased, and Stonehenge is the site of the ancestral dead of the same community (Parker Pearson et al. 2007, 636–637). The River Avon is the water-course in this monument complex, and an earthwork avenue links the sites. Very few Neolithic houses have been identified in England, but Parker Pearson's team excavated at Durrington Walls and located four residences in the main trench that reinforced the relationship of the site to Stonehenge, as the remains of 'box beds and storage units like those crafted in stone in the Orcadian houses' (Parker Pearson 2012, 73).

Neolithic culture and the WRP: cultural success and issues of power

Earlier in this chapter comparisons between prehistoric societies and modern indi-genous cultures were disparaged in the context of WRP textbooks. This is not to say that such comparisons are totally valueless, but to draw attention to the care with which they must be undertaken. Parker Pearson's confirmation of the rela-tionship between Durrington Walls (the living) and Stonehenge (the dead) initially derived from a hypothesis that humans would, across geography and temporality, respond to and understand certain construction materials in broadly similar ways. The Madagascan prehistoric archaeologist Ramilisonina informed Parker Pearson that Madagascan sites associated with the living were typically built in wood (which was transitory, as was human life) and those associated with the ancestral dead were built in stone (which was eternal). Parker Pearson and Ramilisonina then collaborated to establish whether this was a plausible explanation of the relationship between Stonehenge and the timber circles within the great henge of Durrington Walls and a related structure, Woodhenge (Pollard 2009, 337–338). Because Stonehenge's posts and lintels were shaped with mortice and tenon jointing like carpentry, earlier theories posited the timber circles as prototypes for the stone circle (Cunnington 1929). Parker Pearson's new model was that the different functions of the two sites mandated different materials, and he is inclined to the view that Avebury, the next most renowned stone circle after Stonehenge, 'was also built as a place for the ancestors, separated by water from the land of the living', following the recent discovery of 'a series of enclosures surrounded by wooden palisades along the Kennet river, a mile from Avebury' (Parker Pearson 2012, 11).

Thus far it may appear that all that has been demonstrated in this chapter is that Neolithic archaeology is an interesting field of research and that many scholarly interpretations of Neolithic monument complexes conclude that such complexes are 'religious' or at the very least 'ritual' sites. Yet a commonly accepted model of the spread of the Neolithic in Europe is that it spread like a new religion; this explanation was first proposed by John C. Barrett in the 1980s and early 1990s. The lack of written texts, so central to the WRP, is an issue in supporting this interpretation, but Julian Thomas accepts that 'commonalities of artifactual form and cultural practice ... spread over enormous distances and great depths of time in Neolithic Europe', and that oral tradition can preserve and transmit a relatively large body of knowledge over lengthy periods (Thomas 2004, 118). It is not known whether a stable belief system underpinned Neolithic structures, though it is reasonable to conclude that centres for the living and the dead, typically in wood and stone respectively (but both in stone in the Orkneys, due to the shortage of wood), were constructed throughout Neolithic communities, and these centres were linked by avenues located by water sources. This is clear, despite the fragmentary survival of the remains of the wooded structures. The uses to which these ritual complexes were put is clarified by the archaeological deposits excavated at the respective sites:

> considerable quantities of feasting debris ... at Durrington Walls and ... large numbers of cremations and unburnt human bones at Stonehenge suggested these monuments performed different but complementary roles in an extended ritual cycle that saw the translation of the newly dead into ancestors most likely around the winter and/or summer solstices, given the axial orientation of Stonehenge.
>
> *(Pollard 2009, 338)*

As the orientation to the sunrise or sunset on the solstices is common to a large number of Neolithic monuments, it is likely that an annual cycle focused on the length of the days, with the midsummer solstice the time of greatest prosperity, power, and fertility for the community, and the midwinter solstice the turning point in which the darkness began to wane and the light of the sun to wax anew (Cusack 2012, 142). This does not constitute a comprehensive mythology or set of doctrines, but rather a bedrock which underpinned such a worldview.

When teaching about religion using these sites as a case study, the two questions posed in this chapter can elicit very sophisticated responses from students. Class discussion of the Ness of Brodgar in first year tutorials generated the idea that the Ness might also be a university, as the University of Sydney campus was clearly set apart from the outside world by an outer wall, and the university itself was a collection of buildings to which many people came daily but in which they did not cook or sleep. That intriguing speculation drew from well-informed students the suggestion that a university such as Sydney was in fact a religious, or at least religiously derived institution, given the clerical origins of such sites of learning and the whiff of monasticism that survived in them until the late nineteenth century when women were admitted as students. Recalling Zinsser's concerns about gender cited above, the question of women's participation in Neolithic society was canvassed, as there is little in the way of scholarship that clarifies the contribution of both genders. Rather, masculinity is the focus when it is known that the construction of the ditch at Durrington Walls has been estimated at 500,000 hours' labour, and the southern wooden circle at Durrington Walls at 11,000 hours' labour, and these figures are roughly comparable to the level of commitment and cooperative effort required by all major Neolithic complexes (Boyne Valley, Orkney, Avebury and so on). This suggests the existence of a sophisticated system of government and mechanisms facilitating extensive communication in the Neolithic era in Britain. It does not, however, say much about the roles played by women in these construction projects or in the rituals conducted within their precincts. Yet, when comparative evidence is sought, it is undeniable that women contributed in various ways to another comparably vast construction campaign, the building of Gothic cathedrals in medieval Europe, as evidence proves they cleared debris, mixed plaster, and performed other tasks that did not require great physical strength (Martin 2012).

The two questions that this chapter is focused on concern whether the origin of the Neolithic monument complexes, the construction of which involved massive social change, can be conceptualized as 'religious' (the answer being broadly 'yes'), and whether the spread of Neolithic material culture was linked to religious as well as political, technological, and aesthetic, dominance? If the answer to that question is also 'yes', the thematic of the WRP that identifies 'world religions' as successful in extinguishing local indigenous traditions through missionary strategies and their greater sophistication of institutional structures and teachings comes into play. Modern colonialism involved religious conversion and political conquest, both of which were exercises of power, of one culture over another, of one religion over another (Strenski 1998). The study of human history (understood to include prehistory) reveals that some human cultural products (for example religions, technologies, political systems, literary forms and so on) are 'successful' and may extinguish or marginalize other products that are of the same type. This certainly occurred with Neolithic material culture, as Mesolithic patterns of gathering and hunting, nomadic movement, and burial, were entirely eradicated by Neolithic agriculture, fixed sites of habitation, and burial practices (described above). In Foucauldian terms the transition from Mesolithic to Neolithic involved 'the emergence of techniques and practices … to increase the utility of human subjects … to discipline bodies in different ways which [made] them more productive' (Brigg 2002, 425).

Despite the European Neolithic not having involved large migrations of peoples, the material culture spread rapidly and replaced the Mesolithic gatherer-hunter culture more or less totally. The Neolithic began in the Middle East in around 9000 BC and was dominant for almost six thousand years, as the Bronze Age is generally dated from approximately 3000 BC, depending on the region (Parker Pearson 2012, 4). This chapter has aimed to open up questions about the WRP by considering thematics of cultural transmission and domination, technological success, the interpretation of material remains without textual corroboration, and the role of sex and gender in prehistoric societies. When analysing cultures from the distant past, it is important to be attentive to interpretive discourses that may be employed to explain the evidence. For example, what Teemu Taira calls *temporal distanciation*, a discourse that 'makes a distinction between primitive and modern, and describes the other as living in eternal childhood or being child-like' (Taira 2013, 33) is often read backwards (especially in WRP textbooks) to explain the religious conceptions of prehistoric peoples. However, the Neolithic sites discussed in this chapter, and the peoples who erected them, have been fairly scrupulously interpreted by archaeologists without reference to these patronizing stereotypes; in fact, Neolithic culture (if not individuals, as they are unknown) has been identified with scientific enquiry, technological innovation, complex cosmology, calendrical studies and pastoral and agricultural developments, all admirable in Western modernity. Insofar as possible, students should be encouraged to view Neolithic society as being comparable to their own while understanding that the erasure of difference to produce 'sameness' is as much of a problem as the fetishization of difference that produces titillation and 'otherness'. It is also important to note that recent scholarship on colonialism has been concerned with 'colonialism's *attitude* towards the colonized and … its exclusionary discourses and practices', whether racism or the promise of 'false liberalism' (Scott 1995, 192, emphasis in original). In fact, colonialism is a complex of realities that involves delicate dances of negotiation and varies considerably over time and geographical distances (Harris 2004). Thus modern Africans and Asians are often proud Christians and seek to re-evangelize the 'godless' Europeans that brought the Gospel to them, and English functions as a unifying point for India, a country divided by multiple languages from different, unrelated language families.

Conclusion

The WRP has been criticized as a simplified, Western-centric, and exclusionary model of religion that closes down interesting avenues of pedagogy and research.

Yet, as noted earlier in this chapter, such simplified versions of complex bodies of knowledge are routinely used in science education and do not attract the kind of concerned criticism that the WRP has in recent years. It seems that the WRP's historical connection to the West's colonial domination of Africa, Asia and the majority of non-European lands creates discomfort among religious studies scholars, and increased knowledge of the great variety of the world's religions, both extant and extinct, creates a desire to broaden the definitions and models that are used to examine religion and to demonstrate inclusiveness and a lack of racism, discrimination, and other colonial and/or theological hangovers. It has here been argued that directly examining archaeological evidence rather than employing *a priori* religious categories or expounding facts about 'religions' usually listed in the WRP (Judaism, Christianity, Islam, Buddhism, Hinduism) is a productive pedagogic strategy that makes it possible to focus on questions of cosmology, cultural transmission, technological innovation, and practices such as cremation and inhumation that are generally identified as 'religious'. Sites such as the Orcadian Neolithic monuments, Stonehenge, Durrington Walls and Avebury are beautiful and remarkable, and have the capacity to fascinate students and fire their imaginations. By getting them to think about how religious studies relates to prehistory and materiality, and not to texts and belief systems, it is possible to shift the emphasis away from the WRP and towards other models that are non-elitist, fluid and non-normative.

Notes

1 I am grateful to my research assistant Venetia Robertson for her skill and patience in locating materials, photocopying and taking preliminary notes. My thanks are also due to Don Barrett for his sympathetic interest in my researches and his assistance in clarifying my thoughts during the researching and writing of this chapter.
2 See editors' introduction in this volume.
3 The extent to which both Religious Studies scholars and the public conceive of 'religion' as 'special' in some sense, and thus deserving some kind of 'different' treatment to the natural sciences or to other 'unproblematic' humanities disciplines such as History or English Literature, is another problem deserving of attention, but the scope of this chapter does not permit me to address it. My personal view is that Religious Studies is an academic field like all other academic fields and does not require any 'special' methodological approaches or treatment by scholars. To claim otherwise is to accord to Religious Studies an essential nature or *sui generis* status, and would convert this secular discipline into a type of theological enterprise (with theology conceived of in the broadest sense).

References

Brigg, Morgan. 2002. "Post-development, Foucault and the Colonization Metaphor." *Third World Quarterly* 23(3): 421–436.
Card, Nick. 2013. "The Ness of Brodgar: More Than Just a Stone Circle." *British Archaeology* 128: 14–21.
Cobb, Michael. 2006. *God Hates Fags: The Rhetorics of Religious Violence.* New York and London: New York University Press.

Cooney, Gabriel. 1994. "Sacred and Secular Neolithic Landscapes in Ireland." In *Sacred Sites, Sacred Places*, edited by David L. Carmichael, Jane Hubert, Brian Reeves and Audhild Schanche, 32–43. London and New York: Routledge.

Cunnington, Maud. E. 1929. *Woodhenge*. Devizes: G. Simpson and Co.

Cusack, Carole M. 2012. "Charmed Circle: Stonehenge, Contemporary Paganism, and Alternative Archaeology." *Numen* 59(2): 138–155.

Cusack, Carole M. 2013. "Enlightenment Concepts, Medieval Contexts." In *Critical Reflections on Indigenous Religions*, edited by James L. Cox, 68–80. Farnham and Burlington, VT: Ashgate.

Daniel, Glyn. 1962. *The Megalith Builders of Western Europe*. Harmondsworth: Penguin.

Dubuisson, Daniel. 2003. *The Western Construction of Religion: Myths, Knowledge and Ideology*. Trans. William Sayers. Baltimore: Johns Hopkins University Press.

Fuller, Jill E. and Burke D. Grandjean. 2001. "Economy and Religion in the Neolithic Revolution: Material Surplus and the Proto-Religious Ethic." *Cross-Cultural Research* 35(4): 370–399.

Harris, Cole. 2004. "How Did Colonialism Dispossess? Comments from an Edge of Empire." *Annals of the Association of American Geographers* 94(1): 165–182.

Kawahashi, Noriko. 2003. "Feminist Buddhism as Praxis: Women in Traditional Buddhism." *Japanese Journal of Religious Studies* 30(3): 291–313.

King, Richard. 1999. *Orientalism and Religion: Postcolonial Theory, India and 'The Mystic East'*. Abingdon: Routledge.

Kirsch, Arnold. 2000. "Aspects of Simplification in Mathematics Teaching." In *Teaching as a Reflective Practice: The German Didaktik Tradition*, edited by Ian Westbury, Stefan Hoppman and Kurt Riquarts, 267–284. Mahwah, NJ: Lawrence Erlbaum Associates, Inc.

Liebersohn, Harry. 1994. "Discovering Indigenous Nobility: Tocqueville, Chamisso, and Romantic Travel Writing." *The American Historical Review* 99(3): 746–766.

MacWilliams, Mark, Joanne Punzo Waghorne, Deborah Sommer, Cybelle Shattuck, Kay A. Read, Salva J. Raj, Khaled Keshk, Deborah Halter, James Egge, Robert M. Baum, Carol S. Anderson and Russell T. McCutcheon. 2005. "Religion/s Between Covers: Dilemmas of the World Religions Textbook." *Religion Studies Review* 31(1–2): 1–35.

Martin, Therese, ed. 2012. *Reassessing the Roles of Women as 'Makers' of Medieval Art and Architecture*. Leiden: Brill.

Noss, David S. and Blake R. Grangaard. 2011. *A History of the World's Religions*. 13th ed. Boston: Pearson.

O'Sullivan, Muiris. 2012. "The Spirituality of Prehistoric Societies: A View From the Irish Megaliths." In *Archaeology of Spiritualities*, edited by Kathryn Rountree, Christine Morris and Alan A. D. Peatfield, 3–23. New York: Springer.

Owen, Suzanne. 2011. "The World Religions Paradigm: Time for a Change." *Arts and Humanities in Higher Education* 10(3): 253–268.

Parker Pearson, Mike, Ros Cleal, Peter Marshall, Stuart Needham, Josh Pollard, Colin Richards, Clive Ruggles, Alison Sheridan, Julian Thomas, Chris Tilley, Kate Welham, Andrew Chamberlain, Carolyn Chenery, Jane Evans, Chris Knüsel, Neil Linford, Louise Martin, Janet Montgomery, Andy Payne and Mike Richards. 2007. "The Age of Stonehenge?" *Antiquity* 81(313): 617–639.

Parker Pearson, Mike, Andrew Chamberlain, Mandy Jay, Peter Marshall, Josh Pollard, Colin Richards, Julian Thomas, Chris Tilley and Kate Welham. 2009. "Who Was Buried at Stonehenge?" *Antiquity* 83(319): 23–39.

Parker Pearson, Mike. 2012. *Stonehenge: Exploring the Greatest Stone Age Mystery*. London and New York: Simon & Schuster.

Pollard, Joshua. 2009. "The Materialization of Religious Structures in the Time of Stonehenge." *Material Religion: The Journal of Objects, Art and Belief* 5(3): 332–353.

Ravilious, Kate. 2013. "Neolithic Europe's Remote Heart." *Archaeology* (January–February): 39–44.

Richards, Colin. 1996a. "Monuments as Landscape: Creating the Centre of the World in Late Neolithic Orkney." *World Archaeology* 28(2): 190–208.

Richards, Colin. 1996b. "Henges and Water: Towards an Elemental Understanding of Monumentality and Landscape in Neolithic Britain." *Journal of Material Culture* 1(3): 313–336.

Scott, David. 1995. "Colonial Governmentality." *Social Text* 43: 191–220.

Selengut, Charles. 2008. *Sacred Fury: Understanding Religious Violence.* Lanham, MD: Rowman & Littlefield.

Strenski, Ivan. 1998. "Religion, Power, and Final Foucault." *Journal of the American Academy of Religion* 66(2): 345–367.

Swain, Tony. 1985. *Interpreting Aboriginal Religion: An Historical Account.* Adelaide: Australian Association for the Study of Religion.

Swain, Tony and Garry W. Trompf. 1997. *Religions of Oceania.* London and New York: Routledge.

Tafjord, Bjørn O. 2013. "Indigenous Religion(s) as an Analytical Category." *Method & Theory in the Study of Religion* 25(3): 221–243.

Taira, Teemu. 2013. "Making Space for Discursive Study in Religious Studies." *Religion* 43 (1): 26–45.

Thomas, Julian. 2004. "Current Debates on the Mesolithic–Neolithic Transition in Britain and Ireland" *Documenta Praehistorica* XXXI: 113–130.

Tobin, Beth Fowkes. 1999. *Picturing Imperial Power: Colonial Subjects in Eighteenth Century British Painting.* Durham, NC: Duke University Press.

Tylor, Edward B. 1871. *Primitive Culture: Researches into the Development of Mythology, Philosophy, Religion, Art, and Custom.* London: John Murray.

Wason, P. K. and M. O. Baldia. 2000. "Religion, Communication, and the Genesis of Social Complexity in the European Neolithic." In *Alternatives of Social Evolution*, edited by N. N. Kradin, A. Korotayev, D. M. Bondarenko, V. De Munck and P. K. Wason, 138–148. Vladivostok: Far Eastern Branch of the Russian Academy of Sciences Press.

Wickham-Jones, Caroline. 2012. *Monuments of Orkney: A Visitor's Guide.* Historic Scotland.

Zinsser, Judith P. 2013. "Women's and Men's World History? Not Yet." *Journal of Women's History* 25(4): 309–318.

Zwartz, Barney. 2012. "Old Trend No Leap of Faith." *Sydney Morning Herald*, 22 June. http://www.smh.com.au/national/old-trend-no-leap-of-faith-20120621-20r29.html (accessed 29 July 2014).

12

COMPLEX LEARNING AND THE WORLD RELIGIONS PARADIGM

Teaching religion in a shifting subject landscape

Dominic Corrywright

Introduction: a world without world religions?

The intellectual history of the idea of world religions involves a complex interplay of historical, political, cultural and academic discourses (see, for example, Masuzawa 2005a, 2005b; Owen 2011; Segal 2007). It has become a stream of knowledge accepted and implicit in common understanding and curricula. The *Encyclopedia of Religion* includes an entry for 'world religions' which, though it is written by a key challenger to the paradigm, notes its ubiquity (while stating it is not a 'technical term', and identifying different uses of the term; Masuzawa, 2005b). World religions has become a category paradigm in social understanding: it is often used uncritically, occasionally reflectively as a useful shorthand, or a pointer to varied patterns of behaviour and belief. It is an umbrella term for diverse phenomena. In the study of religions, the term 'religion' is also generally understood as an umbrella term, a lexical signifier for diversity.

As will be discussed below, category construction requires such 'shorthands'. But knowledge and understanding require reflexive application – even as we use knowledge to develop greater understanding we critically reflect upon the substance of that knowledge. Academic study requires an eternal return to its foundations, modes and representations. Just so, in the study of religions students and tutors begin, repeatedly with each new year's intake, defining, challenging and investigating the primary category of religion. The study of religions is the subject of study and the cumulative history of a variety of approaches to a subject area. It is also a discourse that critically considers itself as an object, and that is the beginning of the pedagogic enterprise for undergraduates; it is ideally the key topic of the first class of the first module introducing the study of religions.

The study of religions is concerned to critically consider the labels and categories used in discourses on religion. Matters of what these phenomena should be called and who has the authority to decide, insiders or outsiders, are core to this academic project. At a deeper level, the effects of these categories are also a serious area of consideration. To what extent are they accurate representations? How much do they mould disparate phenomena within the boundaries of an external category? How much do the categories exclude? And to what extent are the borders and liminalities an affective part of the category? There is, within this analysis of categories, a linguistic and philosophical question about the relationship between language and the 'world'. Epithetical responses to this question include Ferdinand de Saussure's foundational linguistic observation that the sign is not the signified (1974). Jonathan Z. Smith emphasized this point with the epithet 'map is not territory' (1978). Both de Saussure and Smith provide an important epistemological warning for the study of religions: signs and maps are constructs created by scholars of religion from their (equally constructed) evidence base, that which is signified, or the 'territory'. The substance of knowledge is attained in the field. Perhaps it might be argued that this perspective, simply described, offers an unsophisticated philosophy of language by separating perception of the world from the linguistic bases by which humans bring the world into being – when there is a much more symbiotic relationship between the world and language. As Russell McCutcheon states, in relation to the terms religion and religious experience,

> It could be persuasively argued that the only reason scholars find religions everywhere in the world, and religious experience in everyone's heads, is because those very scholars approach the world – in fact *make* their world – by using this term, defined broadly enough, so as always to find sufficient things that they can deem/group together as religion – suggesting to me that a theory of *deeming* (i.e. a theory of signification) and *grouping* (i.e. a theory of classification) are far more required than theory of religion.
>
> *(2012, 88)*

However, the view that map is not territory includes a moral injunction to treat the objects of study, the territory, as preeminent. Categories such as linguistic signs and maps have a dangerous and bewitching tendency to supersede that which they purport to describe. The World Religions Paradigm (WRP) is a sign that shapes understanding of religion in the world. It does not disinterestedly paint a picture of the world, but helps to construct the picture.

Students should be pointed toward a primary understanding that categories and discourses offer lenses of perception, and that these lenses are subject to change, and to choice. As Craig Martin has observed, 'getting past the common-sense view of language is the first step to high-quality, critical scholarship' (2012, 21). This critical revaluation of terms and categories, such as 'world religion', is an imperative for academic development and pedagogical intent. In common discourse, and still in much of the study of religions, the map of the world is coloured by areas labelled by signifiers from the WRP.[1] The uses of generalized forms such as world religions are obvious when the lens of observation is focused on representing majority religious traditions. But, politically and ethically it is not acceptable to overlook minority voices. Injunctions against omission by oversight according to gender, ethnicity or age, as much as warnings to observe the processes of power, to listen for the voice of the subaltern, as well as challenges for inclusive and wide representation of all, require the scholar of religion to specifically pay attention to minorities. The WRP and focus on majority groupings of religion are open to each of these injunctions and challenges.

In a remarkable text, *The World's Religions in Figures* (2013), Todd Johnson and Brian Grim collate and analyse a significant range of data to examine the global scope of what they term the 'major religions'. Their selection of major religions is: Christianity, Islam, Hinduism, Buddhism, Chinese folk-religion, Judaism and 'ethnoreligions' (2013, 74 fn. 1). They are wary of world religions as a category, stating that listing world religions alongside numerical data for each, 'is valuable as a succinct global summary, but if it is not expanded further, such listings become gross oversimplifications of what is in fact a vast global complex of thousands of distinct and different religions' (2013, 137). Yet, it should be questioned whether 'major religion' is little more than a synonym for world religion. Are these just different ways of describing the same phenomena? Or are they significantly different as means of representing these phenomena? How are scholars to describe and define either major or minor traditions? Undergraduates require a framework by which they come to understand that categories and taxonomies are ways of packing up data – from this point they can begin to unpack, or more accurately, 'unmask' the effective elements and affective consequences of categories such as WRP.

This chapter employs a pedagogical perspective in the critical re-evaluation of the WRP. It describes a process of de-schooling and re-schooling a ubiquitous structure within the discourse. In a radical re-visioning of education, Ivan Illich has described the process of 'de-schooling society' (1971; 1973a). Schools and universities, he argued, are ideologically designed to reproduce a social system that is inequitable, excludes marginality and should on these terms alone be de-constructed. Moreover, 'the school system inculcates its own universal acceptance' (1973b, 97). By analogy it may be that the WRP is in process of being de-schooled, decommissioned, as not fit-for-purpose. It has created its own 'universal acceptance' which must be carefully unpicked from the discourse. Unpicked and unthreaded it may be discarded, or its overarching remit may be demoted to a loose descriptive term. There is also a pedagogical imperative in Illich's prescription to 'question the nature of some certainty' (1973b, foreword), to teach the freedom to challenge – and in the case of this chapter, it is both the freedom to challenge the WRP *and* the freedom to challenge that challenge and assert the value of the category minus its prescriptive characteristics. Students should be encouraged to critically consider the WRP, to imagine a world without world religions, and to evaluate the value of maintaining or discarding this category.

Complex learning: pedagogical processes in category constructions and deconstructions

When I began teaching, twenty-five years ago, to secondary/high school level students in the UK, the programme for religious education lessons was based on a nineteenth-century Tylorean evolutionary approach to religious development. The first year of study examined ancient and dead religions; the second year polytheistic religions; the third year monotheist religions, culminating in Christianity. This model was a strictly hierarchical representation of religious development within a Christian culture. This included an explicit assumption of historical development with the notion of a distinct progress from superstitious worldviews to rational belief systems. Pedagogy is often not about what is taught so much as how it is taught. There is implicit within curricula a model, or series of models, of what is 'out there'. Fortunately, pedagogy at secondary/high school levels of study has improved significantly in the UK with, for example, the establishment of Standard Advisory Councils for Religious Education (SACRE), influenced by useful organizations such as the SHAP Working Party on World Religions in Education and the Religious Education Council. But evolutionary positivism in the study of religions has been superseded by the WRP, and school curricula now have an endemic model of world religions. The model retains its power in undergraduate curricula and the resources that support them. This point is neatly exemplified by a chapter subtitle of a teaching text, *World Religions Today*: 'The great transition: from tribal life to urban life and the emergence of world religions' (Esposito *et al.* 2009, 15). Complex learning in the twenty-first century requires approaches that problematize meta-theories and models such as the WRP.

The model of the WRP is a linguistic sign not only of what is 'out there in the real world' but also of human desire to make meaning, and to structure the multiplicity of phenomena into order to simplify through classificatory systems. This human desire is both social and psychological:

> The models by which meaning is constructed are derived from, and produced within, social bodies, by their members who are themselves shaped by historical and social concerns. Humans develop models by which to encode and comprehend existence. Models allow us to make sense and shape the world(s) in which we live.
>
> *(Juschka 2012, 55)*

The psychology of pedagogic practice recognizes that students seek patterns of certainty and simplicity that such models afford. But challenging the desire for certainty and simplicity is a core ambition for teachers. Thus, as we teach typologies, categories and terminology – those models that provide certainty and simplifying structure – we unmask their effects and bring about uncertainty anew. Even the generic terms by which religious insiders and academic scholars of religion label these traditions have a simplifying structure. Thus when Johnson and Grim identify

Christianity, Islam and Hinduism as 'major religions', they simplify into singularity that which is diverse and disparate. One way of countering this is by simply adopting plurality in the term, to challenge monolithic labels – see for example Corrywright and Morgan, where the discussion of 'grouping religions' both challenges the WRP and presents varied religious groupings as Christianities, Islams and Hinduisms (2006, 18ff.). It is an approach that can have significant social effects – for example in correcting the potentially dangerous, stereotyping monolithic representations of Islam in common media as identified in the Runnymede Trust report on Islamophobia (L. Smith *et al.* 2004). One important facet of complex learning is to emphasize plurality and difference. Another feature is to challenge the desire for simplicity and the concrete.

For the pedagogue introducing the study of religions to new students, there are resources aplenty to prise open the processes of category construction. These can be presented as vignettes, small studies. Outlining the processes, historical and intellectual, of the construction of a model or a category can also be the beginning of a deconstructive process. The tools of deconstruction are manifold. But just as the teacher defines the architecture of construction, so he or she must provide a framework for deconstruction. Some foundational theory that shows the contingent nature of knowledge and intellectual history is necessary. This requires neither a nuanced social constructionist philosophy nor a full-blown relativism, merely some foundations in the constructive effects of human understanding of the world. Possible beginnings may include Marshall McLuhan and Quentin Fiore's influential text *The Medium Is the Massage* (1967, reprint 1996) and the important discussions that arise from their assertion that 'the book is an extension of the eye'. Another departure point may be a consideration of Marxist critique of the social functions of religion and the specific historical and social contexts of these functions.[2] The keystone of such sample starting points is for students to recognize (and challenge) the assumption that there is an external empirical category of 'religion' which is global and a-historical, and composed of world religions. The next cognitive step for students is to recognize that positivist presumptions in the order of knowledge underlie the WRP. The world of religions, it is assumed, is defined by an accumulation of knowledge, out of which the category 'world religion' emerges. Yet, the history of ideas shows that knowledge is contingent on its cultural contexts. What is known is limited not only by the unknown, but manipulated by power relations, through political, economic, social and cultural means, that make representations of the world according to their interests. Thus students must learn to unlearn in a complex interplay of assertion and challenge to the very categories which, in part, construct the subject of their learning.

There is a tension in category construction between groups and individuals, types and specific instances, multiplicity and singularity, and between association and differentiation. Recognition occurs at many levels, inductive and deductive: we recognize types or groups and then specificities within those types, or, from specific instances, we recognize 'types'. Academic study leads to a sophisticated process of recognition which identifies difference and multiple identities and that combats simplistic identifications according to generic categories. However, academic discourse includes varied layers of recognition which accord phenomena varied levels of categorization. We might define these different levels of understanding as orders of knowledge. Recognizing the hierarchical structures of orders of knowledge, and the categories that play within them, is an important facet of complex learning. It is also a key mode in discourse analysis and Foucauldian unmasking. Foucault uses a splendid example of categories from the imagination of Jorge Luis Borges to illustrate how the process of ordering and labelling the world is culturally contingent:

> This passage quotes a 'certain Chinese encyclopaedia' in which it is written that 'animals are divided into: (a) belonging to the Emperor, (b) embalmed, (c) tame, (d) sucking pigs, (e) sirens, (f) fabulous, (g) stray dogs, (h) included in the present classification, (i) frenzied, (j) innumerable, (k) drawn with a very fine camel hair brush, (l) *et cetera*, (m) having just broken the water pitcher, (n) that from a long way off look like flies.' ... the thing we apprehend in one great leap ... of another system of thought, is the limitation of our own.
>
> *(Foucault 2005 [1974], preface, xvi)*

So students come to understand that the WRP offers a classificatory system which arises in a specific social context. But they fall ever again into simple label–object correspondence. They may even repeat a tale from another early seminar class, where I explain the importance of different academic subject areas investigating religions, using the story of the six blind men and the elephant. These students may aver that the blind men represent differing classificatory systems but they are all *of* the elephant. Three ripostes may scotch this naïve theory of correspondence. First, a brief consideration of the taxonomical system of biological sciences of classification according to domain, kingdom, phylum, class, order, family, genus, species, seems to offer a very robust taxonomy. But, as biologist Stephen Jay Gould has shown, different systems of identification can result in radically different categorizations within the taxonomy (in McCutcheon's measured and careful consideration of religion and classification; 2007, 65–71).[3] A second response may be to consider Ludwig Wittgenstein's duck-rabbit and what kind of thing it is. From different perspectives and depending on the prevailing identificatory system it is a duck or it is a rabbit. Lengthy class discussions may ensue on classification and taxonomies. But it is not either thing at all. It is a board squiggle, a representation, which is either, both or none of these things. Representation is not reality, neither are classificatory systems such as the WRP. Third, we do not challenge the existence of real elephants for the issue is not ontic, to do with their existence or non-existence, but epistemic, what we know about them and how we respond to their existence. The lenses of perception, such as the WRP, structure what is perceived and how it is accorded significance.

Classificatory systems and taxonomies provide paradigms of understanding phenomena that are, in fact, representations, and which are subject to change.

Thomas S. Kuhn provides the seminal outline for the notion of paradigm creation and subsequent shifts (1970) which is appropriate to understanding the historical role of the WRP and its functions as a representation of religiosity. The WRP is in fact an example, *par excellence*, of a paradigm in the process of changing. The notion of a paradigm is also well exemplified by the shift in pedagogy itself, from a model of didactic delivery of concepts and knowledge (where learners are consumers) to one where students at undergraduate level are encouraged to be producers of knowledge, even co-contributors to learning.

Teaching and learning in the twenty-first century is a complicated *melange* of partially effective old models, such as the lecture format – see Bligh (1971) and Gibbs (2013) – and varied novel teaching strategies – see, for example, Ronald Barnett's notion of a 'learning-amid-contestation' epoch in pedagogy (2011). Complexity in teaching approaches is met by complexity of learning. In the lecture-seminar-class room, the WRP is a paradigm that can be discussed and challenged in multifarious and nuanced ways. But among historical and current resources in academic study of religions the WRP resonates as a common universal category. It is, as noted above, commonly found in textbooks for the study of religions. Moreover, a quick Internet search reveals wide usage of the WRP. Teachers in the study of religions must be careful curators of the resources on the Internet. Students are efficient navigators of this territory, whose trajectories of discovery are constrained by their own (lack of) knowledge and the curious, and instrumental, algorithms of search engines. Internet search terms and associated links use 'shorthands' such as 'world religions' that can undermine the careful pedagogy of the classroom. For teachers of religion in the new world of learning it is a challenging process of leading students through a super-abundance of information and providing direction against a dissipating category. For students of religion the complexity of perspectives and the lack of firm knowledge bring about uncomfortable uncertainty in a shifting landscape of knowledge.

Complex learning then arises from the pedagogic assumption that key changes in sources and access to them, and changing modes of delivery, from globalized opportunities for travel to e-learning and Massive Open Online Courses, point to new kinds of learning experience in higher education. Equally, greater levels of student engagement and increased emphasis on students as knowledge producers lead to a model of complex learning and require a review of pedagogical approaches.[4] It is in this context that the overarching trope of the world religions model is dissolving in academic literature and yet requires further unmasking as it is asserted and then unpicked by students.

Two object lessons in the study of religions are presented here as examples of topics and teaching tasks that unmask the WRP. The first task can be completed within the space of a single lecture/seminar session in the first year of an undergraduate programme. The second topic is designed for an honours level class, reiterating the importance of course structure to return to the task of unpicking the WRP throughout a curriculum over each level of study. Such teaching tasks are of course layered and complex – they are lessons about the broader academic study of religions and opportunities to introduce and discuss concept schemes, terminology and tropes within the tradition of the study.

In practice: formations

The students are presented with fifty laminated cards. The cards are each labelled from an apparently arbitrary set of 'names' of religious traditions, worldviews, titles and descriptors of religions. The students are asked first simply to organize the cards according to whatever taxon they deem appropriate and to reflect on the cognitive processes they adopt in deciding which category system to adopt. The first, often unconsciously adopted system is simply based on recognition between known/ unknown, that which is recognized and that which is alien. Other first systems of organization are binary – live/dead, major/minor, monotheist/polytheist, religious/ non-religious. The pile of 'unknown' religions or groups is often quite significant (an object lesson in itself of the amount students have to learn in the course of their studies). Quite quickly most groups of students will move towards the overweening model of world religions gained through lower level studies or the implicit deep presence of the WRP. Thus they will find titles of world religions and begin to group labelled cards under these category headings. This category system is most frequently offered by students as the most robust system, though they are con-founded by where to locate the term 'Orthodox' (under Christianity or Judaism), or 'Tantra' (under Buddhism or Hinduism), are not sure at all where to put either 'Mormonism' or 'Latter Day Saints' and profess failure at the significant pile of other labels from 'Candomble' to 'Marxism', 'Orphism' to 'New Atheism'.

One purpose of the exercise is made explicit to students at this stage in the seminar: card-sorting is a sorting not of the things themselves but of categories. A secondary point, one core to the project of research in the study of religions, is elucidated by Craig Martin's binary that 'the process of labelling or naming is a secondary process, and one that does not change the nature of the thing named' (2012, 19). It is a pedagogical imperative that students understand the constructed nature of such category systems. It is also vital that students in the study of religions are introduced early to the contested areas of category construction and the implications of taxonomic systems, and that these labels and categories have real functional impact on those they purport to describe. The issue is particularly well described by Clifford Geertz:

> As to whether particular analyses (which come in the form of taxonomies, paradigms, tables, trees and other ingenuities) reflect what the natives 'really' think or are merely clever simulations, logically equivalent but substantially different, of what they think.
>
> *(1973, 11)*

In a teaching conceit the seminar leader assumes that there are world religions and discussion focuses on which are the world religions and what characterizes them.

At this stage in undergraduate studies the primary criteria presented are often, simply, size and spread. The students are provided with a map of the world and asked to place labels onto the areas where they originated. The question-begging consequences of the task are clearly evident in the limited locations of the origins and the significant empty spaces across the world. Key questions about *who* is not represented, and *why* these religions and cultures are not represented, powerfully undermine the apparently global model of the WRP. It will be suggested that world religions have historically become so, that origins do not define a world religion, but rather the dispersal and growth of a religion accorded the title 'world religion'. The importance of synchronic and diachronic representations can be introduced to this process of concept mapping and category construction. The snapshot of world religions at their origins or in their current existence belies their existence as 'world religion'. At what point in its historical development does a religion become a world religion? Who decides? Historicizing the establishment, growth and end of a religious tradition makes the category of world religion lose its descriptive efficacy. Moreover, a diachronic perspective which examines the growth of a religion through evangelism and colonial expansion provides a hermeneutic of suspicion regarding the hidden authority and authenticity accorded to religious groupings that self-define as world religions.

There are many possible extensions and further directions to this seminar task. Three example areas include: firstly, discussion of possible alternative categories and labels that could replace 'world religion'. The constitutive elements of a definition of 'religion' are also, in part, those of 'world religion'. Thus, discussion of Ninian Smart's notion of 'worldviews' and his permissive structure of the varied 'dimensions of religion' are appropriate to critical reflection on the WRP (1998; 1999). Equally, the notion of 'family resemblances' between religious groupings and within groupings can be examined as the key mode within which criteria are defined for the category of religion. The idea of a world religion becomes obsolete with these foci. Secondly, this can lead to a consideration of the Weberian/Troeltschean Church–denomination–sect–cult typology widely used in sociology of religion. The typology provides both a synchronic representation on the varied elements within a major religious grouping and a diachronic perspective that can show how a sect or cult becomes a 'Church'. Flawed though this typology can be, the concept of a 'Church' does not require the WRP. Thirdly, the hermeneutic of suspicion regarding the self-defining element of world religions leads to an unmasking of historical and contemporary religious expansion, (neo)-colonial appropriations and hegemony over the discourse of religion itself.

In practice: locations

Examining the locations of religion also provides an inroad and challenge to the WRP at a higher level of undergraduate study. A series of seminar sessions examining contemporary religious contexts and practices provides an opportunity to reconsider some important concepts in the study of religions and to challenge the universalizing tendency of the WRP. Locations are defined for students as both the 'materiality of place' and 'social contexts'. Students are asked to discuss and identify the locations of the 'sacred' in contemporary 'secular' cultures. Two responses are common to this question of location: first, everywhere, or anywhere humans are to be found (in societies and cultures); second, specific places, constructed and deemed 'sacred' by religious traditions – both are points to be developed in the subsequent discussion (below). Students are then provided with two short readings, from *Black Elk Speaks* (1932) and *Dover Beach* (1867).

A useful illustration of this dual perception of universality (everywhere and in specific religiously nominated places) is exemplified in the first reading taken from John G. Neihardt's *Black Elk Speaks*. Black Elk is describing his mystic vision:

> I looked ahead and saw the mountains there with rocks and forests on them and from the mountains flashed all colours upward to the heavens. Then I was standing on the highest mountain of them all, and round about beneath me was the whole hoop of the world. And while I stood there I saw more than I can tell and I understood more than I saw; for I was seeing in a sacred manner the shape of all things in the spirit, and the shape of all things as they must live together like one being.
>
> *(1932, 42–3)*

Neihardt adds a key footnote to this section, that while Black Elk stated he was on Harney Peak in the Black Hills of Dakota he added, 'But anywhere is the center of the world' (1932, 42–3). This perennialist notion of essential religious unity is usefully exemplified by essentialist scholars such as Mircea Eliade, whose concept of *hierophany* suggests that any place can be the location of the sacred. It is a theme which also underpins the WRP – that there are entities, world religions, which have the same essential identity, regardless of place or time.

Despite the many valid critiques of Eliade's universalizing tendencies, the universal perception of the place of the sacred is a common trope for both religious insiders and in common discourse about the WRP, which assumes that transportation, or diaspora, may affect borderland structures and expressions, but does not affect the essential criteria of the WRP. The perennial perspective implied by the notion of 'world religions' is usefully challenged by the formations and locations of contemporary 'alternative spiritualities'. There has been a shift in focus for many in alternative spiritualities from the other-worldly transcendental to this-worldly self-transformation. As Peter Berger has suggested – contra his own significant model of 'the sacred canopy' (1990 [1967]) – 'the other world, which religion located in a transcendental reality, is now introjected within human consciousness itself' (cited in Heelas 2008, 237). Alongside this 'inward turn', there has been a movement away from the salvific emphasis of some traditional religions to a this-worldly internal focus on transformation (see Chen 2008). Moreover, there has also been a shift from religious practice in religious buildings to more diversified locations, including virtual- and social media-based locations.

In studies of religions, those indicators that serve to maintain the WRP – events such as pilgrimages, calendric religious observances, festivals and holy days, and places such as shrines, temples, buildings, edifices and sites – indicate the regular practical observance of religious ideology in the 'traditional' world religions. Yet much of the phenomena of religious practice and expression is hidden, a dark matter outside the construction of the WRP, comprising informal networks, diffuse, non-localized communities and dissipating structures.

Students are asked to consider how religion and secularity stand in relation to each other in contemporary culture. Some background reading and discussion about secularism, secularity and secularization is required. Students are then presented with the second text. When Matthew Arnold wrote about the tidal withdrawal of the 'sea of faith' in *Dover Beach* in 1867, he was reflecting a social and intellectual *Zeitgeist* of fear about the declining role of religion:

The Sea of Faith

Was once, too, at the full, and round earth's shore

Lay like the folds of a bright girdle furl'd.

But now I only hear

Its melancholy, long, withdrawing roar,

Retreating, to the breath

Of the night-wind, down the vast edges drear

And naked shingles of the world.

(From Dover Beach*)*

A century later secularization theory was in its heyday, with Bryan Wilson's strident claims about the steamroller of secularization in his publication *Religion in Secular Society* (1966). Yet even then, there were challenges by other sociologists of religion on the meaning and significance of secularizing processes (see, for example, Fox 2005). Equally there were a range of new formations, or new theories about religious formations, that suggested differentiated religious expression in secular society. Secularization itself, it should be recognized, has been a universal category in sociology of religion, now effectively differentiated in many ways according to local, social, historical and cultural contexts. It is in these contexts of place within secular culture that the growth of communities of alternative religiosity is a significant indicator of change in the practices of religious adherents and the locations of their practice.

Students are asked to consider how religious communities function, how they establish traditions, how they are inter-linked and in what ways they create order. Notions of hierarchy, traditions, law and power are evident in early discussions of the structure of communities within religions. This is one aspect of the prevailing model of the WRP. But many non-traditional, historical and contemporary communities do not conform to the model. The notion of 'diffuse communities' is a significant concept in understanding the informal networks of new formations of religion such as those on social media, and new and alternative spiritualities. These religious 'communities' are often fragmented non-localized networks. The network connections of diffuse communities are not as strong or easily identifiable as formal and geographically specific communities. Relationships in these diffuse communities, between individuals, organizations, and even systems of belief, are not clearly identifiable as nomothetic 'facts' or rules. The relationships of the diffuse communities of alternative spiritualities are subject to flux, development and change; they appear to be structurally weak. The relationships of formal systems and communities of the WRP are more static and fixed; they appear to be strong. One might analogize that this theory of the difference between the structured, established communities evident within the WRP and diffuse communities is similar to the physicists' search for a unified field theory — where once the distinction between 'weak forces' and 'strong forces' led scientists to prioritize strong forces and overlook the highly significant weak energetic forces.

In comparison to the bold existence of world religions, these diffuse communities may seem to be fading communities. But the paradigm of thought for this perspective is entropic. That is to say, communities are considered to be in dissolution and the diffuse communities of the new and alternative spiritualities merely exemplify this process of dissolution. Theorists of postmodernity, who rely on the concepts of 'fracture', 'fragmentation' and 'dissolution', function in an entropic world view which, ironically, is a feature of the paradigm of old positivist science. However, an alternative scientific paradigm is available in Ilya Prigogine's notion of 'dissipative structures' (1997). In essence, Prigogine's argument, which was applied to chemical processes (and for which he won the Nobel Prize in 1977), explains the movement from simple to higher order structures. Certain structures are 'closed' systems, where there is no internal transformation. Other structures, such as living beings and cultural systems, Prigogine has noted, contain continually transforming energy. This energy and the complexity of these structures lead to instability, but instead of collapse and entropy, the systems move into a higher order. These systems are 'dissipative structures'. The diffuse communities of the alternative spiritualities can then be seen as potentially indicative of such a shift to a higher order, or we may simply say, non-hierarchically, *different* order structures of community.

Conclusion: charging at windmills

We may take our proverbial horses to water, but they may not drink. When Wilfred Cantwell Smith suggested in 1962 that the word 'religion' be discarded in favour of 'tradition', his reasoning was very sound. But, over half a century later, the word resonates with as much vigour as it ever has. Might it be that challengers of the WRP are Quixotically tilting at quintains; moreover, which spin in eternal return? Insiders of the major, and even minor, religions have vested interests in identifying their tradition as a 'world religion', while the shorthand 'world religion' in common discourse seems to point to a recognizable thing. It may be that, akin to Prigogine's dissipative structures, the paradigm and the term world religion are adapting to a new theoretical environment that challenges the old model. 'The WRP is dead, long live the WRP!' We may further deduce that use is meaning or the Lewis Carroll Humpty Dumpty principle – "'When *I* use a word," Humpty Dumpty said, in rather a scornful tone, "it means just what I choose it to mean – neither more nor less"' (Carroll 1871, Chapter VI). The WRP is a model that can be stripped of its pejorative historical elements, its usage limited to shorthand for major traditions and religions with global spread. But to do this requires a sophisticated and complex understanding of the historical functions of the WRP. What appeared clear and concrete is in fact muddy and contested. As Jeppe Jensen has expressed, 'Even the seemingly simple class of "world religions" has turned out to be a matter of ambiguity and religious apologetics' (2014, 50). It is indeed a tricky time to be a student.

Notes

1 Examples of such coloured maps, which are defined by most adherents in each region, can be found in Johnson and Ross (2009, 6–7), Esposito, Fasching and Lewis (2009, xvi–xvii and 4), and Ellwood and McGraw (2009, 6–7).
2 See Tremlett in this volume.
3 McCutcheon is decidedly less mealy-mouthed in his description of taxonomic schemes in the study of religions as a 'dog's breakfast' (2003, 83–97).
4 For a fuller discussion of these transforming modes of pedagogic practice in the study of religions see Corrywright (2013).

References

Arnold, Matthew. 1867. *Dover Beach.* http://www.victorianweb.org/authors/arnold/writings/doverbeach.html (accessed 1. 04. 2014).
Barnett, Ronald. 2011. "Learning about Learning: A Conundrum and a Possible Resolution." *London Review of Education* 9(1): 5–13.
Berger, Peter. 1990 [1967]. *The Sacred Canopy: Elements of a Sociological Theory of Religion.* London: Anchor Books.
Bligh, Donald. 1971. *What's the Use of Lectures?* Exeter: D. A. & B. Bligh.
Carroll, Lewis. 1871. "*Through the Looking Glass* and *What Alice Found There.*" http://www.gutenberg.org/files/12/12-h/12-h.htm (accessed 1. 04. 2014). Project Gutenberg: Chapter VI.
Chen, Shu-Chuan. 2008. *Contemporary New Age Transformation in Taiwan: A Sociological Study of a New Religious Movement.* Lampeter: Edwin Mellen Press.
Corrywright, Dominic. 2013. "Landscape of Learning and Teaching in Religion and Theology: Perspectives and Mechanisms for Complex Learning, Programme Health and Pedagogical Well-being." *Diskus* 14: 1–20.
Corrywright, Dominic and Peggy Morgan. 2006. *Get Set for Religious Studies.* Edinburgh: Edinburgh University Press.
Ellwood, Robert S. and Barbara A. McGraw. 2009. *Many People, Many Faiths: Women and Men in the World Religions.* 9th ed. New Jersey: Pearson Education Inc.

Esposito, John L., Darrell J. Fasching and Todd Lewis. 2009. *World Religions Today*. 3rd ed. Oxford: Oxford University Press.

Foucault, Michel. 2005 [1974]. *The Order of Things: An Archaeology of the Human Sciences*. eBook. London: Routledge.

Fox, Judith. 2005. "Secularization." In *The Routledge Companion to the Study of Religion*, edited by John R. Hinnells, 291–305. London: Routledge.

Geertz, Clifford. 1973. "Thick Description: Toward an Interpretive Theory of Culture." In *The Interpretation of Cultures: Selected Essays*. London: Fontana Press.

Gibbs, Graham. 2013. "Lectures Don't Work, but we Keep Using them." *Times Higher Education Supplement*. 21 November. http://www.timeshighereducation.co.uk/news/lectures-dont-work-but-we-keep-using-them/2009141.article (accessed 27.03.2014).

Heelas, Paul. 2008. *Spiritualities of Life*. Oxford: Blackwell.

Illich, Ivan D. 1971. *Deschooling Society*. New York: Harper and Row.

Illich, Ivan D. 1973a. "The Futility of Schooling." In *Celebration of Awareness: A Call for Institutional Revolution*, 89–101. London: Penguin.

Illich, Ivan D. 1973b. "School: The Sacred Cow." *Celebration of Awareness: A Call for Institutional Revolution*, 103–114. London: Penguin.

Jensen, Jeppe. 2014. *What Is Religion?* Durham: Acumen.

Johnson, Todd M. and Brian J. Grim. 2013. *The World's Religions in Figures*. Malden, MA: Wiley-Blackwell.

Johnson, Todd M. and Kenneth R. Ross. 2009. *Atlas of Global Christianity*. Edinburgh: Edinburgh University Press.

Juschka, Darlene. 2012. "Fixed Geomorphologies and the Shifting Sands of Time." In *Failure and Nerve in the Academic Study of Religion: Essays in Honour of Donald Wiebe*, edited by William E. Arnal, Willi Braun and Russell T. McCutcheon, 50–61. Sheffield: Equinox Publishing Limited.

Kuhn, Thomas. S. 1970 [1962]. *The Structure of Scientific Revolutions*. 2nd ed. Chicago: University of Chicago Press.

Martin, Craig. 2012. *A Critical Introduction to the Study of Religion*. Sheffield: Equinox Publishing Limited.

Masuzawa, Tomoko. 2005a. *The Invention of World Religions; or, How European Universalism Was Preserved in the Language of Pluralism*. Chicago: University of Chicago Press.

Masuzawa, Tomoko. 2005b. "World Religions." In *Encyclopedia of Religion*, edited by Lindsay Jones, 9800–9804. 2nd ed. Vol. 14. Detroit: Macmillan Reference USA, Gale Virtual Reference Library. Web. (accessed 27 March 2014).

McLuhan, Marshall and Quentin Fiore 1996 [1967]. *The Medium Is the Massage*. London: Penguin.

McCutcheon, Russell. 2003. *The Discipline of Religion: Structure, Meaning, Rhetoric*. London: Routledge.

McCutcheon, Russell. 2007. *Studying Religion: An Introduction*. London: Equinox Publishing Limited.

McCutcheon, Russell. 2012. "Everything Old Is New Again." In *Failure and Nerve in the Academic Study of Religion: Essays in Honour of Donald Wiebe*, edited by William E. Arnal, Willi Braun and Russell T. McCutcheon, 78–94. Sheffield: Equinox Publishing Limited.

Neihardt, John G. 1979 [1932]. *Black Elk Speaks*. London: University of Nebraska Press.

Owen, Suzanne. 2011. "The World Religions Paradigm: Time for a Change." *Arts and Humanities in Higher Education* 10(3): 253–268.

Prigogine, Ilya. 1997. *The End of Certainty: Time, Chaos, and the New Laws of Nature*, in collaboration with Elizabeth Stengers. London: The Free Press.

Saussure, Ferdinand de. 1974 [1916]. *Course in General Linguistics*. Trans. Wade Baskin. London: Fontana/Collins.

Segal, Robert. 2007. "The Invention of World Religions: Or How European Universalism was Preserved in the Language of Pluralism." *Journal of Religion* 87(1): 146–148.

Smart, Ninian. 1998. *Dimensions of the Sacred: An Anatomy of the World's Beliefs*. Berkeley, CA: University of California Press.

Smart, Ninian. 1999. *Worldviews: Crosscultural Explorations of Human Beliefs*. New York: Scribner.

Smith, Jonathan Z. 1978. *Map Is not Territory: Studies in the History of Religion*. Leiden: Brill.

Smith, Laura, Hugh Muir, Richard Stone and Robin Richardson. 2004. *Islamophobia: Issues, Challenges and Action: A Report. Runnymede Trust. Commission on British Muslims and Islamophobia*. Stoke on Trent: Trentham Books.

Smith, Wilfred Cantwell. 1991 [1962]. *The Meaning and End of Religion*. Minneapolis: Fortress Press.

Wilson, Bryan. 1966. *Religion in Secular Society*. London: Penguin Books.

13

AFTERWORD

On utility and limits

Russell T. McCutcheon

> Indeed, I've often argued when teaching in the social science Core that, if I could
> only have the first week of Chemistry 101, my job would be infinitely easier because
> at least we would have raised the possibility that one wears eyeglasses when one
> gazes at these naked facts.
>
> *(Smith 2007, 76)*

In Prague in 2006, the members of the International Astronomical Union (IAU)
voted, as part of their 26th General Assembly, on two resolutions that, unlike the
work accomplished at most scholarly conferences, made the headlines.[1] The first
was *Resolution 5A: Definition of 'Planet'*. They agreed, by a resounding majority (so
much so that the votes didn't even need to be counted) that a planet is an object
that (1) orbits the sun, (2) has enough mass so that its own gravity can ensure that it
maintains what they call 'hydrostatic equilibrium' (in layman's terms, it stays
round), (3) has cleared the path of its own orbit of smaller orbiting bodies, and
(4) is not itself a satellite of another planet (ruling out our moon, for example, from
being a planet). There were also some other parts of this resolution, such as creating
the new category of 'dwarf planet' – a celestial body that meets all the criteria of a
planet but one: it has not sufficiently cleared its orbit of neighbours. As mentioned
above, the astronomers who comprise this international group voted on a second
noteworthy resolution that year, this one passing with 237 votes for and 157 votes
against (with 17 abstentions). Called *Resolution 6A: Definition of Pluto-Class Objects*,
it dealt explicitly with what made this all news to people like you and I: in light of
the other resolution, Pluto – that merely 1,400 mile wide planet with several
moons of its own, finally discovered in 1930 after being long predicted to exist
(prior to its discovery it was just called, in suitably sci-fi terms, Planet X), and
whose orbit takes it to the furthest edge of our solar system – *was not a planet*. And
just like that, we no longer had nine planets but, instead, eight so-called 'classical

planets', a variety of newly minted 'dwarf planets',[2] along with everything else floating around out there in our local night sky, i.e. what they named 'small solar system bodies'.

What may be even more curious to those who are troubled to find that the so-called facts of science are open to debate and voting is that about 11,000 members of the IAU[3] were not present for the 237 to 157 vote that prompted us not only to recalibrate how we understand the night sky but also which forced publishers to issue new editions of their science textbook. How would those absent astronomers have cast their ballot if they had attended the conference or stayed for the business meeting (lending new meaning to the old saying that the world is run by those who go to the meetings)? Might Pluto still be a planet? But there are other things that could attract our attention about this recent episode in cosmic classification; for, as far as I can tell, no one seems to be able to agree on what counts as a planet's 'neighbourhood' let alone how free of debris it must be in order to be judged sufficiently cleared (how small does something have to be to count as debris worth noticing and thus tracking?). After all, not only does every so-called shooting star that briefly streaks across the night sky signify an invader into our neighbourhood (that it's 'shooting' means we've cleared it out of our way, I guess) – something that got a little too close to us for its own good (come to think of it, why does the path even have to be cleared for it to count as a planet?) – but, as mentioned above, there are plenty of objects that we call moons (another question: how big does something have to be before we stop calling it 'debris'?) cluttering up the orbits of lots of planets – we have one, of course, whose reflection of the sun lights up our night sky, but Jupiter has 67 varying sized objects orbiting it that we call not debris (to be cleared) but moons (to be studied); in fact, it even had a monolith orbiting it in the film version of Arthur C. Clarke's *2001 A Space Odyssey*. And, come to think of it, Saturn is literally ringed with what we estimate to be billions of objects, thought to range from just a centimetre to ten metres in size, but that hardly counts as an unclear orbit for what, I guess, we somehow are already certain to be obviously or self-evidently a planet ....

Not unlike the certain knowledge we once had, for almost a hundred years, that Pluto was not only one of the ancient Greek names for the god of the underworld (named in early texts as Zeus's brother Hades) but also the name of a planet – a rather tiny, extremely distant planet but, yes, a planet all the same.

As an aside: did you know that Ceres – orbiting in what we now know as the asteroid belt between Mars and Jupiter and which was first seen in 1801 by the Italian astronomer and Roman Catholic priest, Giuseppe Piazzi (1746–1826) – was originally classed as a planet, but, by the mid-nineteenth century, was demoted to an asteroid (a term for 'star-like' objects, coined around 1802)? And did you know that the larger ones were once called planetoids (what we now know as dwarf planets)? Did you also know that for much of human history, stretching from antiquity to the European Middle Ages, the sun was, yes, also understood to be a planet? (Of course Nicolaus Copernicus's [d. 1543] critique of the so-called geocentric, or Ptolemaic, view of the universe, with the earth presumed to be its centre, put an end to that.) And did you know that, as our star-gazing methods have become increasingly refined and sophisticated, we keep finding more and more stuff out there, some of it an awful lot like what we already knew to exist (like Eris, for instance, the roughly Pluto-sized object first spotted in 2005 and which, as you may be able to predict, played a role in prompting scientists to recalibrate their definitions, for if Pluto is a planet, then why not Eris …?). And so, with each technological advance, we are put in the position of either continually expanding the number of planets whose names, many poached from ancient Greek and Roman gods, we teach school children or, instead of seeing this list as open-ended, seeing it as a delimited family, which then requires the creation of whole new, and more easily expanded, subtypes (e.g. asteroids, dwarf planets, trans-Neptunian objects) into which we can place the miscellany of those newly found objects that, in our estimation, fail to match up to our planetary prototypes.

In 2006, the members of the IAU took the latter path, thereby declaring the canon of planets to be closed.

And voilà, headlines about Pluto that once read, 'Scientists spy planet hunted for 25 years: astronomers believe it's big and cold' (*Chicago Daily Tribune*, March 14, 1930) were replaced by signs that read 'Size doesn't matter' at a protest on September 1, 2006 (taking place at New Mexico State University, at which colleagues of the late Clyde Tombaugh [1906–1997], who is credited with discovering Pluto, contested the IAU's vote from just a week before); and now, Pluto is no longer a planet – at least for some. For others, such as those of us who grew up knowing – that's right, not believing or thinking or assuming, but *knowing* – that there were nine planets, we'll always have a soft spot for that careful little object, so far out there in space, that crosses Neptune's path but never collides with it.

The moral of the story?

Votes. Assumptions. Criteria. Judgements. Social interests. And, yes, technological advances. Contrary to how we normally think of science, as dealing with the objective, cold hard facts of the case, all of these contingent, historical factors make possible our ability to devise and authorize a system, a structure, that helps us to make sense of the world, such as, in this one case, describing and thereby under-standing those twinkling things in the night sky – and, as a result, understand something about our own place in a cosmic pecking order. But who would have thought that such certain knowledge about the heavens, let alone who we are in relation to it, would hinge on a vote?[4] For now you don't have to be a conspiracy theorist speculating on secret sound stages and actors dressed in astronaut suits to come to hear the seemingly simple, straightforward statement 'We landed on the moon' as being far more than just an idle description of an obvious or disinterested fact. After all, should we propose another resolution and hold another vote, then 1969 might have marked not a 'moon landing' but, rather, our inaugural adventure in interplanetary travel, making hopes to get to Mars in the near future somewhat redundant.

But now for the question that some, or all, readers are probably asking themselves: what has all this got to do with world religions?

Perhaps some of the preceding chapters have already made all too apparent just what the relevance is: like our definition of 'planet', the 'world religions' category performs a service, as our editors inform us, for it is part of our modern conceptual grid, a pair of those eyeglasses that Smith mentions in the epigraph we opened with, that we use not just to make sense of *the* world but, more specifically, *our* world – doing so in a very particular and always self-beneficial manner. It strikes me that what this book has been about is not religion and certainly not about how best to teach a World Religions course but, using this thoroughly modern notion of world religions as its starting point, it seems to me that its chapters have been a series of studies on how a particular group of people (those people being *us*) have developed a way of identifying and organizing not the heavens but their world (or, more specifically, arranging the people in it, the ones who are said to 'have a religion' or 'to be religious'), so as to understand themselves in light of the relations they could establish with others (for these two are interconnected, of course – who I am, and who I'm like, is just code for who I'm not and from whom I differ, and vice versa). They've done this by placing select actions, associations, symbols and claims (and in that placement that groups things together *as* religious or not, we have all the evidence that we need for seeing the world as comprising the choices and distinctions that have been made by invested social actors) into highly controlled, structured relations with each other, relations of similarity and difference, much as our predecessors once decided that Pluto, though small and distant, was sufficiently like Mercury and our own home here on the earth to be classed a member of the family of planets – a judgement which, as we've seen, can be changed, all depending on who shows up to vote, and which can also prompt a reaction, such as a series of online petitions, inviting us to wonder when it might be returned to the planetary ranks. After all (with an even more recent classificatory headline in mind), despite paleontologists deciding in the very early twentieth century that the well-known *Brontosaurus* (you know, the one Fred Flintstone slides down when the whistle [correction, bird] blows to end the work day at the quarry?) was, in fact, not a distinct genus at all, but a mistakenly classified species of *Apatosaurus*, some[5] now argue that what scholars have ever since been calling *Apatosaurus excelsus* really ought to just be renamed *Brontosaurus* once again.

The bones haven't changed, of course, but, like lens-grinding advances that presented to our ancestors' senses more and more celestial objects in need of names as well as a place not in the universe but in *their* representations and schemes, the way we identify, study and then classify them has changed. This point was made so nicely not only by Ramey's contribution but also in Baldrick-Morrone, Graziano and Stoddard's co-written chapter, focused as both are on what the latter authors term 'the arbitrary and contested nature of representation itself'; this is also nicely evident in the case of those newly named dwarf planets: classification is therefore all about us, the classifiers ('classification is a political act!' as students in our department have lately come to phrase it), and our continually changing practical situations (our interests, priorities and technologies). So, contrary to common sense, it is not driven by the need to fit or account for the so-called stable or obvious facts on the ground (or in the sky), which makes it all the more interesting that our changing definitions for what counts as a planet seem, in an unplanned way, to have much to do with where we got that word 'planet' in the first place: from ancient Greek, meaning 'to wander'.[6] For those so-called concrete, objective facts – i.e. what's worth paying attention to and what can just be overlooked altogether – turn out to be the products of our own meandering, contingent (read: historical) definitions and thus situations. So while the objects we name may themselves wander, our criteria for what counts as something worth watching and tracking wander as well.

But, come to think of it, this seemingly self-evident opposition between facts and lenses, between things and our possibly skewed viewpoint of them – the old distinction of subject and object – is part of the problem we have to reconsider if we take classification (whether applied to stars or people) seriously as an inevitable cognitive and political act. Take Pluto, for example, yet again; just as was the case with, as we say, 'discovering' Neptune, we only knew to go looking for Planet X because of a hypothesis we had concerning our observations of other planets (in the case of finding Neptune it was observations, from the early nineteenth century, of what seemed to be deviations of Uranus's orbit and in the case of what eventually was named Pluto it was subsequent observations of Neptune's orbit failing to conform to our predictions of what it ought to be doing out there in the dark). Lacking those observations (and the technological means to make them) and without a systematically arranged set of assumptions, aka a theory, of how objects of mass move and, more importantly, affect each other's movements, no one would have gone looking for Planet X – like the tree falling in the forest with no one around to witness its demise, it didn't exist for us and was therefore not an item of discourse. It only became something worth looking *for* (long before something worth looking *at*) once we devised a way to imagine it, making the it, the object, of the observing subject the product of our own imaginations and thus our ability to distinguish (to return to another earlier example) what will now count as *this* ancient beast's petrified remains as opposed to those of *that* one; lacking the criteria, without the theories and assumptions, and thus in the absence of the curiosity we feel to resolve anomalies in how the world appears once we arrange it however we might, we just have piles of indistinguishable bones (making evident that no matter how closely we look at the so-called archaeological facts in the ground, we can't make sense of them without those *a priori* categories); but *with* the criteria, *with* the attempt to explain why things don't fit together as *we* think they should, we suddenly again have the *Brontosaurus* in our museums and textbooks and we are compelled to search for whatever object of mass *might* be out there causing what we see as that unexplained wobble in Neptune's orbit. But until the moment when we can imagine their existence (long before ever even having a name for them, let alone seeing them) and thereby obtain a point of purchase that allows us to draw an imagined boundary or establish a fictive relationship, the objects that we only later come to take for granted – so much so that we end up anachronistically assuming that they were there all along, like the Americas prior to Europeans setting sail west, as if they were just patiently waiting to be discovered by those early explorers – were not part of our system of knowledge, were therefore not an 'it' that could be named or could *attract* our attention (and there we see the subject/object distinction reintroduced, as if the subject's disinterested gaze is irresistibly drawn to objects due to their own gravitational pull and not, instead, due to *our* assumptions, *our* need to resolve what *we* see as anomaly, and *our* technological innovations).

So it's not so much about the way we look at the world, about a viewpoint that we happen to have that can be critiqued in light of how it does or does not fairly represent the world as it really is, but, rather, about the way we create the impression of a world worth looking at. At least considering that we wear eyeglasses when looking at the naked facts is, as the epigraph suggests, an important first step, but pressing this considerably further (as Smith's use of 'at least' suggests he was game to see happen) means that we need to take seriously that without our prescription lenses there's nothing to see. And when that *we* who are actively constituting our world is expanded to include the imaginative acts of the very people we're studying – for, unlike celestial bodies that remain silent when we decide what they are or are not, the human bodies that we, as scholars, name and group together or distinguish from one another, end up talking back to us and have interests, investments and goals of their own, and thus are engaged in their own strategic groupings and identifyings – it makes our effort to say who is or is not a Hindu or a Jew, and which tales are myths and which are history, so much more complex than the astronomical analogy with which I've set this afterword's table.

But again, I should ask: what has all this got to do with world religions?

The same question is probably posed by my students when, in my own intro-ductory course on the study of religion, we spend a class discussing a short, but nonetheless significant, 1893 US Supreme Court judgment on whether a tomato is a fruit or a vegetable,[7] sooner or later also citing D. G. Burnett's fascinating book, *Trying Leviathan* (2007), on an 1818 New York state federal course case on whether a whale is a fish or a mammal. That we classify to establish and manage relation-ships and identities might be obvious but, as the editors note in their introduction, that issues of power and rank are woven into the very fabric of the classificatory act may not be so evident – not, that is, until, as a newly arrived visitor, you stand before a sign in the customs area of any international airport that distinguishes citizens from aliens. Or until we learn that under the US Tariff Act of 1883 all imported vegetables were taxed while imported fruits were not. (Is not the tomato a fruit, botanically speaking? Could you leverage a return of the duty you paid on the tomatoes that you brought in from the West Indies by means of an argument anchored in botany rather than in their popular use?) Or perhaps once we under-stand that there might be an incentive to try to recoup the tax paid on the whale oil your early nineteenth-century ships brought to port once we question whether the import tax on fish oil ought to apply to those sea creatures that, at least in

Europe two centuries ago, were being dissected systematically for the first time, to reveal just how unfish-like they were on the inside. (There's no tax on importing mammal oil, after all.) That much of my course is a subtle argument to treat naming something *as* religion, seeing something *as* a world religion, as no more or less mundane a moment, and thus no less intertwined with practical issues of power and identification, as these other examples might escape some students, but I'll guess not many; for once we address issues of tomatoes and whales (and that's where we learn of the judge's interest in a stipulative definition, by the way, for he wasn't concerned with what tomatoes *really were* but, instead, what they would be for purposes of trade and tariff) we soon turn our attention to the US's Internal Revenue Service's ongoing efforts to define what counts as a church – a specific type of non-profit organization, for purposes of taxation.[8] And not long after that we end up considering something like the host of news articles that, depending on what is going on in the world, appear almost daily, on whether this or that 'radical' group is legitimately Muslim or not. In fact, keeping in mind the variety of classificatory moments and boundary calls that, collectively, constitute our field (e.g. at what point does Buddhism become something other than Hinduism and if Jesus was actually a Jew then what do we make of Christian origins?), I'd go so far as saying that the story of Pluto is directly relevant to any course on world religions since such a course is actually a study in classificatory ingenuity and thus a class on the utility – or, dare I say, lack of utility – of what was originally a late nineteenth-century way of dividing up the world and identifying oneself within it (e.g. 'they are/are not like us because …'). That the global divisions we know as modern nation-states date from around the same time should make clear that just because it is old doesn't make it old-fashioned or outdated, but if we see classification as an all-too-historical, and thus situated, human act, then we ought not only to be curious about the ramifications of cutting the cake this way rather than that (as was evident in those 237 votes for and 157 against at the IAU), but we should also ask whether any of these particular slices, as time-honoured as they may appear, suit our tastes today.

So why do we persist in thinking that a distinct part of human action is or is not religious? Why do we think the globe is organized in terms of large, international groupings – making them, perhaps, the first transnational corporations – called world religions? Why are they good to think with today?

After the previous chapters, followed by this afterword opening with a tale of planetary identities and then briefly touching not just on ambiguous dinosaurs but also on tomatoes (the fruit we use as a vegetable) and what we now confidently know to be seafaring mammals (despite all of our predecessors knowing whales to be fish), I'm hoping many readers have already started asking these questions for themselves, becoming interested in such things as whether our views on a category's shortcomings are linked to – as evidenced in Tremlett's critique of Mircea Eliade's 'extremely narrow notion of religion' – the number of things able to gain admission to the grouping (e.g. do we criticize a textbook for not having a chapter on primitive religion, or what we later reclassed as tribal religions, and what was eventually reformulated as the now more acceptable primal or small scale or what some may now even term indigenous religions?). Or, instead, can we entertain being curious not about how we either encourage or police entrance to the club, thus quibbling over what's worth calling or being treated as a world religion, but, instead, shift the ground entirely and study why such a 'members only' club exists in the first place? Such a shift would have us following Craig Martin in examining 'how people use their cultural inheritance to advance a social agenda', studying whose interests are served by continually tinkering with the admission policies (to borrow some of the words of our volume's editors). For while private golf clubs across the US have increasingly debated whether to admit members who were different from their, in most cases, exclusively white male founders and present owners, what exactly has been accomplished by opening membership to more diverse groups? Sure, the board of directors may have been expanded, which is likely to be a noble goal to many, but it is not difficult to imagine someone whose interests were, say, economic rather than gendered or racial, and thus a person who would see the very existence of class-based private associations as the curious item worth studying, rather than investing our energy in advocating for expanding the membership to other no less affluent groups.

A case in point: will the recent two-volume *Norton Anthology of World Religions* (Miles 2014) attract debate on its editor's possibly controversial choice to include *only* six entries – Hinduism, Buddhism, Daoism, Judaism, Christianity, Islam – or will the controversy be that in the year 2015 a major publisher has invested its time and resources in producing a classroom anthology that reauthorizes this conceptual holdover from the height of the colonial era?

What's noteworthy to me about the preceding chapters is that I could imagine some of their authors being divided over which of the two preceding options to pursue; for while some are interested in the implications of even thinking that there are such coherent and distinct things as world religions, let alone religion itself, others seem more concerned with problematizing this now commonplace category by critiquing the level of inclusion/exclusion evident in its dominant uses (i.e. for some, the problem with the term 'world religions' is that we define it too narrowly). It's as if members of the latter grouping were voting on whether Pluto was or was not a planet, debating the limits of the family and thereby assuming that there just are, or ought to be, such things as planets and that our job, as scholars, is to arrive at the definitive list, while those in the former group strike me as akin to those 17 abstentions in that astronomical exercise in democracy, a move that could be understood as registering one's dissent from assuming that some cognitive tool, such as 'world religions', ought to be used to create the impression of cross-cultural unity and shared identity among otherwise diverse people. And so, much like that 2006 IAU meeting, where the disagreements of the pros and cons were repre- sented alongside those exempting themselves from having to make the choice, I see in this very volume evidence of the same debates and stances – with some chapters fine-tuning the World Religions Paradigm (WRP) by offering better ways to study the real religion of people's lives or of the past, while others are trying to figure out ways to make the designation itself their object of study – such as Suzanne Owen's interest in examining not whether something is sacred but, instead, how discrete groups work to make things seem sacred.

Finding this distinction in one volume is not to be lamented, however; rather, it suggests to me that our field is at a rather interesting moment in its history; for it is not difficult to imagine the creation of such a book being tackled just twenty years ago, which would probably have produced a set of essays in which these abstentions – such as Teemu Taira's interest in a discursive analysis of the very act of using the world religions category, however defined and managed – would not have been represented at all since they were hardly heard in the academy of that day. (Did we even call something in our field 'discursive analysis' back then?) Sure, some could cite what James Cox and Dominic Corrywright describe as Wilfred Cantwell Smith's either ground breaking or very sound reasoning, from as far back as the early 1960s, when Smith critiqued the category religion by first historicizing the word itself. But I don't think it takes too close a reading of Cantwell Smith's work to understand that his critique was concerned with the inadequacy of the word to convey the deeper significance of what he speculated to be the prior, inner, personal, and thus immaterial no-thing called *faith*, which he then distinguished, in typically idealist fashion, from the observable *traditions* that those of us relying on nothing but our five ordinary senses have no choice but to study – don't think you're studying religion's source and true meaning just because you've described a ritual, recited a myth, or understood a set of ecclesiastical rules, he might as well have said, for (in a typically phenomenological manner) the timeless essence (*the faith of men* [sic], as he often called it) is not to be conflated with its various historical and thus tangible manifestations. And so we arrive at a moment when (in a move reminiscent of Friedrich Schleiermacher's [d. 1834] much earlier rhetorical distinctions) original and immaterial faith was strategically differentiated from subsequent tradition, yet another handy division of labour (much like subject/object) that lives on to this day, being but one variation on the now popular 'I'm spiritual, not religious' stance that some now use to authenticate, and thereby authorize, themselves. (That there's nothing novel or unique about this bold attempt to individuate is the great irony, of course; in fact, this contradiction is among the few things that make such claims interesting to study.)

It is this very ability to see an author, such as Cantwell Smith, as being involved in authorizing a position, a situation, perhaps even a speaker, by how he framed, divided, ranked, and thereby talked about the world, rather than reading him as talking dispassionately, descriptively, about some obviously existing and thus real sentiments and affectations in the world, which marks what is new in our field – and I find it encouraging that some of the preceding chapters entertain this as an approach worth adopting.

But, like all orbits, I must now return to the opening to this afterword, for Pluto and Neptune have even more relevance for the topic of this volume: economic advantages and technological advances led not only to discovering more and more objects in the sky (prompting us to redefine 'planet' as a regulatory mechanism that governs the economy of newly found objects) but such advantages and advances also made possible sailing ships with ever-increasing range and thus more and more ambitious expeditions ensued, funded by private and public wealth's search for even more wealth, setting off for the known world's periphery from a variety of centres of power and knowledge across Europe. This was an ambitious exercise of the people who, for a few centuries, had already quite successfully been refining that ancient Latin word *religio* for purposes that were hardly religious (at least as we today define and use that term). For instance, as noted in the introduction and also by Owen, the terms sacred and secular have a long history, of course, but, contrary to how many now tell this story, we'd be in error to assume that all along they were specifically *religious* concepts, just as we today use them (even the Latin antecedents of the modern word 'religion' aren't religious); instead, we might avoid self-serving anachronism in our history writing by assuming that they simply functioned as a conceptual grid to distinguish the domains and thus duties of church officials (who should themselves be understood not as specifically religious people, working in a specifically religious institution, but, rather, as officials of one among many social institutions in, say, the medieval European world): some worked within 'the world' or 'among their generation' (from the Latin *secularis*), as did a parish priest; others were 'set apart' from the world and carried out duties inside the walls of the institution itself, say, living and working within a convent or a monastery (people once referred to a monk as 'a religious'). Thus, while these terms are deeply embedded in our discourse on religion today, we would be well advised to see them as once having simply named a practical division of labour within a specific institution. How they were then gradually resignified and spiritualized to mean a deeply personal, private affection that transcends time and space – a use that functions as a no less practical division of labour today – is then the interesting question.[9]

But keeping in mind those technological wonders that we once called sailing ships and celestial navigation, in the moments of contact that ensued ('contact' being a euphemism for all sorts of scenarios that unfolded once those ships came ashore all across the so-called New World or the Mystic East) the local and known was inevitably used (by all parties) as the model to assimilate information on the distant and the unknown – we today, in the European intellectual tradition, happen to have just inherited the results of one side's deliberations, of course, making our pre-occupation with religion an historical accident. And, like our necessarily wandering definition of planet, so too those early explorers', traders', soldiers' and missionaries' understandings of what was sufficiently like them also changed over time (e.g. the term 'Orient' keeps moving eastward, from once being used to name what we now call the Middle East to now designating the so-called Far East), all of which was prompted by increasingly bold journeys over land and water, repeated greetings, trade, conquest and yes, even subjugation and domination. So, as David Chidester told us some time ago (1996), we would be wise to consider not only our term 'religion' but also the later 'world religion' to have developed from out of this particular historical confluence, always keeping in mind the practical reasons for and effects of classification. This awareness might in turn prompt us to look anew at those late nineteenth-century scholars who first coined *Wereldgodsdiensten* in Dutch and *Weltreligionen* in German, both of which were in contradistinction from what they thought to be merely ethnic or national religions (which, for whatever reason, had failed to find what these scholars understood as worldwide converts beyond their own original kin groups), the ones who first identified just two members of the world religions family (read: world class) – Christianity and Buddhism (Masuzawa 2005, 108–9). But since then the category has spread worldwide while being repeatedly repurposed – as with all language, mind you – and, like the family of planets, the world religions kin group has steadily grown, regularly assimilating the newly familiar, and ending up so large today that any world religions map will now inform you, as if conveying neutrally and thus innocently descriptive information, that every human being on the globe can be plotted somewhere within this now universal taxonomy – in fact, even atheists are now regularly placed on such maps, perhaps because (thanks in part to Ninian Smart) some now see that thing we call a worldview as the genus of which religion is but one of several species. And so now, much like astronomers working out the details of dwarf plants vs. asteroids, many scholars of religion are working to make this classification scheme more precise and total ('If it names a deeply transhuman trait then shouldn't we expect to see it everywhere?'), so that it is truly able to encompass everything, past and present; for where there were once just two world religions as opposed to a host of local or national religions there are now lived religions and global religions, major or international religions as opposed to folk religions, elite versus popular, vernacular, material, and embodied religions and, of course, there are those the sociologists have recently grouped together as 'the Nones', who scholars of religion seem to feel compelled to study as a group, despite these people's adamant claims, via their answers to just a couple of questions on questionnaires, that they have no religious affiliation whatsoever.

And so we arrive at a moment when a taxonomy originally developed about 150 years ago, used to identify those who some Europeans once thought shared their own globalizing ambitions, in distinction from those who were merely local (and thus no threat?) – it was, after all, an us/them device – has become so successful in helping us to deal with what Jonathan Z. Smith once called the 'explosion of data' that attended the imperial exercise (Smith 1998, 275) that, like stargazers using their now self-evident grids, many of us can't imagine *not* talking about the world religions, however defined, as not just constituting coherent, transnational communities of people (e.g. the Taoists, the Zoroastrians, etc.) but also as naming deeply human, universal characteristics and timeless motivations shared by all social actors. A case in point: 'Muslim and Hindu riots turn deadly ...', began the *Daily Mail* headline on September 8, 2013, reporting on a conflict in the Indian state of Uttar Pradesh; we seem unable to make sense of the world, and thereby understand why people do whatever it is we see them doing, without these designations and the deep motivations we imagine them to signify – or, rather (and is this why the category continues to be used?), dropping them would mean that we'd have to entertain using alternative systems to make that sense. Because that might risk understanding human action as motivated by something other than timeless affinities and the stands we assume people take on existentially Big Questions, we more than likely prefer to group people in this old manner, as if knowing that the eighteen-year-old Tenzin Choezin is a *nun* and thus a *Buddhist* will provide newspaper readers with essential information as to why, in early February of 2012, they may have seen a news photo of her on fire in Aba Prefecture (also known as Ngawa) in the western Chinese province of Sichuan (a region that, historically and culturally, might also be termed Tibet). Knowing something instead about the complex relations between modern China and the nation we once called Tibet (or what, since 1965, has been renamed by the Chinese government as the Tibetan Autonomous Region), and thereby making sense of the graphic event by referencing historically specific and continually changing geo-political situations, would be likely to prompt us to talk about a very different set of relations and identities when confronting the shocking image of that burning woman. But, as I argued almost two decades ago with regard to how scholars write about what we generally name 'self-immolation' (McCutcheon 1997), for those unwilling, for whatever reason, to take issues of conflict and conquest into account in their studies, those who are unable to make the Copernican shift that, judging from some of the chapters in this collection, some colleagues now see to be a viable option in our field, there is something to be gained by continuing to understand human behaviour by devising a few epicycles[10] to help make an old scheme work, continually coining some new subspecies (such as how we got from heathens to primitives and eventually to indigenous religions), publishing lightly revised editions of decades-old textbooks, continuing to offer these courses to undergraduates, and thereby drawing upon the world religions model to make sense of the world and our place in it.

But my hope is that more of us in the academic study of religion can learn something from the arc of Pluto's rise and fall as a planet – if nothing else, at least to see that it is *we* who do the classifying, revealing such acts to be choices of agents whose situations are governed by wide structures and local interests. If so, then despite disciplinary divisions, the humanities and the so-called soft sciences might be understood to share much with the natural sciences and we may come to see scholars in all of these areas become equally invested in devising taxonomies to make sense of that part of the world that they find curious; that is to say, despite their sometimes overly confident claims about reality, none are studying obviously existing items and none are free of *a priori* assumptions, but, instead, as a group they are all implicated in fabricating the places where they carry out their own work. That few in our field seem to recognize this, instead seeing objectively existing Sikhs and Christians whose compelling doings seem to produce a gravitational field all their own, thereby demanding our careful description and comparison, turns out to be little different from the tendency in the hard sciences, from where so many of our World Religions enrollees come (at least in the US, where so many of our students first stumble across our field as an elective that satisfies a Core Curriculum breadth requirement). But if what we're teaching these diverse students in our World Religions courses is not just the names and dates that these students are probably focused on but, instead, we are subtly demonstrating to them how scholarship happens, how historically-situated people make sense of their settings by naming and distinguishing and ranking, then perhaps there's something to be gained by making reference to astronomy in one of our classes, making reference to botanic classification, or perhaps using a chemistry experiment in distillation, in which we boil away the water to see what remains, as a way to explain what we mean by reduction in the study of religion. For it seems to me that we ought to be teaching our students (especially in such broad, lower level surveys as a World Religions course) not just names and dates specific to our material but skills that are relevant across the disciplines, skills that are useful in unanticipated settings, skills such as how social actors make the worlds they happen to find themselves in – complete with twinkling lights in the sky and people making references to immaterial beings who govern their fates – sensible and thus habitable. And one of those skills is always being on the look out for the grids any group, including scholars themselves, impose and then authorize, those historically and culturally discrete systems of order that sanction interests but also produce anomalies when released into the wild of an unruly world. The WRP is one such imposed structure that, of course, has uses, but like anything with utility, it probably also has a limited shelf-life and thus an expiry date. Are our students aware of this or has the designation taken on such a life of its own that we, its makers, fail to recall that we find religions in the world only because we're the ones who have defined them in such a way that enables us to go looking for them?

And so, to conclude by returning one last time – slowly and elliptically, perhaps, but returning nonetheless – to where we started: if some in the field could teach just the first week of not only the Chemistry 101 class, where students are introduced to what seem to them to be eternal principles, but also the omnipresent survey of world religions that is still taught by so many of our colleagues, or maybe have the luxury of inserting a foreword into the surely planned tenth edition of Mary Pat Fisher's *Living Religions* (2014) or perhaps writing a crafty preamble to what will sooner or later probably be published as the fourteenth edition of the late Lewis Hopfe's *Religions of the World* (2015), then our job as scholars and teachers would be infinitely easier because, as Smith rightly observed, 'at least we would have raised the possibility that one wears eyeglasses when one gazes at these naked facts'. For then, to build on a point nicely made by Baldrick-Morrone, Graziano and Stoddard, but reinforced by Michel Desjardins and David McConeghy, the students would learn that not only the textbook 'participates in the construction of the objects it references' but they and their instructor do as well.

Notes

1 See http://www.iau.org/news/pressreleases/detail/iau0603/ for the press release. Accessed April 11, 2015. I also appreciate helpful conversations on this topic with Raymond White, Chair of the Department of Physics and Astronomy at the University of Alabama, and member of the IAU.
2 Pluto is now also seen as the prototype for this new designation, as well as being an example of the class of what they now term trans-Neptunian objects, i.e. a planet-like object that orbits the sun but at a greater distance away than Neptune, the planet whose trajectory now sets the solar system's limit.

3 See http://www.iau.org/administration/membership/individual/ for the organization's own self-reported membership number.
4 Come to think of it, the course of modern liberal democratic nations is determined by casting a ballot, sometimes with a surprisingly low voter turn-out, and always with profound implications ('Should we go to war?') – making the consequences of the IAU's vote seem commonplace by comparison.
5 As stated in the paper's abstract, 'This resulted in the proposal that some species previously included in well-known genera like *Apatosaurus* and *Diplodocus* are generically distinct. Of particular note is that the famous genus *Brontosaurus* is considered valid by our quantitative approach.' See Tschopp *et al.* (2015).
6 Greek: *(asteres) planetai*, meaning 'wandering (stars)', from *planasthai*, meaning 'to wander'. It is thought to betray the distinction of nearby celestial objects moving more quickly across the night sky as opposed to the far slower arcs of more distant stars.
7 Nix. v. Hedden 149 U.S. 304 (1893).
8 For example, see Spiritual Outreach Society v. Commissioner of the Internal Revenue, No. 90–1501. United States Court of Appeals, Eighth Circuit (Submitted Nov. 15, 1990. Decided Feb. 27, 1991) for a particularly good example of the IRS's use of a 14 point definition of church which it used to determine that, for purposes of taxation, the SOS did not constitute a church.
9 McCutcheon (2003), notably the final chapter, 'Religion and the Governable Self', explored this very topic.
10 Epicycle is the term for hypothetical and necessarily unseen orbital deviations that early astronomers speculated celestial objects performed so as to account for how far their own geocentric-based predictions were from the observations they made of planets' movements.

References

Burnett, D. Graham. 2007. *Trying Leviathan: The Nineteenth-century New York Court Case That Put the Whale on Trial and Challenged the Order of Nature*. Princeton, NJ: Princeton University Press.
Chidester, David. 1996. *Savage Systems: Colonialism and Comparative Religion in Southern Africa*. Charlottesville, VA: The University Press of Virginia.
Fisher, Mary Pat. 2014. *Living Religions*. 9th ed. New York: Pearson.
Hopfe, Lewis and Brett Hendrickson. 2015. *Religions of the World*. 13th ed. New York: Pearson.
Masuzawa, Tomoko. 2005. *The Invention of World Religions; Or, How European Universalism Was Preserved in the Language of Pluralism*. Chicago: The University of Chicago Press.
McCutcheon, Russell T. 1997. *Manufacturing Religion: The Discourse on Sui Generis Religion and the Politics of Nostalgia*. New York: Oxford University Press.
McCutcheon, Russell T. 2003. *The Discipline of Religion: Structure, Meaning, Rhetoric*. New York and London: Routledge.
Miles, Jack, ed. 2014. *The Norton Anthology of World Religions*. 2 vols. New York: W. W. Norton.
Smith, Jonathan Z. 1998. "Religion, Religions, Religious," in *Critical Terms for Religious Studies*, edited by Mark C. Taylor, 269–284. Chicago: University of Chicago Press.
Smith, Jonathan Z. 2007. "The Necessary Lie: Duplicity in the Disciplines," in *Studying Religion: An Introduction*, edited by Russell T. McCutcheon, 73–80. New York: Routledge.
Tschopp, Emanuel, Octávio Mateus and Roger B. J. Benson. 2015. "A specimen-level phylogenetic analysis and taxonomic revision of Diplodocidae (Dinosauria, Sauropoda)." *PeerJ* 3:e857 https://dx.doi.org/10.7717/peerj.857 (accessed April 11, 2015).

INDEX

 Taylor & Francis eBooks

Helping you to choose the right eBooks for your Library

Add Routledge titles to your library's digital collection today. Taylor and Francis ebooks contains over 50,000 titles in the Humanities, Social Sciences, Behavioural Sciences, Built Environment and Law.

Choose from a range of subject packages or create your own!

Benefits for you

» Free MARC records
» COUNTER-compliant usage statistics
» Flexible purchase and pricing options
» All titles DRM-free.

Benefits for your user

» Off-site, anytime access via Athens or referring URL
» Print or copy pages or chapters
» Full content search
» Bookmark, highlight and annotate text
» Access to thousands of pages of quality research at the click of a button.

Free Trials Available
We offer free trials to qualifying academic, corporate and government customers.

REQUEST YOUR **FREE** INSTITUTIONAL TRIAL TODAY

eCollections – Choose from over 30 subject eCollections, including:

Archaeology	Language Learning
Architecture	Law
Asian Studies	Literature
Business & Management	Media & Communication
Classical Studies	Middle East Studies
Construction	Music
Creative & Media Arts	Philosophy
Criminology & Criminal Justice	Planning
Economics	Politics
Education	Psychology & Mental Health
Energy	Religion
Engineering	Security
English Language & Linguistics	Social Work
Environment & Sustainability	Sociology
Geography	Sport
Health Studies	Theatre & Performance
History	Tourism, Hospitality & Events

For more information, pricing enquiries or to order a free trial, please contact your local sales team: www.tandfebooks.com/page/sales

 Routledge
Taylor & Francis Group

The home of
Routledge books

www.tandfebooks.com